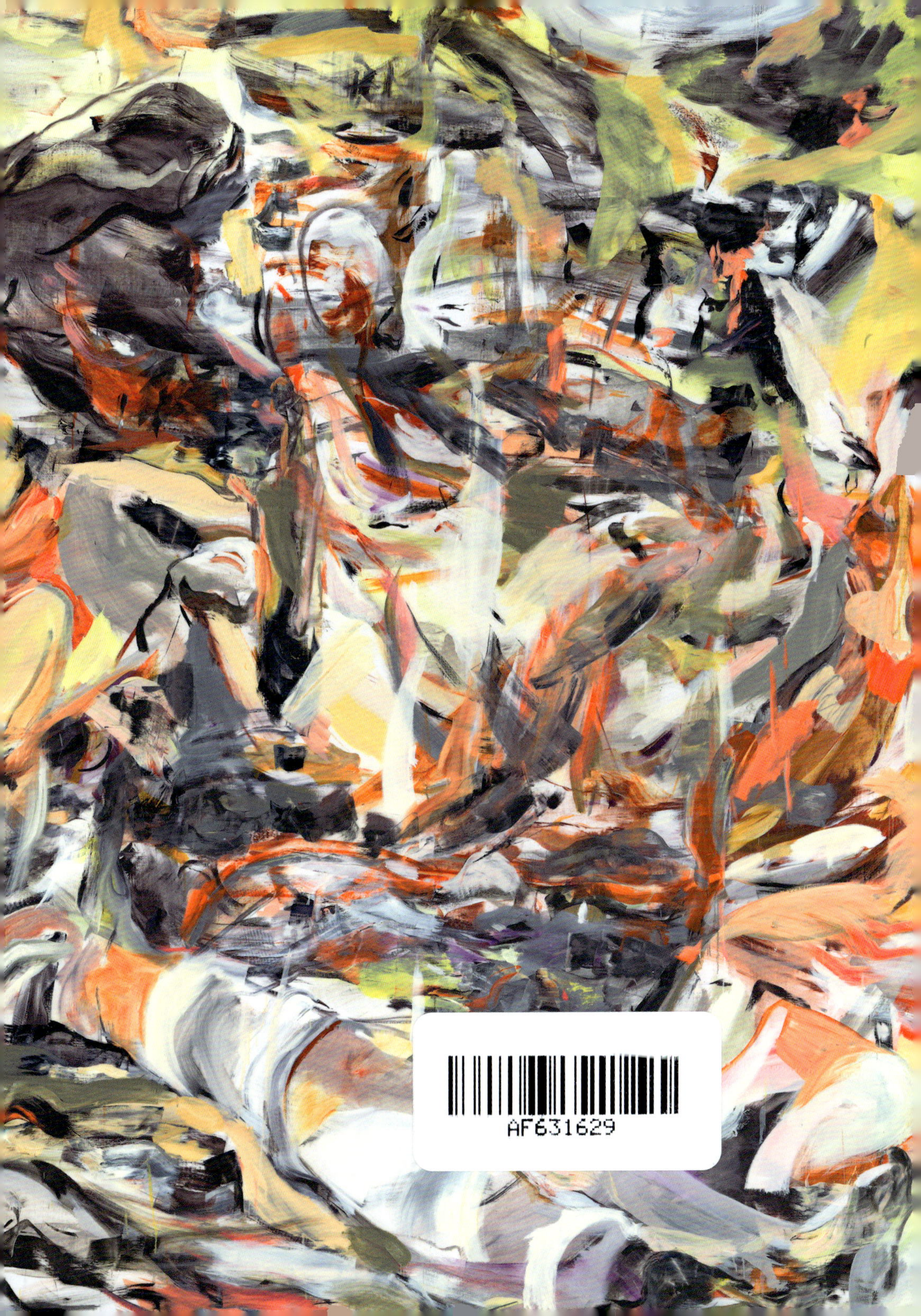

WHERE, WHEN, HOW OFTEN AND WITH WHOM

LOUISIANA MUSEUM OF MODERN ART

CECILY BROWN

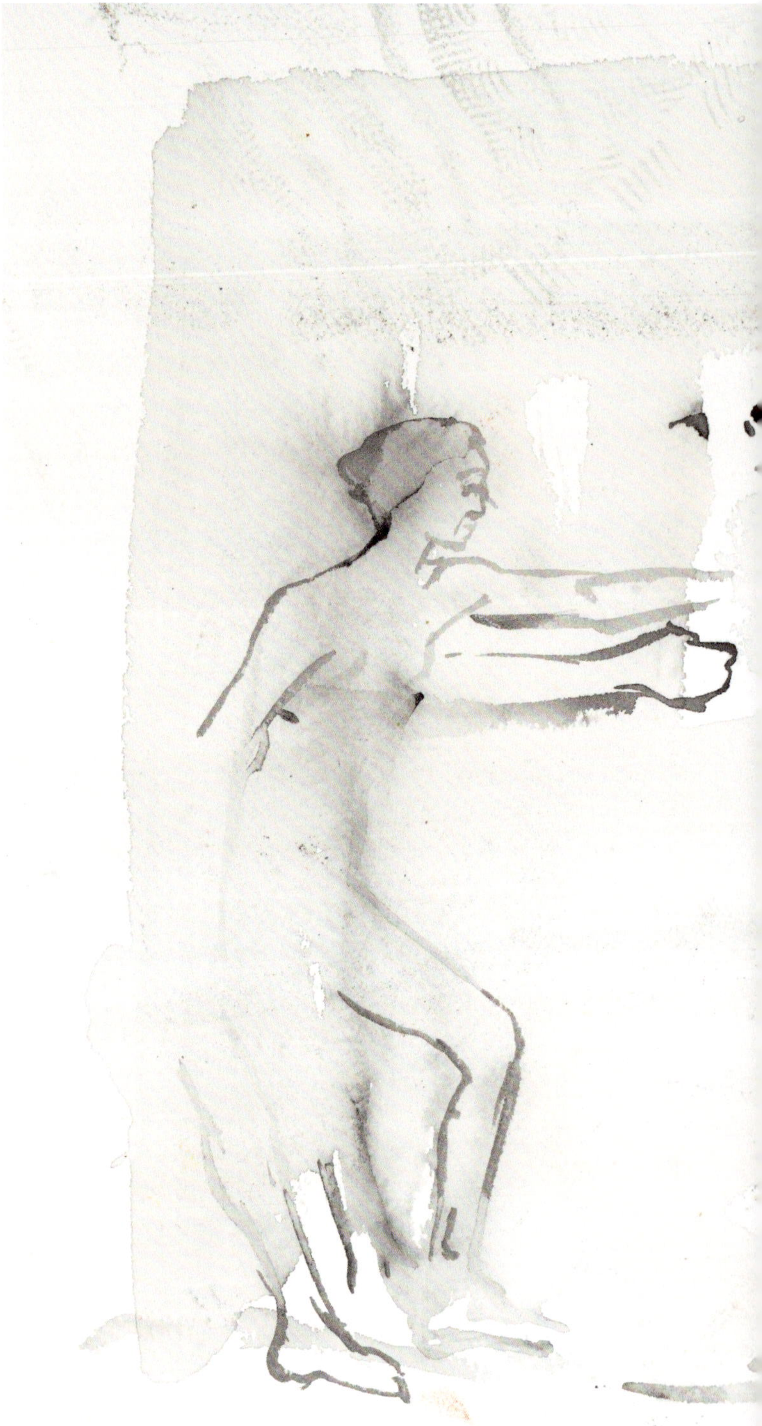

Young Spartans (After Degas), 2013

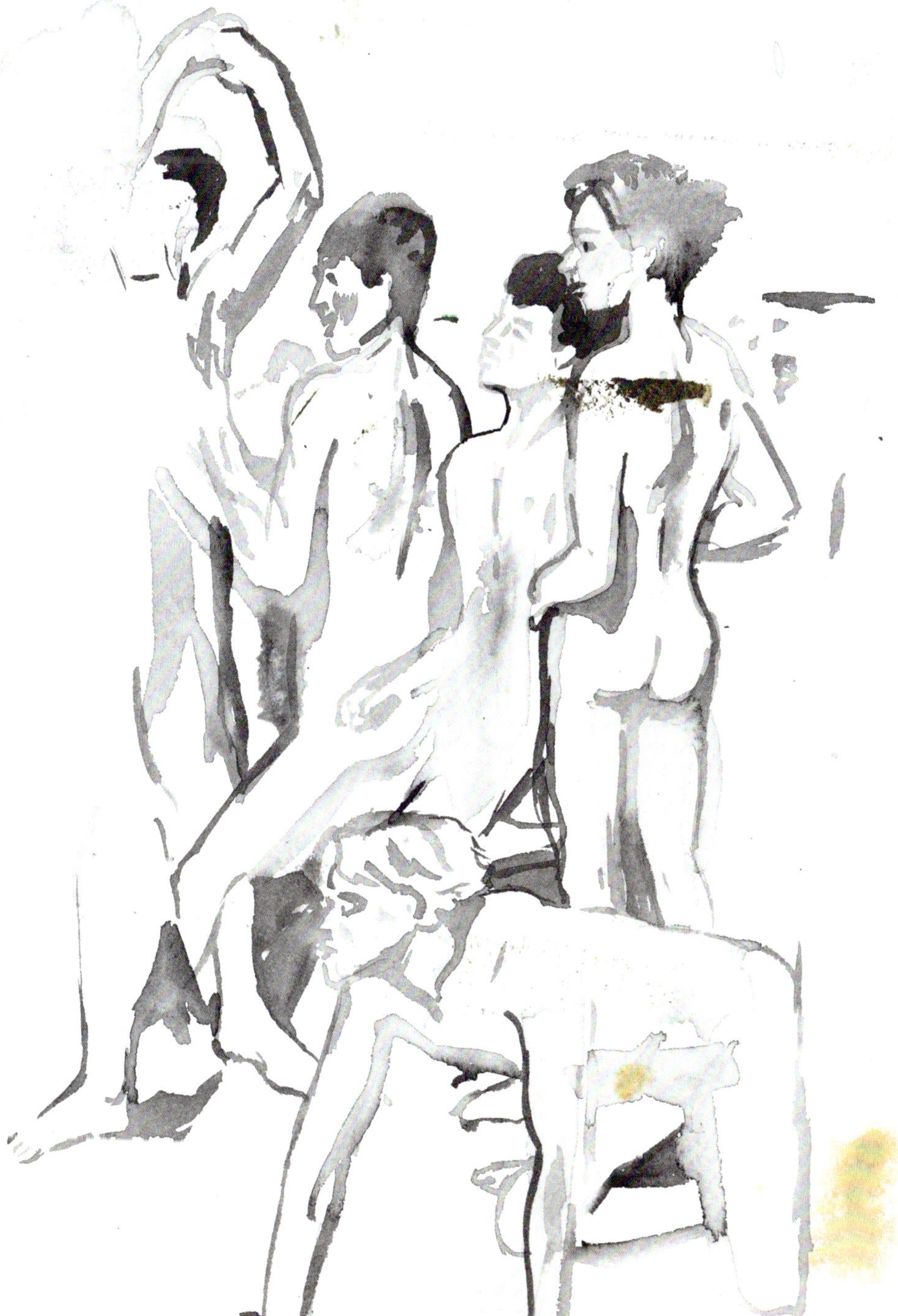

CONTENTS

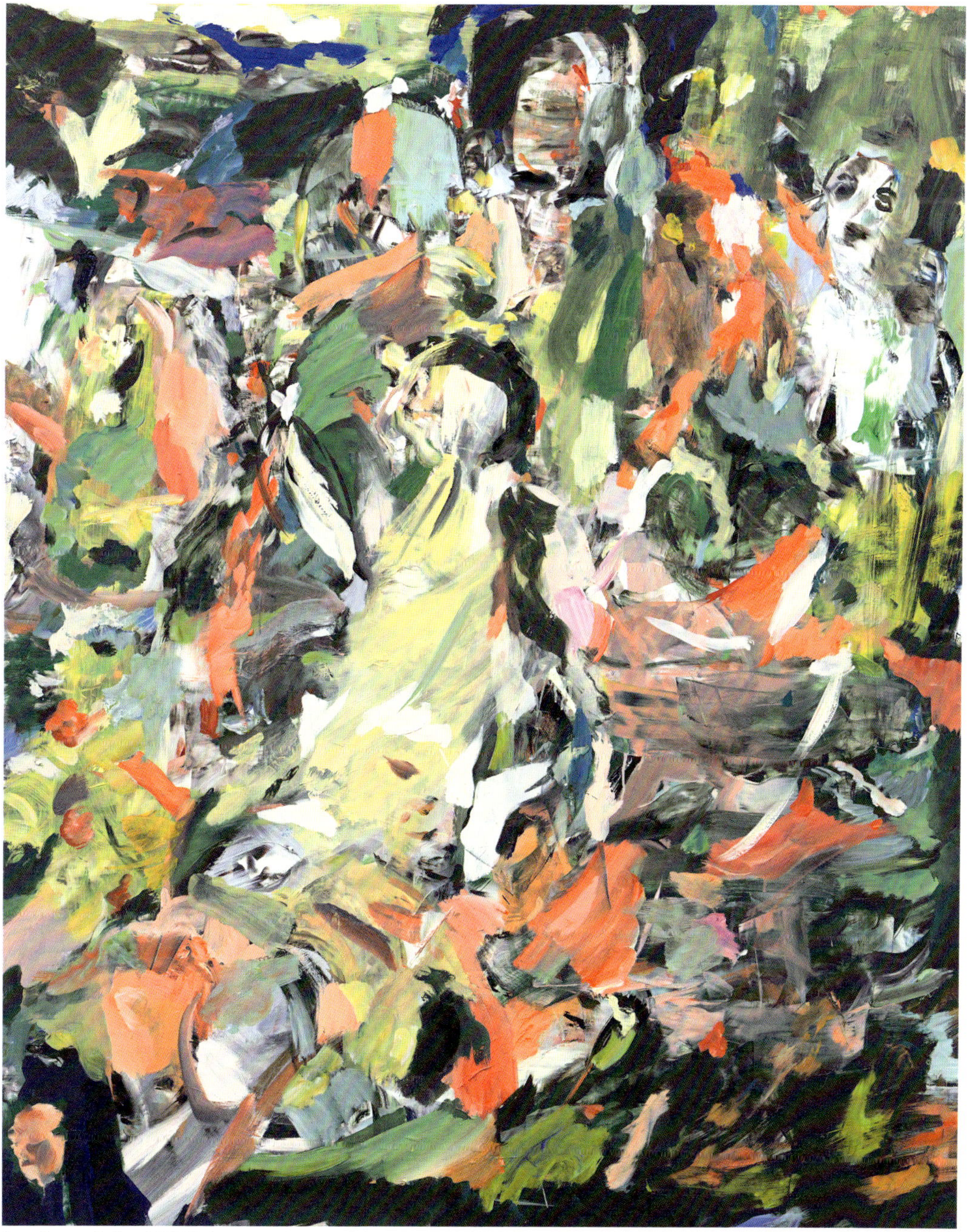

Frenchy on a Swing, 2017-2018

FOREWORD

Many painters, among them Cecily Brown, describe painting as possessing the ability to sometimes override the painter. While some see this as the greatest joy, a momentary flow of aesthetic integrity beyond the artist's intentions, for Brown it only steps up the need for intervention. She resists, often latching on to figures or narrative fragments amidst the storm, as she puts it in the interview in this catalogue. The artist's comments are lucid, unequivocal and hard earned, making it immediately clear that the game between the apparently abstract and the apparently figurative in her art is not an academic issue but a vital sign that painting, for Brown, is physical.

The physicality of painting – not choices, or the lack of them – is what creates this dynamic between the abstract and the figurative. A painting is not separate from the process that created it. It lives by constantly unfolding its own history. The painting and the act of painting it are sometimes the same. A finished work by Cecily Brown contains all the magic of the initial mark-making. The viewer can tell that the painting comes from "somewhere," which here, for once, refers not to a relocation from one place to another, but to time itself. Brown's paintings are actions on canvas, time, at once extended and stopped. Beholding her paintings is to unspool that time again, backwards and forwards, seemingly bringing the painting to life before us.

Painting materialized as in Brown's work accentuates the potential union of artist and viewer. The artist mentions her concern with painting observers into the spaces of her pictures, placing us at once inside and outside the picture. The artist is a viewer as well. The artist might even be the viewer's viewer. The fact that sight, the seeing eye, is painted into what we see proves to me that painting is not just about seeing but about doing. The painter does not reproduce the world, she produces it. A painting is a field of physical action – Brown's painterly world is full of bodies. The point of a painting is that it is painted. We relate differently to the painted image than to so many other kinds of images. It is both farther away – rarely fooling us as photography's cinematic effects can do – and closer, because it involves perception bound to a sensation of physicality.

There are many ways of painting. Painting can be as pure as mathematics, but rarely is, because the moment a programmatic aesthetic is revealed as an artistic intention, matter strikes back. Even in Mondrian's work, lines shimmer. Painting can also be as impure as an experience we would rather be without. But even then, the image does the work of fiction: visiting the worst of places, being there, but not inescapably – Brown mentions her fascination with art-historical hellscapes. For many years, critics claimed there was only one way for painting to go – straight down the drain. They felt safe making that claim because they themselves only operated in one way, inheriting a philosophy of history that only went one way, as well as a thinly veiled contempt for the sensory image. A lot of that seems oddly irrelevant when painted images actually occupy spaces. As Peter Doig's paintings did at the Louisiana in 2015, Daniel Richter's in 2016 and Tal R's in 2017.

It is my great pleasure – and privilege – to add the work of Cecily Brown to the unfinishable story of everything that painting is, can do and be. I want to thank the artist for working so actively with Louisiana curator Anders Kold – for the benefit of all of us viewers, who will shortly leave words behind in favour of deeds – on canvas and paper. A big thanks to all the lenders, institutions and individuals alike, for their generosity. Thanks as well to the writers of this catalogue for their insight, and the artist's galleries for their engagement.

Poul Erik Tøjner

Director, Louisiana Museum of Modern Art

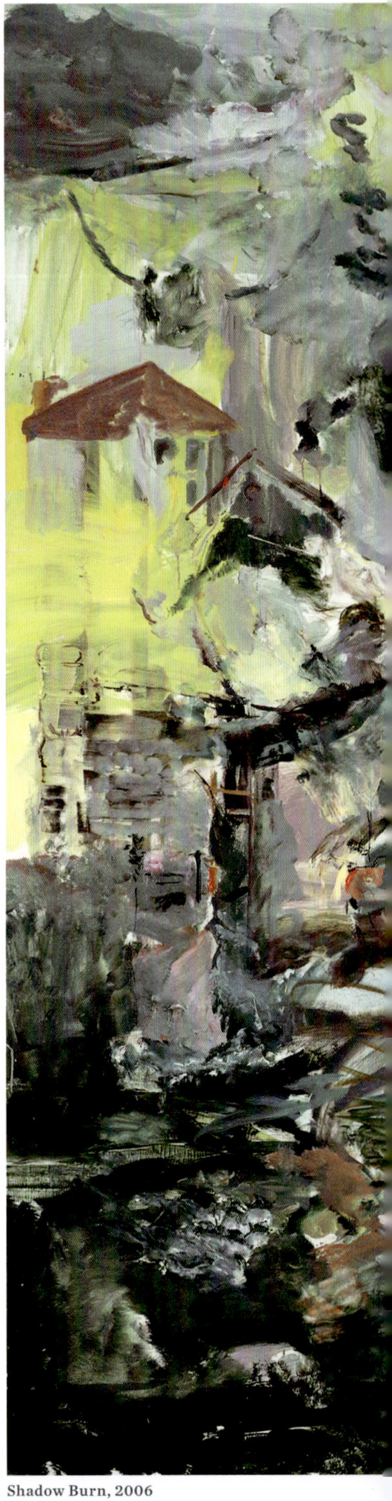

Shadow Burn, 2006

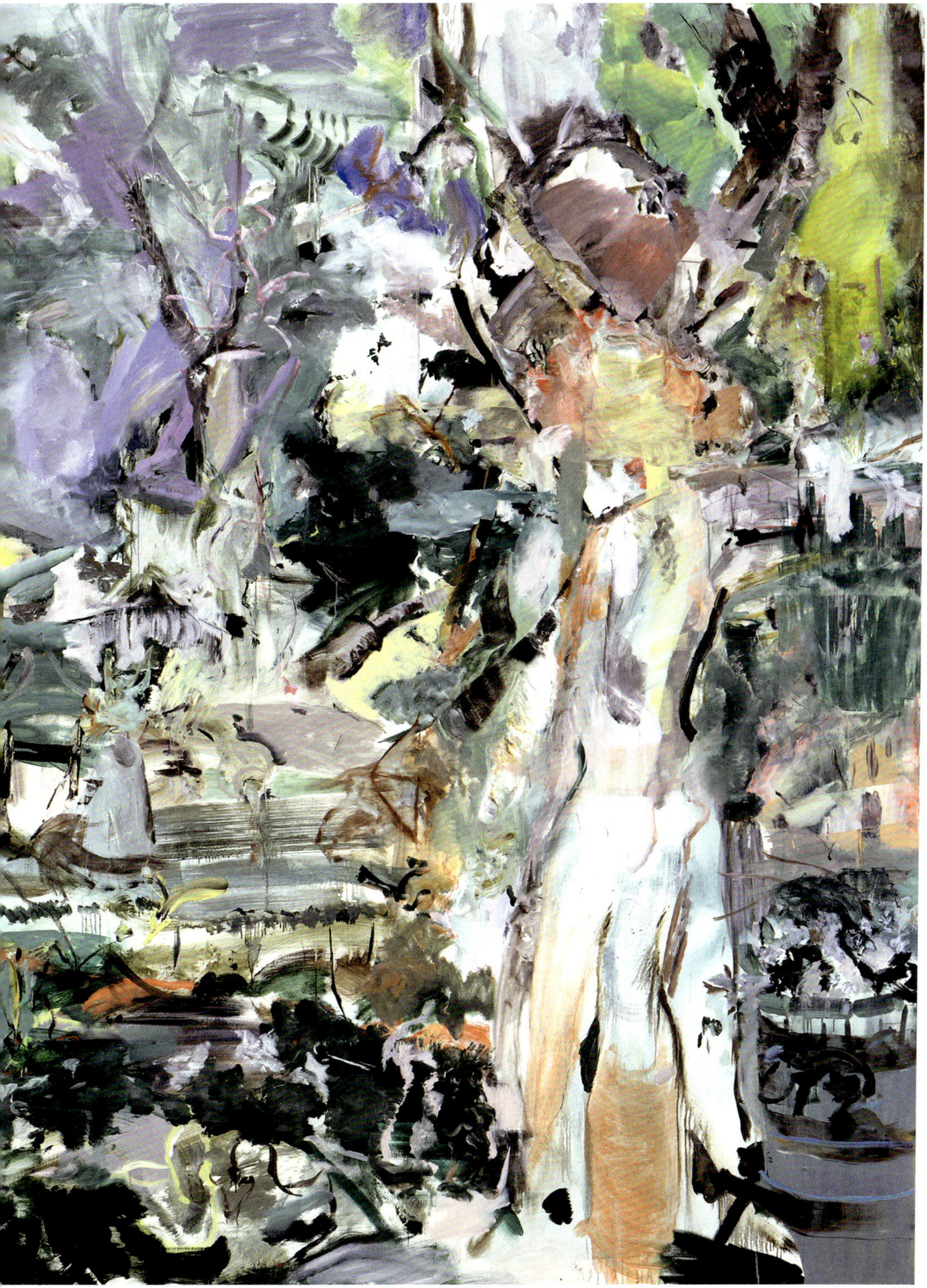

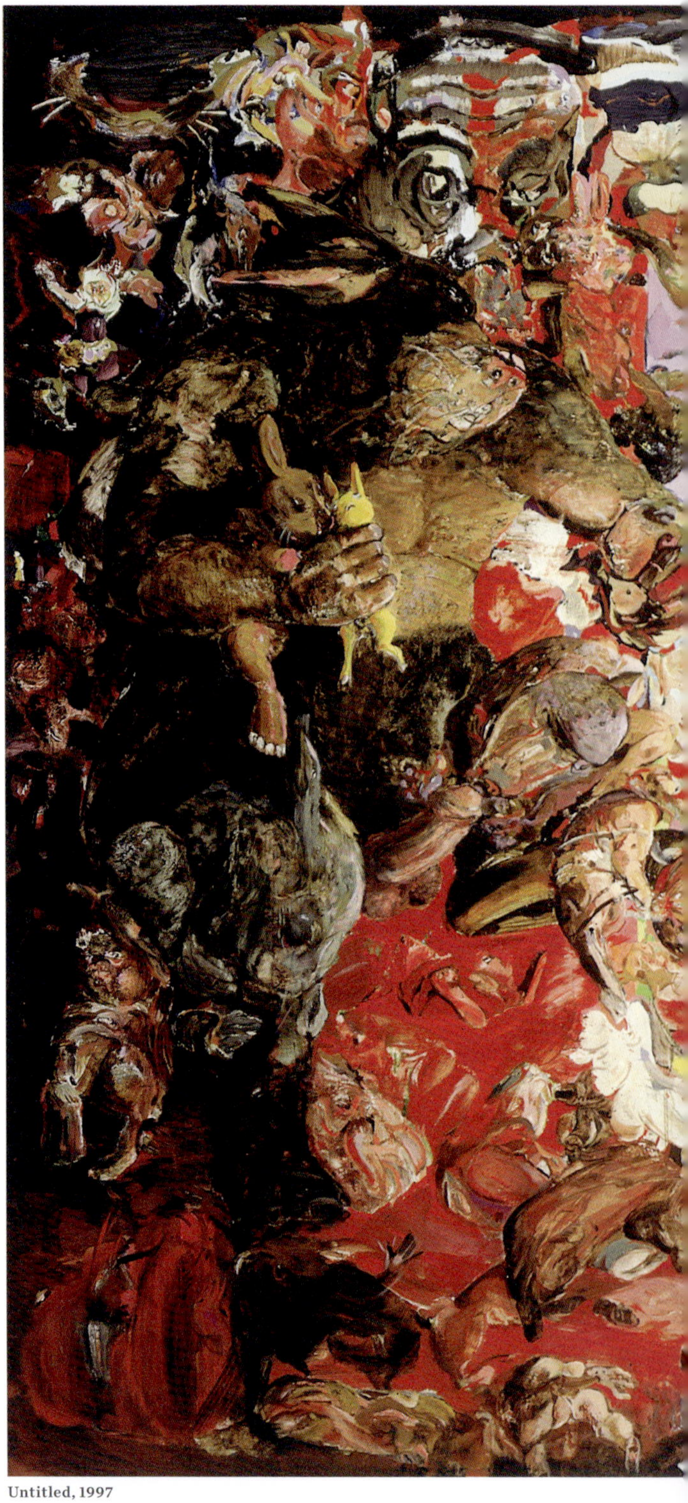

Untitled, 1997

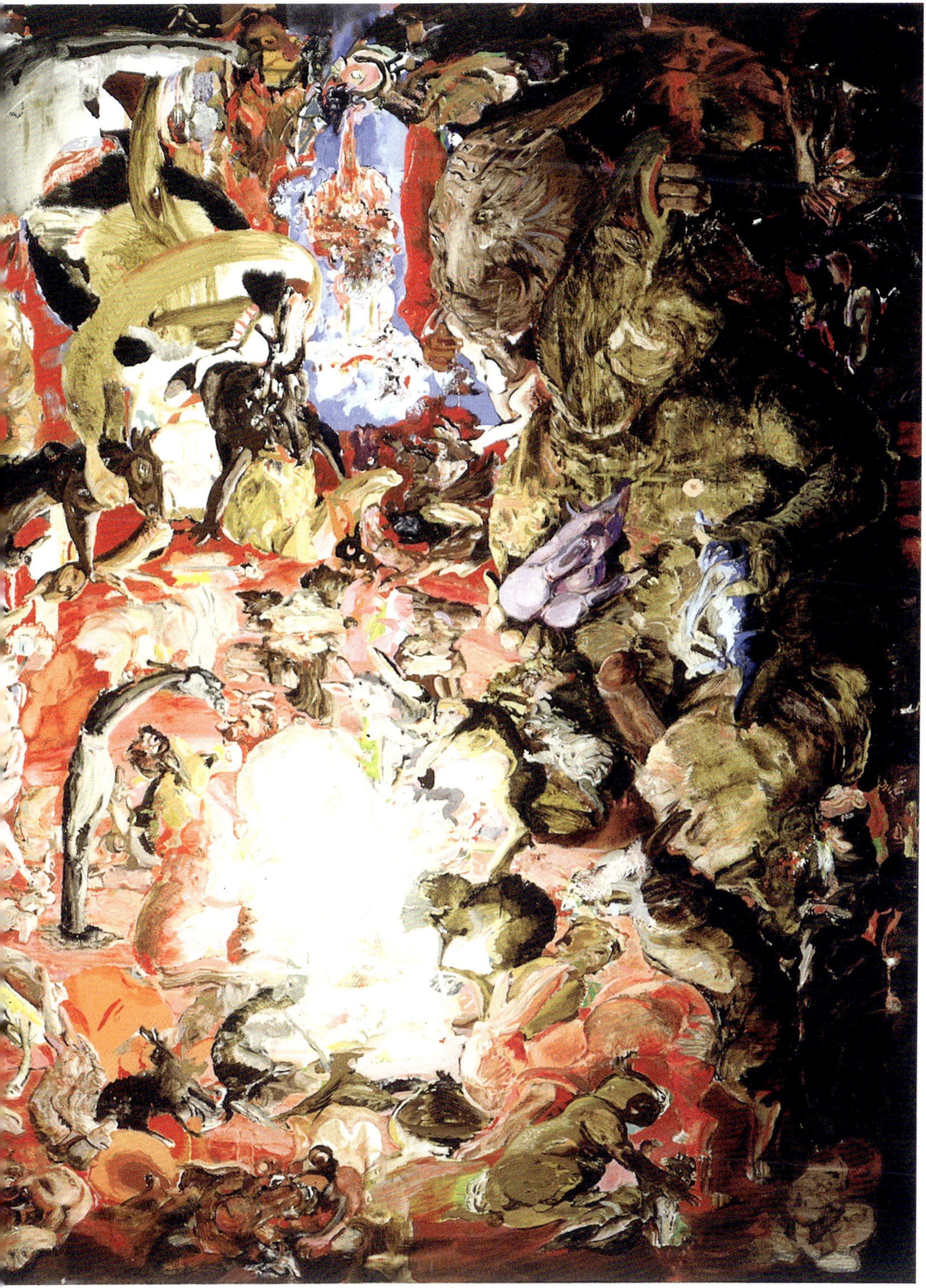

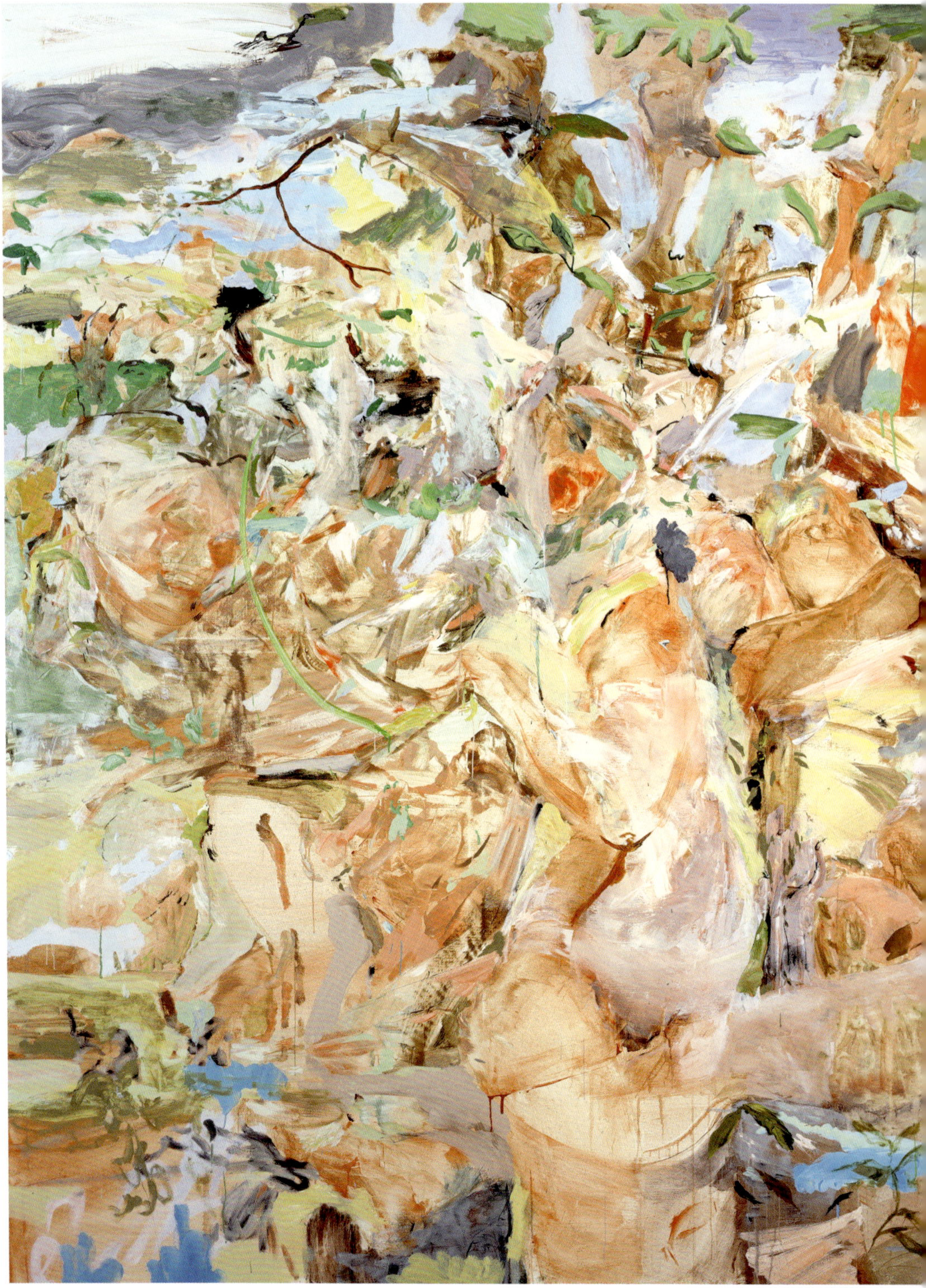

Figures in a Landscape 1, 2001

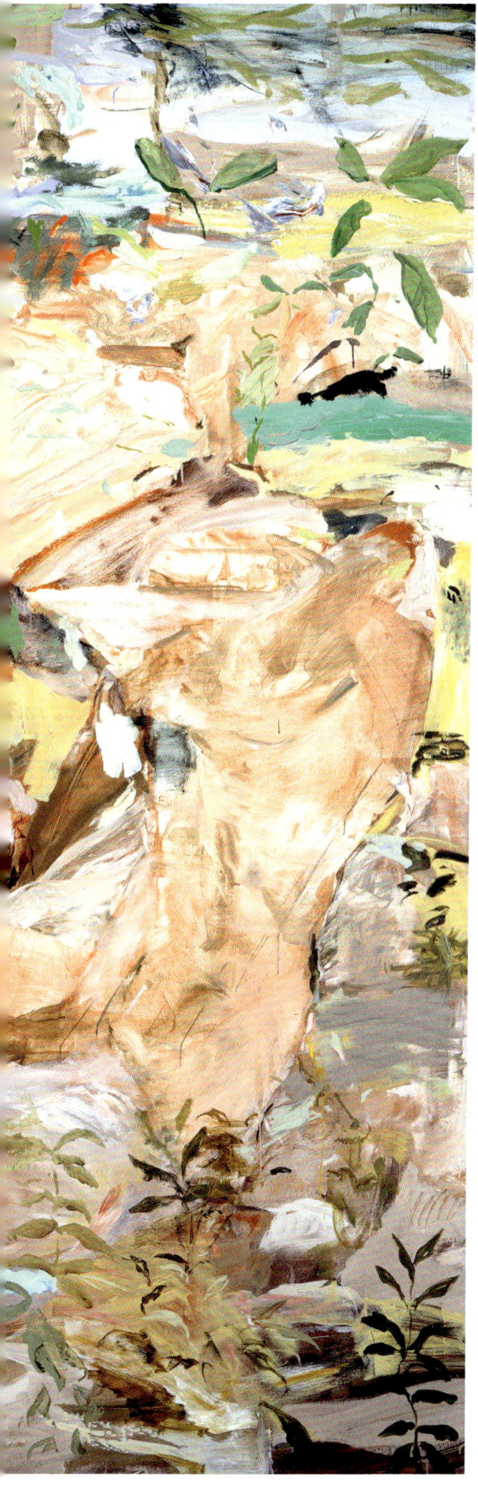

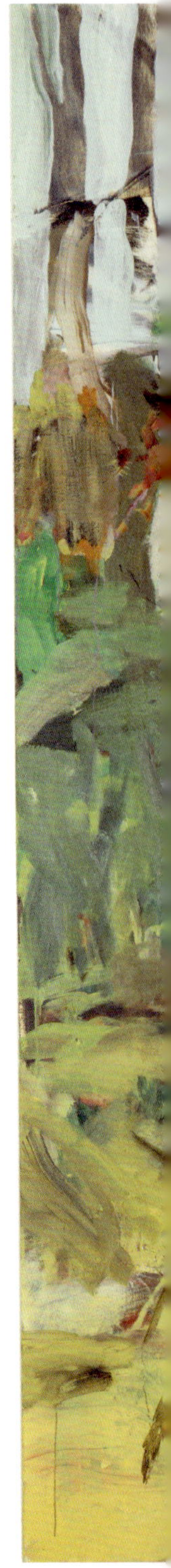

Couple, 2004

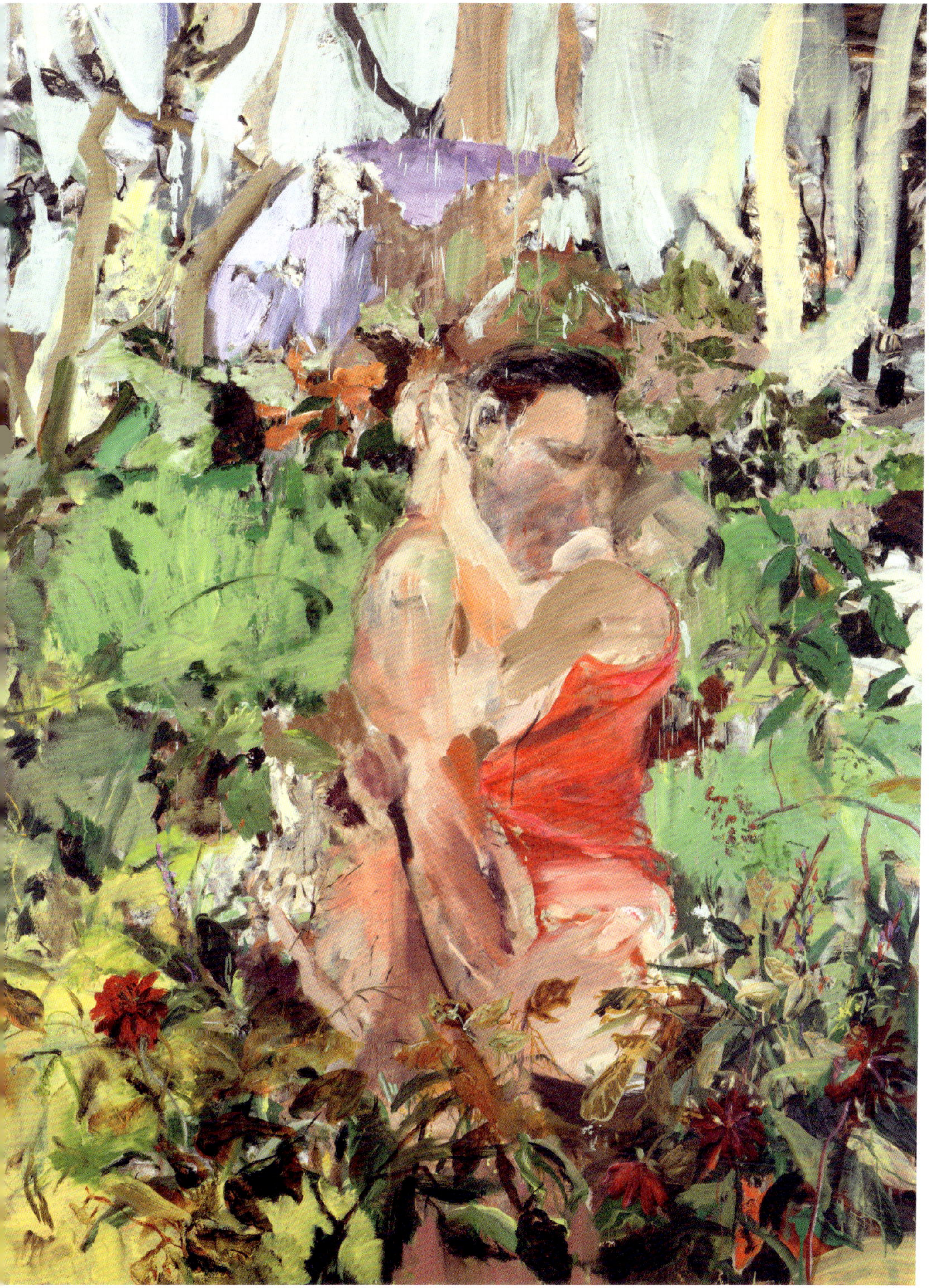

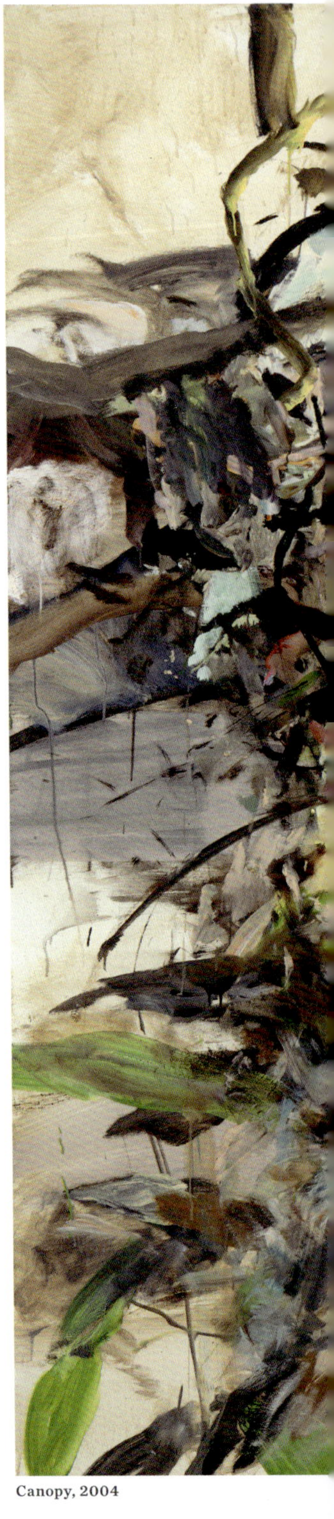

Canopy, 2004

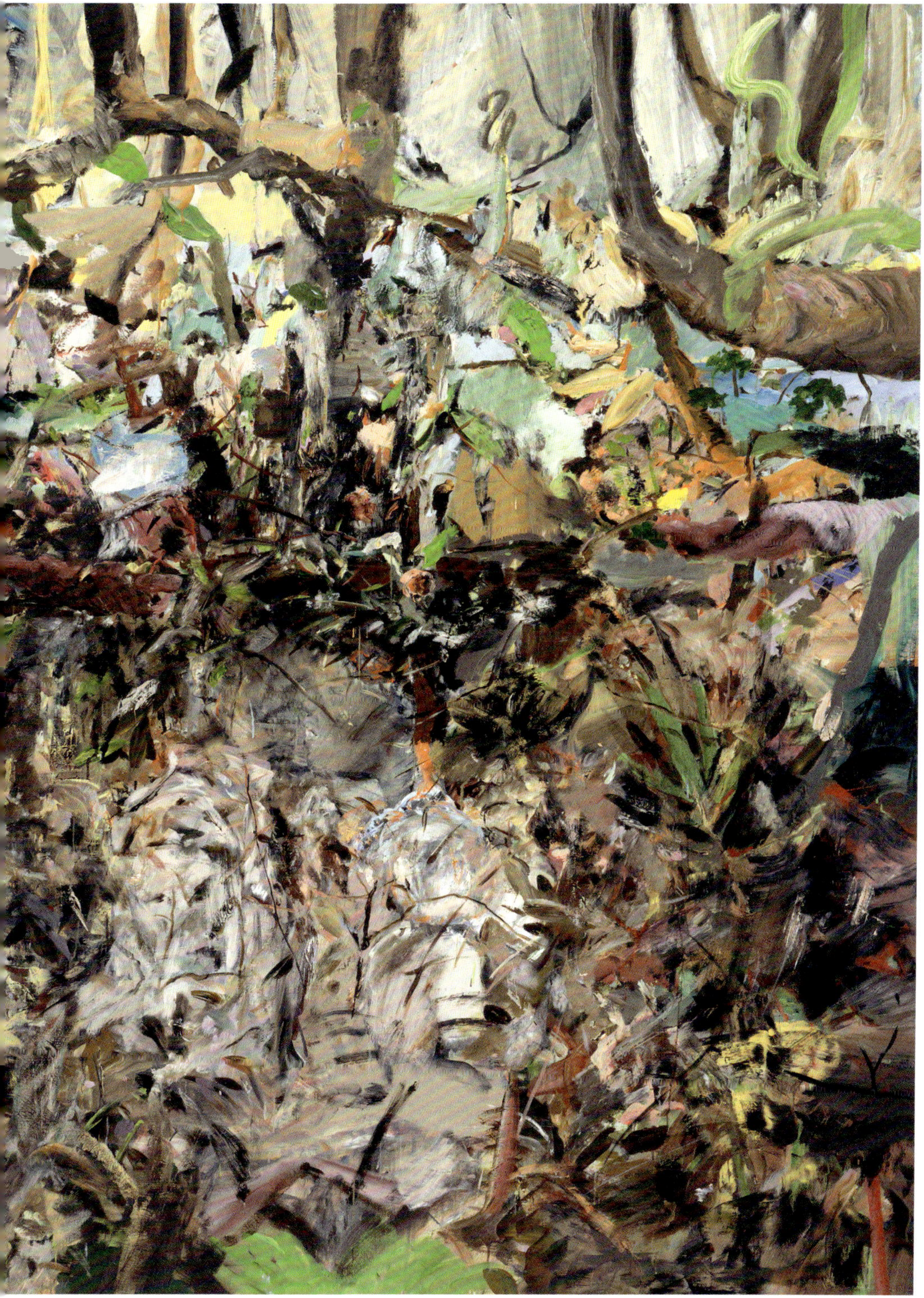

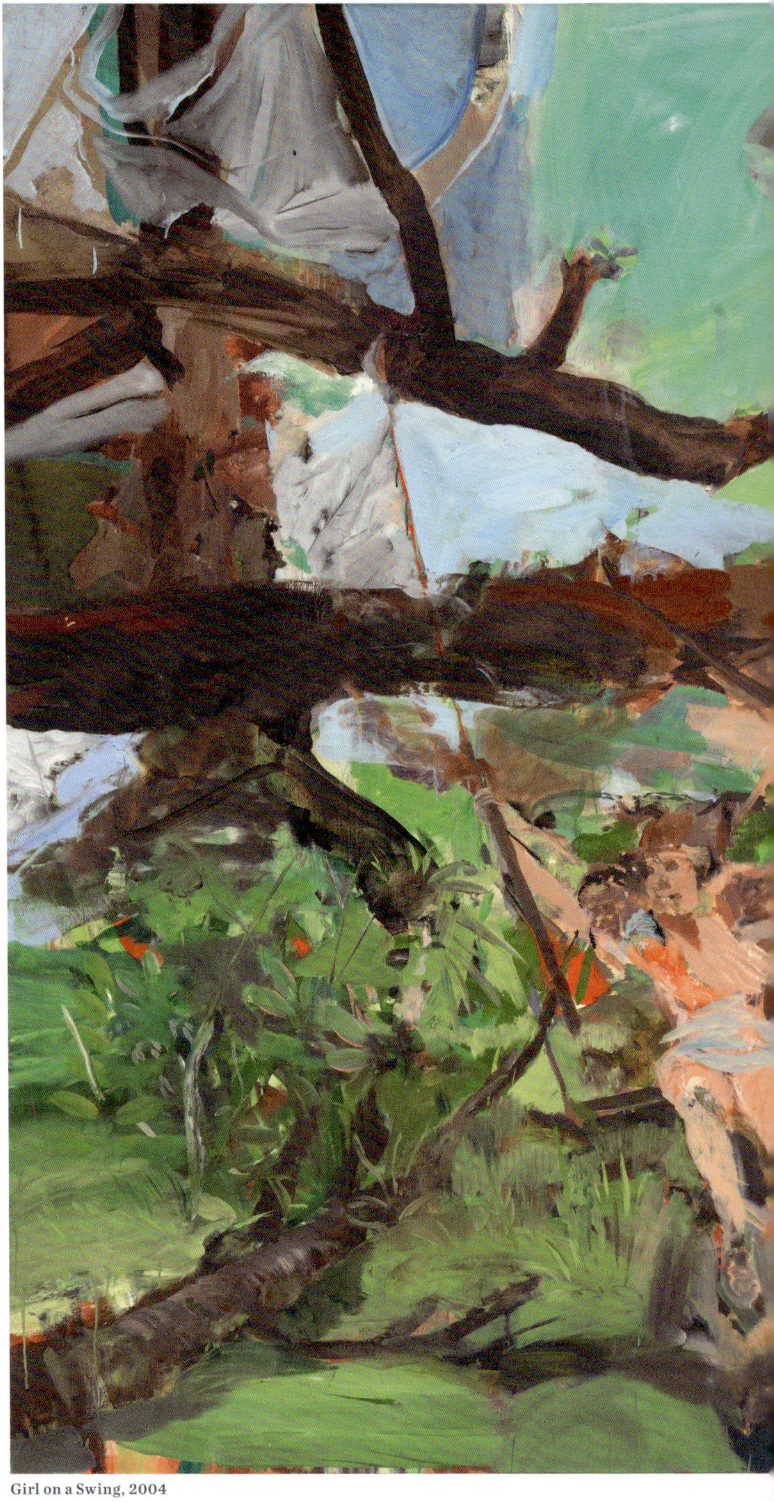

Girl on a Swing, 2004

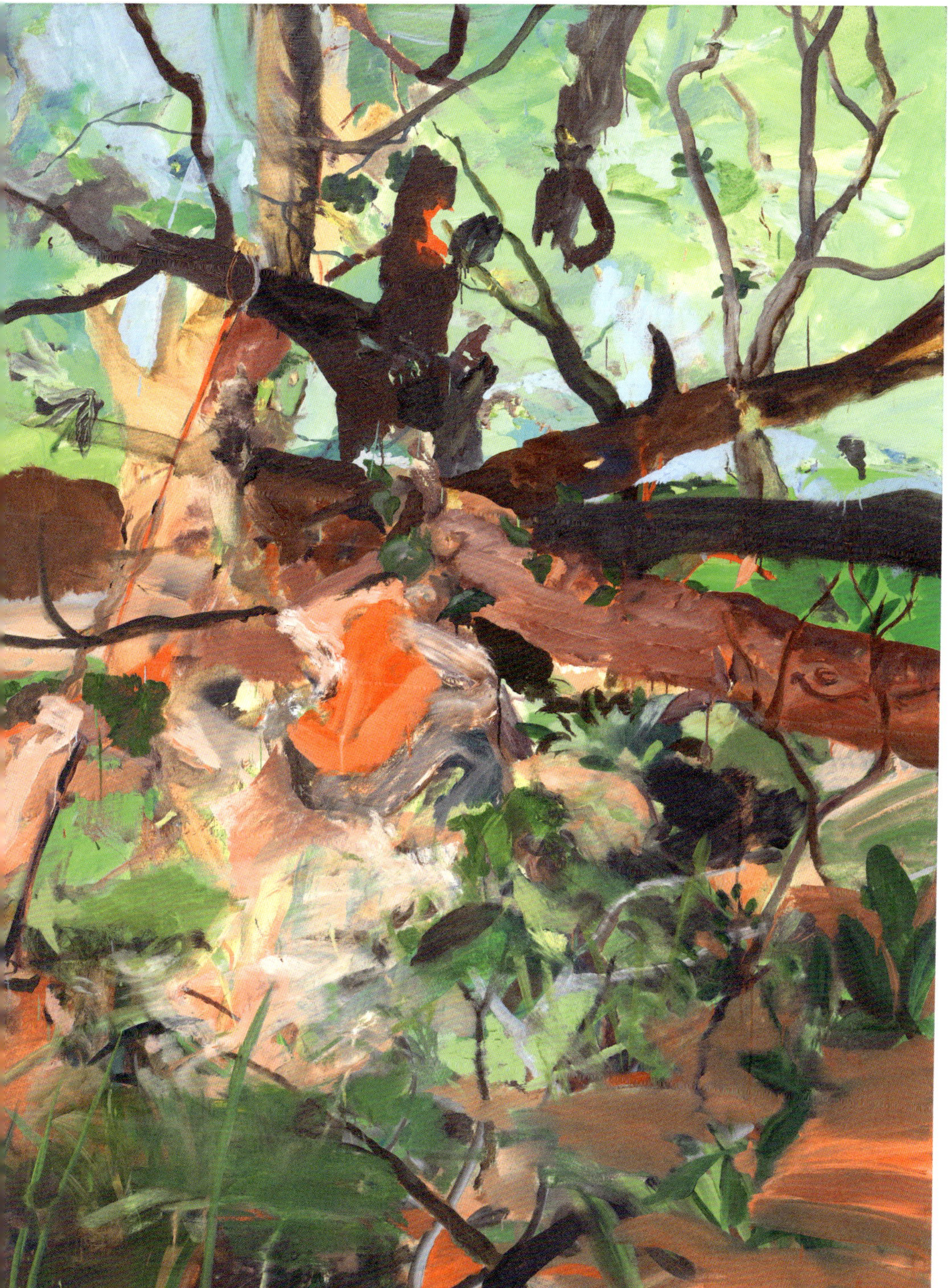

HEROIC-PORNOGRAPHIC

Anders Kold

The history of recent art has often cast painting, especially of the figurative kind, in a rather unflattering light. There is by now a long-standing and familiar tradition of death threats against painting. The critique commonly involves a comparison with other artistic practices, and painting, with its long history, seems to confound the notion of art as an unbroken progression building on what came immediately before. While the actual reality of artistic practices, of course, may not always conform to that image, there are historical reasons why so many contemporary art chroniclers are not only sceptical but clueless when it comes to paintings, like those of Cecily Brown, whose *raison d'être* depends on the outcome in oils between figuration and abstraction. All the same, Brown's work meaningfully connects to older pictorial traditions, while acutely materializing current crises and observations.

The issue many have with figurative painting like Brown's derives from the fact that it manifests neither Pop art's stencilled repertoire nor a critique of the representational premise per se. She is a painter in the traditional sense, so forget about unlearning the craft and outsourcing the artistic impetus. But she is also undisputedly a voice of today. Her relationship to past art has nothing to do with retrospection. Polemically, we might even say that her art causes bewilderment precisely for that reason – because, in contemporary art history writing, it is hard to connect with anything going back decades. And because the notion of an impact history that is presumed to reach meaningfully from modernism into our time is invariably misguided. Painting *is* a slow medium, and it has a singular way of interacting with reality. A lot can be said about that, though few today have said it more aptly than American critic James Lawrence describing Brown's work as "an antidote to electronic refinement. It has all the pleasure of being imperfectly real."[1]

Linking back three centuries while not ignoring the existence of other art histories then or now, works by Brown, alongside a key Rococo work and contemporary photo-based practices, will here be addressed to describe the entanglement and disjunction that make up such a vibrant continuum for her painting.

Where, When, How Often and with Whom

An analytical approach of some kind may be appropriate when facing scenes of great complexity, as so often is the case with Brown's paintings. To avoid falling into an abyss of pictorial description, we might, to gain an initial overview, apply the template of where, when, how often and with whom. Potential targets for such analysis include Titian's *The Rape of Europa*, Watteau's *The Embarkation for Cythera* and Manet's *The Luncheon on the Grass*, to indicate the range, alongside Brown's 2017 triptych[2] *Where, When, How Often and with Whom*, which also furnishes the title for this exhibition.

More than 10 metres long (32 feet), the painting presents a landscape in a frieze-like composition, with groups of figures weaving in and out of a turbulent pictorial space. The light, greyish ground and the central massif are joined at the top by delicate yellow formations, interspersed with red, white and chalky rose tones. It is a grand composition, insofar as the many figures actually have anything to do with one another. Typically, it is hard to make a coherent narrative out of Brown's disjointed moments and actions, including not least the figures' interrelationships. From left to right, we see a clot of figures floating over a masted boat, a small group of women directing their attention at us from behind a spread-out blanket, two female figures, front and centre, shielding each other as they seem to be headed out of the picture, a heavy, seated woman and, at the far right, a supine, perhaps lifeless body and a female figure kneeling alongside. Heroic? Perhaps, though in fact our present-day unfamiliarity and discomfort with heroisms is asserted.

The lack of careful alignment between the elements on the three canvases is probably not accidental, either. While the left and centre panels match up at the bottom of the picture, the figuration warps into misalignment as it moves upward: a spread-out blanket and, behind it, a bag and possibly a leg, but as if taken from different episodes of the same story. Note also that Brown's title does not end with a question mark. Nor are any answers forthcoming. Moreover, we might bear in mind that, since the turn of the century, her titles have only to a negligible degree been descriptive of the works. "Titles need no paintings," the artist says. Occasionally ready-mades, the titles are stuck on at the end.[3] In their half-random, half-associative nature, they sometimes function almost as a kind of party game. That does not make the works dishonest or any less interesting, however. On the contrary, she and we are fully aware that what we have before us is art, and that the pursuit of honesty in painting is necessarily a lie.[4] Yet, artfulness is at the core of her work. The jocular and horrifying plot-scenography does get at something central about the human relationships in Brown's art.[5] "In flashes, or by squinting," as she puts it, we can tell what the playing field is.[6]

For years, the artist has been reworking some of art history's greatest, most heroic wrecks, including those in works by Delacroix and Géricault, particularly the latter's *The Raft of the Medusa*. But how do such subjects as the castaways on the far left and the possible washed-up body on the right tie into the other groups of figures in Brown's painting? The blanket, the bag and the huddle of women behind it do not come from the world of art. In August 2016, four police officers took action against a Muslim woman on a beach at Nice. Wearing a burkini, a bathing suit respecting Islamic rules of female modesty, the woman had lain down to sleep. The image went worldwide, fatefully pitting the recent French ban on face covering against Islam near the very spot, the Promenade des Anglais, where an Islamic terrorist

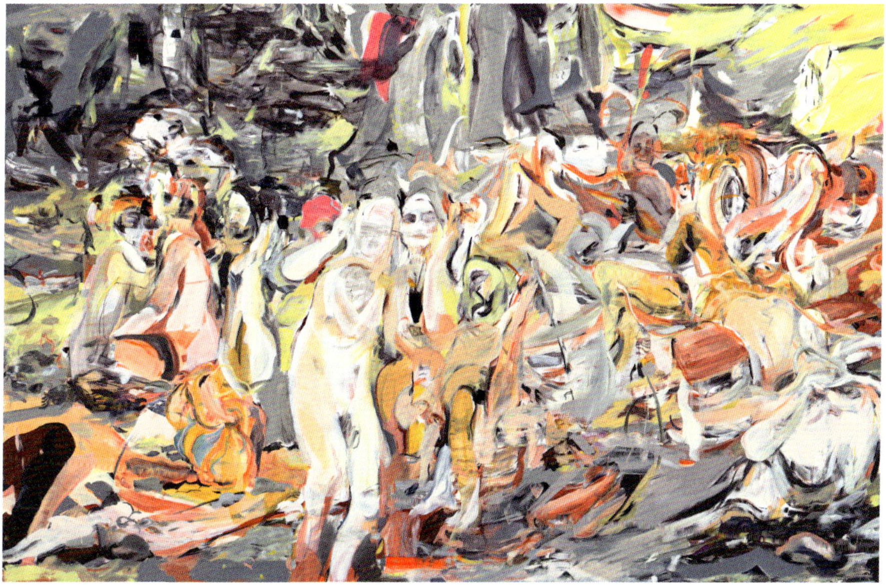

Detail of Where, When, How Often and with Whom, 2017

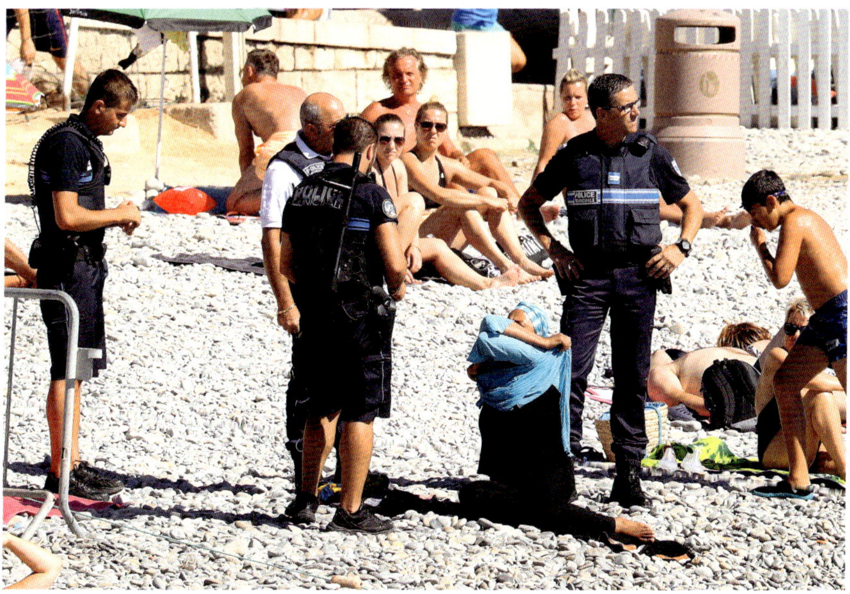

Police patrolling the Promenade des Anglais beach in Nice fine a woman for wearing a burkini, 23 August 2016. Photo: Vantagenews.com

shortly before had driven a truck into a crowd of people, causing a massacre. Sunshine and noir, an affinity usually associated with Los Angeles narratives, is certainly in play in Brown's art.

The bag, the blanket and the seated woman on the right side of the central panel are sourced from that episode. In addition to the police surrounding the woman, the press photo shows beachgoers, whose highly unflattering stares make the image a minefield of interpersonal relationships. In the painting, which dissolves the woman's face in brushwork, rendering her faceless, we clearly see the three female figures behind the blanket turn and look out at us or at the two central figures, blurred and piercing at once. Appearing to lean against each other for support and looking out in our direction, the two resemble nothing so much as the naked, suffering couple in the Renaissance master Masaccio's *Expulsion from the Garden of Eden*, which also fuels the discussion of Brown's use of references. Whatever is happening on this beach, the story can be seen structurally as a series of figurations with widely different origins and effects.

Human conflict is indisputably a central theme of Brown's art – the fact, as she describes it, "that good and evil can exist in the same place at the same time. Whether it's bunnies being gang raped in the most beautiful bucolic landscape, on a day with scudding clouds and sunshine or something like this."[7]

Over Board

At this point, we will pull up alongside Jean-Antoine Watteau's masterful *Embarkation for Cythera* from 1712-16. An academic piece originally listed in the protocols as depicting a pilgrimage to the island of Cythera, it was soon retitled *Fête Galante*. Presumably, Watteau chose the first title to better honour the institutional demand for history painting.[8] However, as the art historian Michael Levey finds, Watteau's work is a modern one of the genre by exercising considerable freedom from conventional mythological and historical subject matter. Universal rather than conventionally learned, it represents not heroicism but love and natural human emotions. As Levey writes, the work is free of moralizing and "like Goya in the other end of the period, Watteau was concerned with reason and passion"[9] – components of a worldview that, as the century unfolds, strikes the first note of true modernity. *Fêtes Galantes,* as an almost self-made genre borrowing from the Italian *commedia dell'arte* tradition, is one thing, but beyond that two additional conditions emerge. As Levey points out, the picture shows not an embarkation for somewhere but the preparations for a *return* from Cythera, the Island of Love. In this work, Watteau, with tremendous engagement, depicts various stages of human emotion, ultimately a sense of loss.

Watteau's composition is serpentine, practically an unbroken frieze. The embarkation from the island is underway on the left. Unreal, almost ethereal, the work is a study of three stages of the consciousness of the end to all things, reaching a thematic climax in the right half of the picture.

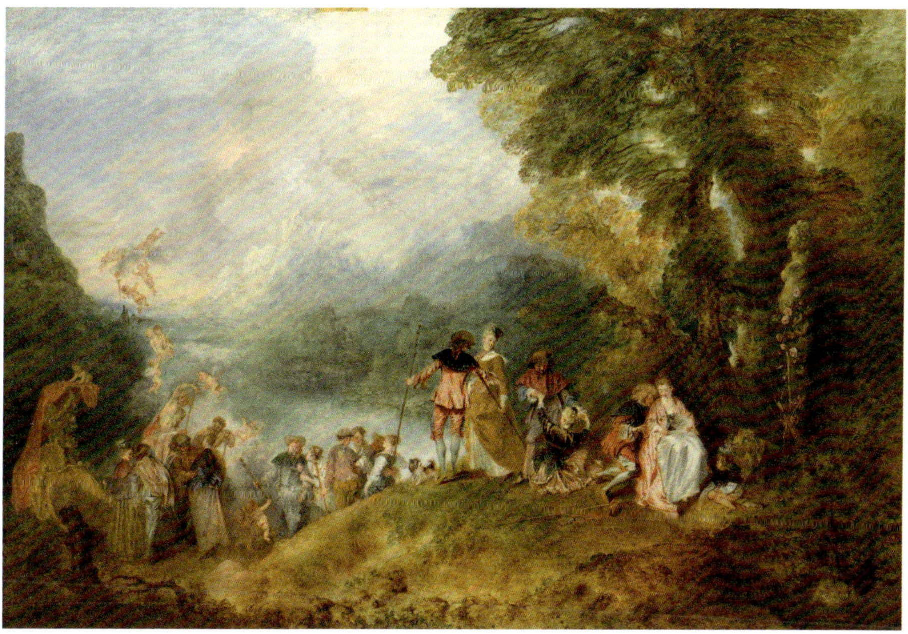

Jean-Antoine Watteau: L'Embarquement pour Chytere, 1712-17
Oil on canvas, 129 x 194 cm. Musée du Louvre

While *putti* gracefully and playfully flitter about, another *putto*, seated at the far right, is urging the two lovers for whom the idea of departing has not yet become real. From this point, in separate movements as in a film strip, the notion of an ideal world of love falls apart. With just a toe in the 18th century, this is radical and modern, and as the subject of an academic piece, it marks a genre departure at the highest level.

It is this representation of transformative departures, in academic registers and human relationships alike, that connects Brown's triptych to Watteau's work, not the fact that they have compositional features in common. In the Watteau, the story may still be coherent, but the party is over. Not just Goya, as Levey notes, but also the subjects in Manet's pictures, who both act in the scene and address the beholder, are only a moment away. This is the beginning of the cognitive space in which Brown works. "There's never really one story. There are different incidents within a painting. I think more of flashes of story,"[10] the artist says.

In Western art history more generally, Brown's triptych and its title hold truths about the time *after* the time when the grand narratives of the history-painting format could still credibly be held up and kept in place. Today, however, the world is terrifyingly our own. There are actors in the tableau, but the story is missing. *And with Whom* – genders and roles are unstable, and at no point do the gazes and bodies converge in a way that makes the action comprehensible to us. It is simply not clear why these people are together. Again, Brown works from a wealth of different realities: from her head, from contemporary social and political events, from pop culture, art history and the no less real object field of oil paint and brushwork. For Brown, things emerge on the artwork's own material terms.

Homeless and Faceless

Like many painters, Brown has a fondness for historical works. She has made studies – rehearsals of sorts, on paper[11] – from the old masters up to the advent of modernism in the mid-19th century. Almost nothing after that, interestingly. The time *after* Bosch and *after* Degas, as she titles her drawings, also effectively becomes *her* epoch, the afterlife where she lives alongside painters like Max Beckmann, Willem de Kooning, Joan Mitchell, Philip Guston and Francis Bacon, as well as those of her own generation. Generally speaking, she shares with these artists the premise of being left with mere rudiments of grand compositions, with restless gazes, mad laughter, occasional heroism and bodies whose disjointed desire no longer describes a complete situation. Hence this essay's openly theatrical title, "Heroic-Pornographic." Hence also, I would venture, the tableau format Brown employs, whether setting her scenes in pastoral English landscapes, in various interiors or near water, as in her big triptych.

A few years back, working from the famous cover photo of the Jimi Hendrix album *Electric Ladyland*,[12] Brown did a series of paintings of women looking out at the viewer. This at once condensed and spatially nebulous group of nude women, she says, was still haunting her when she made *Where, When, How Often and with Whom*. These women, too, appear to be near water. But while the figures in the triptych are spread across the whole scenery, the opposite principle reigns in the *Ladyland* works. This very boudoir version of Géricault's *The Raft of Medusa* takes us much closer to the figures, though, symptomatically, not in terms of their characterization. In a common Brown move, their faces are in various states of motion, masking, dissolution or outright facelessness. As in the case of the seated figure on the beach in the big triptych, with its hasty brushwork where the face should be, the gesture is active, miles from the defacement of an existing, photographically mediated representation.

Name That Tune, from 2012, like the other works in the *Ladyland* series, is like an erotic party game with implicit dead seriousness, the figures entangle and untangle in a Noël Coward-ly bacchanalia slash-massacre of gender and persona. The restlessness is reflected in our reading of the work. Almost impossible for the viewer to nail down and memorize, it veers dramatically between momentary, local clarity and the afocal – not unlike the experience of looking at a classic Pollock drip painting.

The 20th-century back catalogue of course includes countless depictions of distorted faces, among them some that inspire Brown, Bacon more than anyone. But by expressing something central about her own time, Brown's works – *Name That Tune* is an excellent example – constitute "a general mood of accidental commonality."[13] Linking to her early works, as well, we could say that her art derives its character not from its erotic content but from its evocation of physical instability, fragility and transfiguration. While her variously shipwrecked figures of ambiguous intent loosely approximate Watteau's frieze of figures, the non-places of pornography rudely situate us in our own time. Nowhere more than in porn do the sensations of facelessness and homelessness so profoundly come together.

The Valley is a series of photos by the American photographer Larry Sultan, showing various locations in California, where the American porn industry shoots its films. While Brown's paintings, as mentioned, pack a wallop in today's world, in part by being imperfectly real, Sultan's behind-the-scenes look, his take on the industry, is perfectly unreal. He documents homes

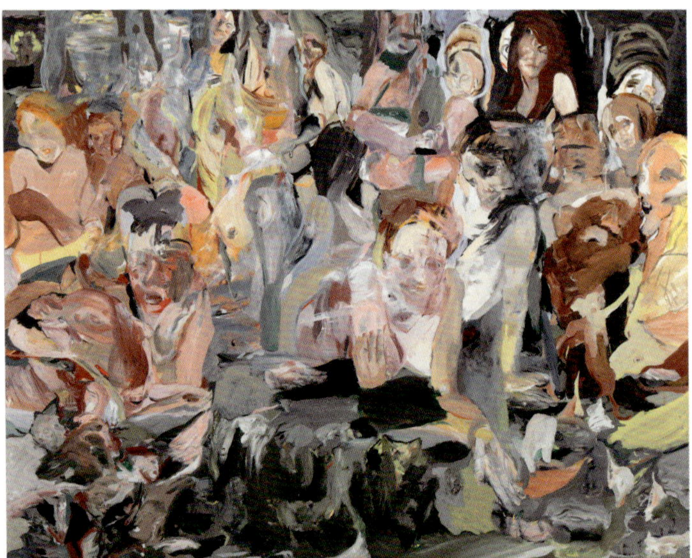

Name That Tune, 2012

where “it’s as if one family went on vacation for a few days, leaving everything in the house intact, and another family, an odd assembly of unrelated adults, has temporarily taken up residence.”[14]

Fallout and Invasion

The homelessness pervading Sultan’s work runs deeper than his restless souls in generic mansions. Specifically, Sultan exposes a person’s inability to recognize themselves and appear whole and undivided, and to establish firm connections between mind and body. In Brown’s triptych, and many of her other works, something is clearly missing or omitted, while something else has bluntly been inserted into the field of vision. Incidentally, that is the *ur*-relationship of collage to the world and a condition of modernity. Here, we will briefly spotlight two photographic works: Sultan’s *Havenhurst Drive* (1999) from the aforementioned series *The Valley* and Thomas Hirschhorn’s *Pixel-Collage n°14* (2015).

Sultan’s image conveys ordinariness but also a pervasive mood of dissonance – a tragicomic and placeless moment, as if the invisible man from the H.G. Wells novel of that name were assigned a lesser role, culminating in the lower left corner of the picture. A tableau, but almost a collage, as well, in which body parts taken from somewhere “else” are intertwined and taken apart, ironically-heroically-pornographically.

Hirschhorn’s pixel collages present an expanded view of pictorial construction. In his view, today’s use of filters for blurring parts of images creates an interesting grey area between different levels of reality. Blurring in general, he points out, lends images a new kind of authenticity, despite their omission of information. In their horrific, painterly blurring of slick fashion shots, juxtaposed or intervening with raw realities, often including bullet-riddled corpses, his pixel collages open up a new layer of interpretation. Something is missing, while something is suddenly, insensitively layered on top of something else. As Brown remarks, “visual inconclusiveness is symptomatic of contemporary experience. Something that’s just glimpsed seems more real than something that's fully described."[15] Plainly, the photographic practices of Sultan and Hirschhorn touch on some of the same things her work manifests in painting.

Handsome Stranger will be a final insert here. This gory, painterly tour de force by Brown is yet another jocular and horrifying image of dissonance as a fundamental premise of the story of the human condition. The painting has everything: severed body parts, erotic drive and arrested narratives, both as subject matter and in the painting's physical expression. When, where, how often and with whom, to be sure, but also a unique, new facelessness creating distance everywhere in daily, social life, between real faces and all the faces we cannot see. There is an imminent risk that this digital facelessness will dominate human relationships, now and in the future. In Brown's oil-based vortex of glazy strokes and aspects of human anatomy – including, prominently, eyes – old-world remnants, among them Hieronymus Bosch monsters, can be discerned alongside the fragmented desire of pornography and, notably, figurative painting in its modern arena.

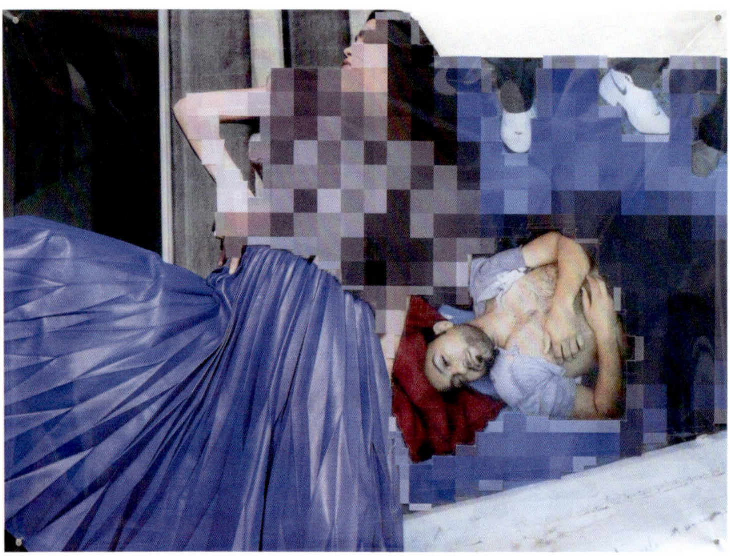

Thomas Hirschhorn: Pixel-Collage n°14, 2015. Prints, plastic sheet, tape, 33 x 45 cm
Courtesy of the artist and Galerie Chantal Crousel, Paris

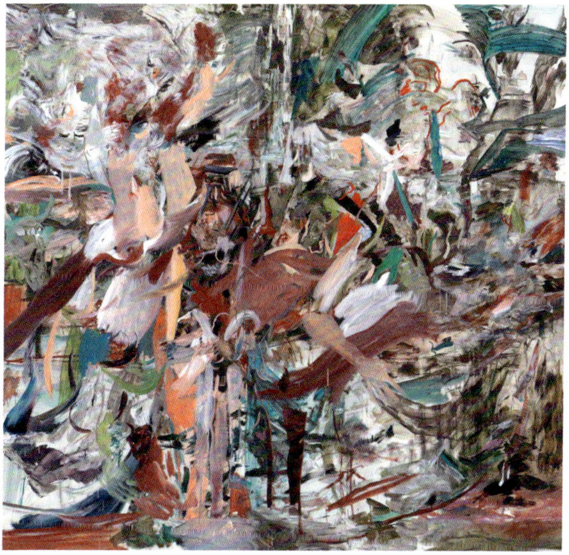

Handsome Stranger, 2010

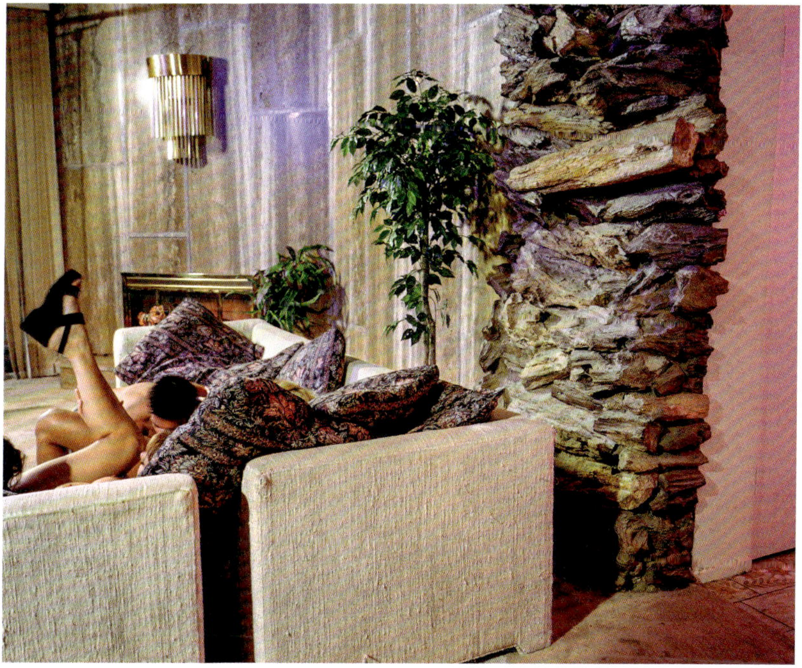

Larry Sultan: Havenhurst Drive, 1999. From the series The Valley
Chromogenic print, flush-mounted, 73.3 × 88.6 cm

An Odd Assembly of Unrelated Adults

Embarkations, luncheons on the green and the highly topical disruption on the edge of water, as well as, inevitably, the universal migration crises, are all at odds with reason. The 18th-century battle between reason and passion never ended. Considering the ongoing sense of meltdown, collapse and disjunction, as the artist describes the relationship between figuration and abstraction in her painting,[16] it is not hard to see Brown's art, in Terry R. Meyers' words, "as the beneficiary of these struggles (of the past), but she hasn't taken them lightly or, worse yet, as a progression. That, today, is a limitation, a capitulation to a desire for art historical order that important painting always resists. She has stuck to painting, reminding us in no uncertain terms why it will not go away."[17]

The old masters are obviously a source of inspiration for Brown, and the modernist impact history remains an active presence in her art, as well. Just as plainly, in and with her painting, she is constantly transfiguring contemporary observations and crises. In *When, Where, How Often and with Whom*, restlessness and politics collide with the familiar presence of painting. Using the image of the suffering victim at Iraq's Abu Ghraib prison as subject matter would not be like her, but a woman exposed in public space and later vanishing has its place. Identity politics is not an obvious discourse for Brown, whereas facelessness is an all but overriding concern of her art. Gender politics are not subject matter for her, while in her tableaux the ongoing dissolution and performance of gender roles is always in play.

On the beach, where the present and something of the past are brought together and derive meaning from each other, even as both are distorted on the spectrum between figuration and abstraction, Cecily Brown's world is insane and terrifyingly normal.

1. James Lawrence, "Time Laid Bare," in *Cecily Brown*, Gagosian Gallery, 2013, p. 21. **2**. Alongside *A Day! Help! Help! Another Day!*, another painting from 2017, this is Brown's biggest work to date. *Where Do We Come From? What Are We? Where Are We Going?* is the title of a famous and equally panoramic painting by Gauguin, which Brown is obviously familiar with and which she plays with, as she puts it, in this context. **3**. See the interview by Lærke Rydal Jørgensen and the author in this catalogue, p. 80. **4**. Brown's fellow painter Daniel Richter, in conversation with Poul Erik Tøjner, in *Lonely Old Slogans*, Louisiana Museum of Modern Art, 2016, p. 76. **5**. In the interview with the author, in Piermont, 8 August 2018, the artist exclaimed, "I can't believe I actually said those three words" ("the human condition"). **6**. Terry R. Meyers, in a 2015 essay on Brown, refers to Willem de Kooning's statement about being "a slipping glimpser," in *The Sleep Around and the Lost and Found*, CFA, Berlin, 2015, p. 7. **7**. Interview with the author, Piermont, 8 August 2018. **8**. An older engraving from Watteau shows an unmistakable scene of embarkation for Cythera. **9**. Michael Levey, in *Rococo to Revolution: Major Trends in Eighteenth-Century Painting*. Thames and Hudson, 1986, pp. 57-64. **10**. Lawrence, 2013, p. 9. Lawrence is citing Robert Enright, "Paint Whisperer: An Interview with Cecily Brown," *Border Crossings*, Vol. 24, No. 1 (February 2005), p. 49. **11**. Clair Gilman describes Brown's practice, in the *Rehearsal* catalogue from the Drawing Center, New York, 2016, including how Brown's works offer fragmented moments rather than coherency. **12**. British edition of the album. **13**. Lawrence, p. 10. **14**. Larry Sultan, artist statement in connection with the exhibition *The Valley*, SF MoMA, 2004. **15**. Lawrence, p. 12 13. **16**. Interview with the author, Piermont, 8 August 2018. **17**. Meyers, in *The Sleep Around and the Lost and Found*, CFA, Berlin, 2015, p. 16.

Anders Kold is curator and Head of Acquisitions at the Louisiana Museum of Modern Art. He has curated numerous exhibitions at the Louisiana, among others David Hockney, Asger Jorn & Jackson Pollock, Tal R, Edward Kienholz, Yael Bartana, Rineke Dijkstra, Ed Ruscha and the current exhibition with Cecily Brown.

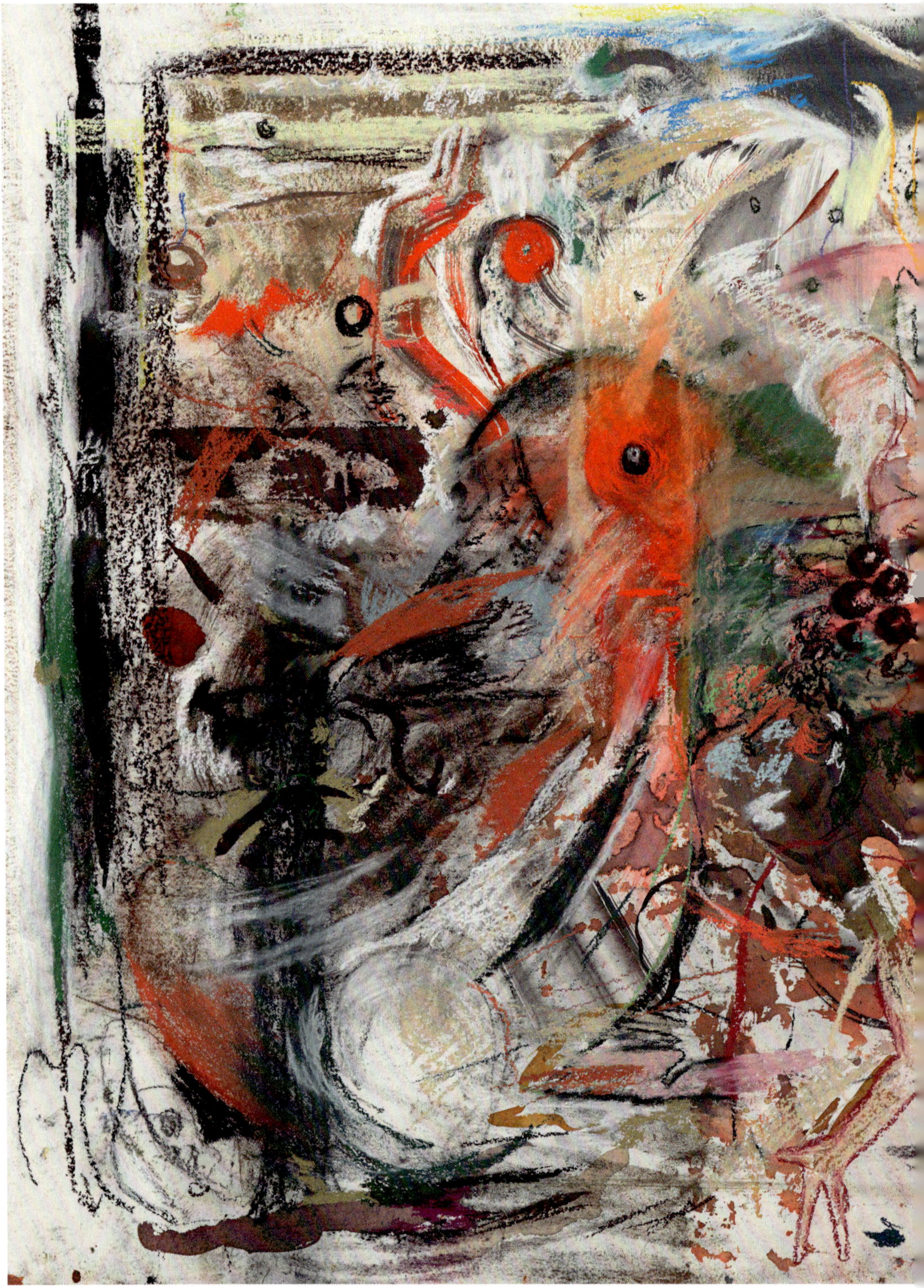

Untitled (After Bosch), 2015

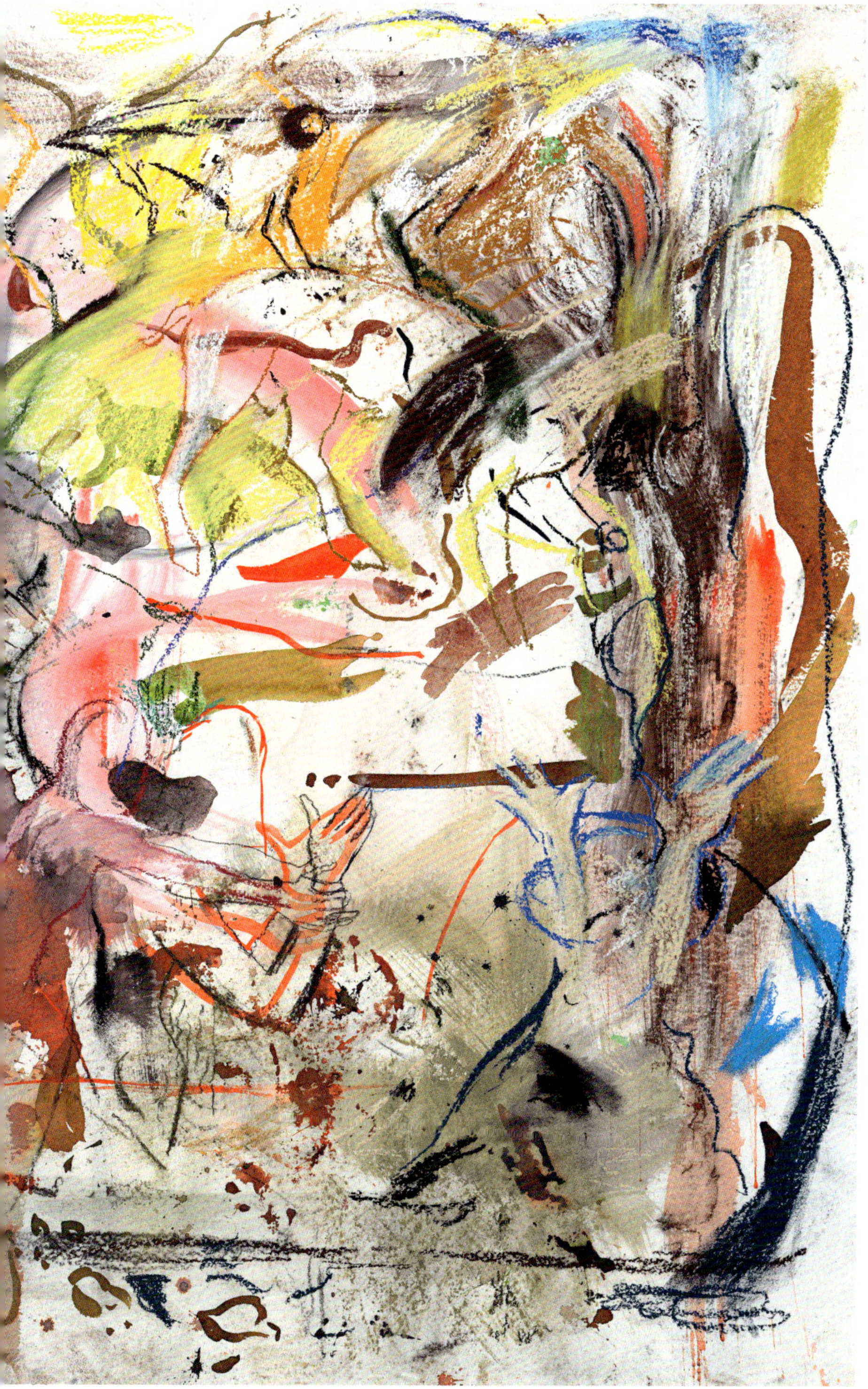

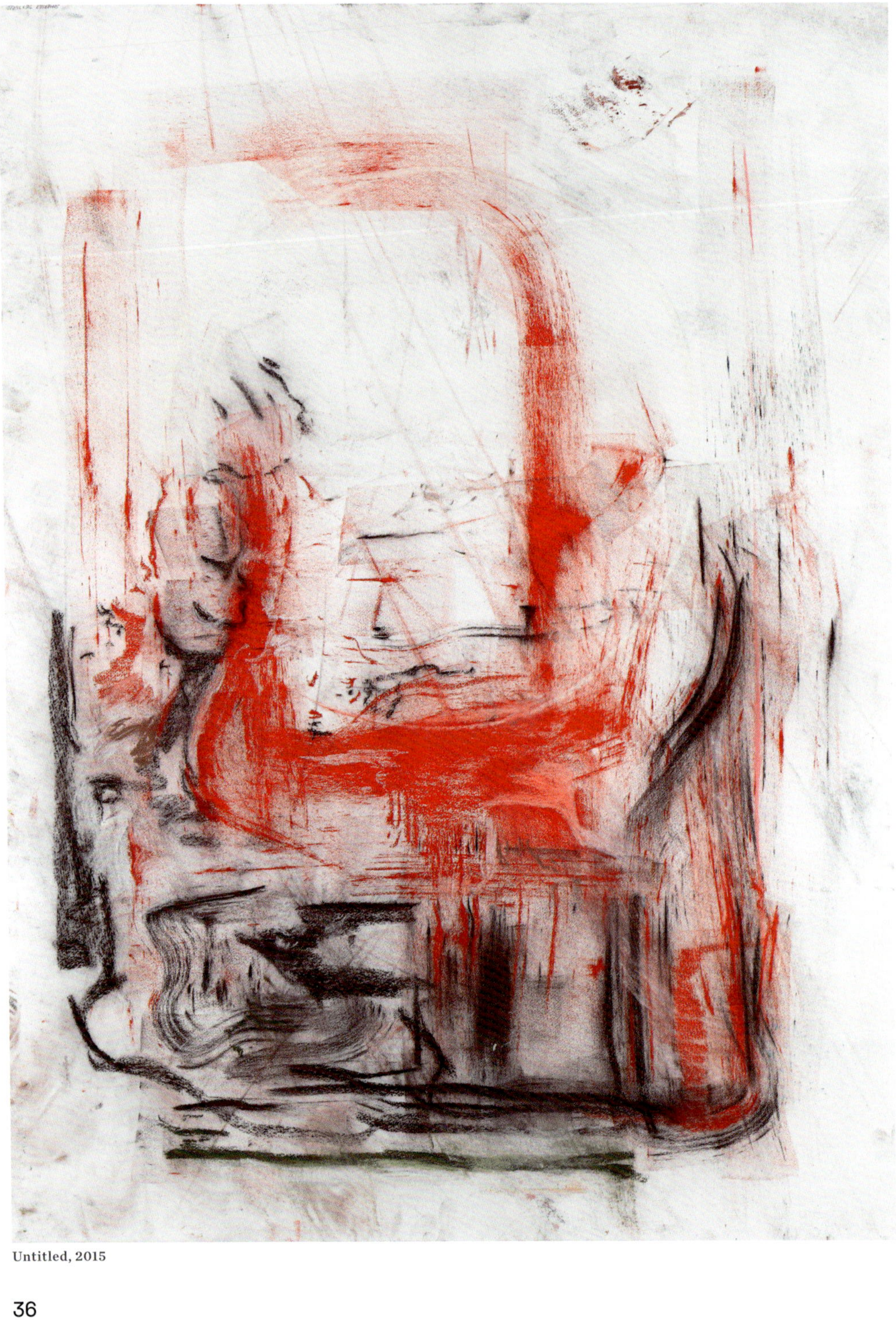

Untitled, 2015

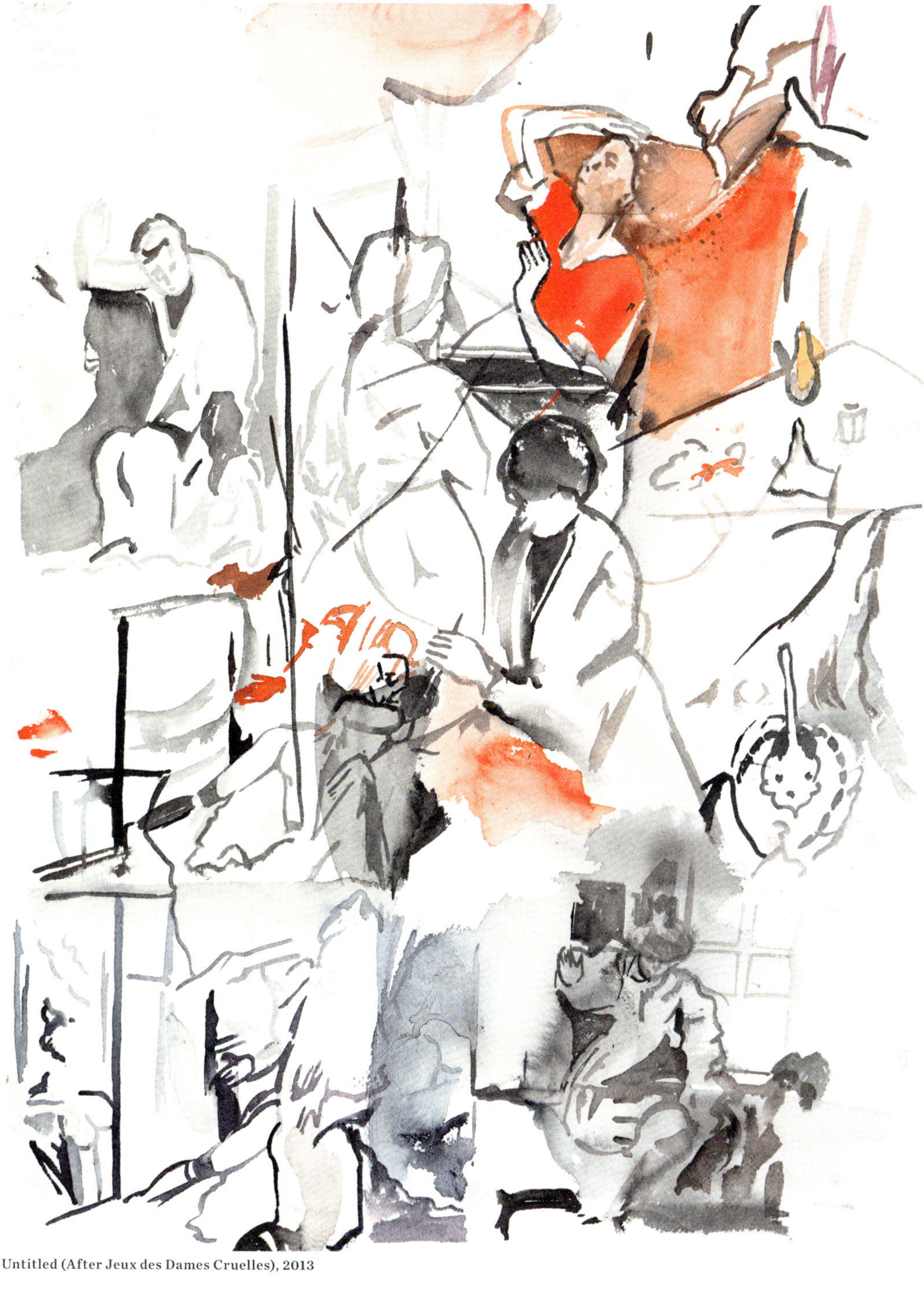

Untitled (After Jeux des Dames Cruelles), 2013

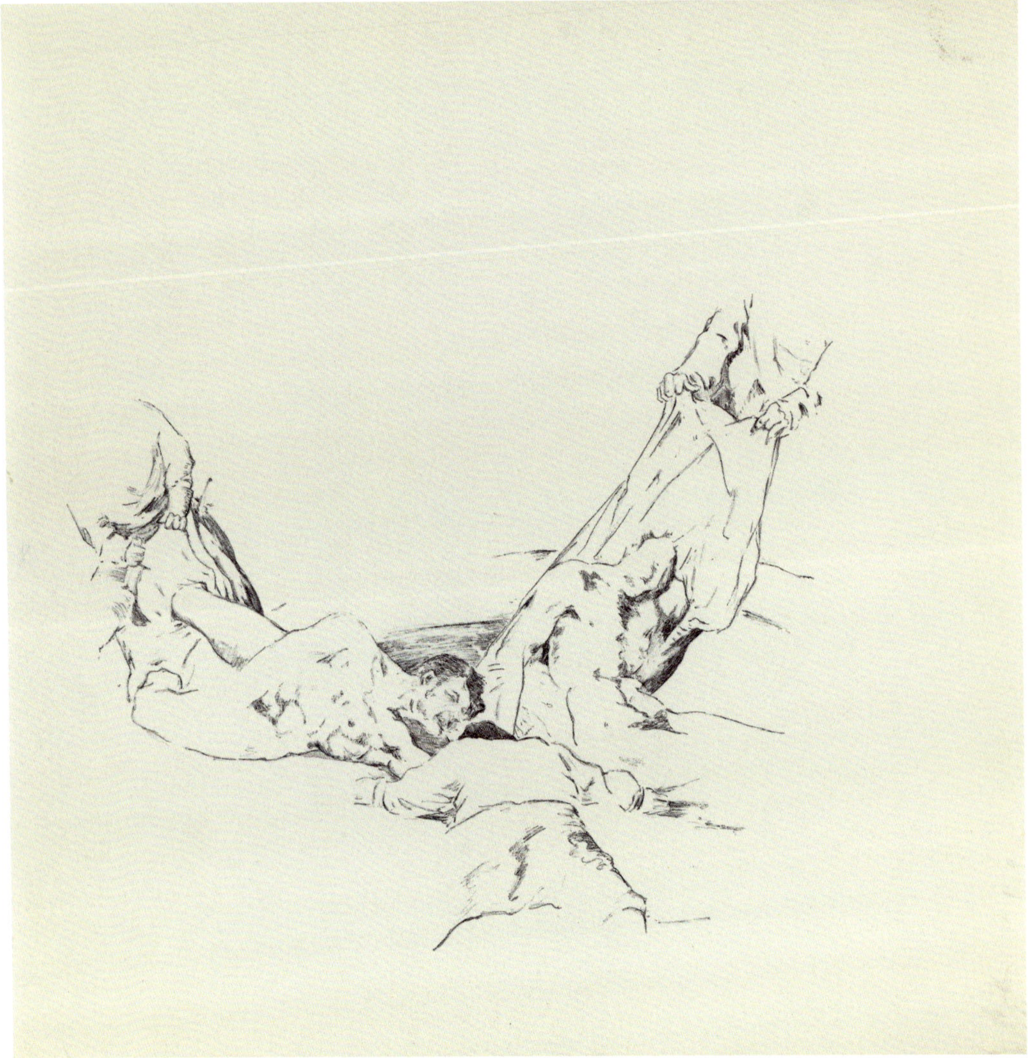

Untitled (After Goya), 1997-1998

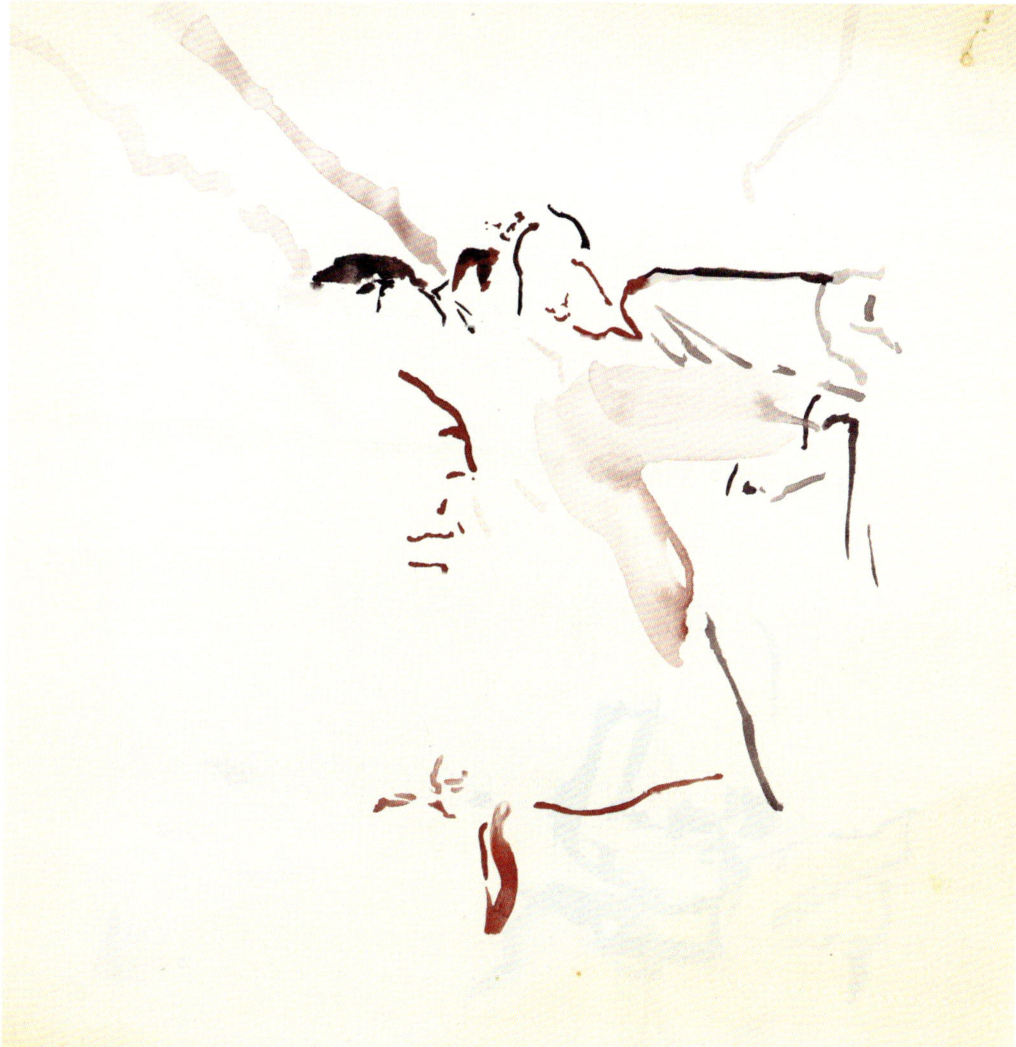

Untitled (After Jeux des Dames Cruelles), 1997-1998

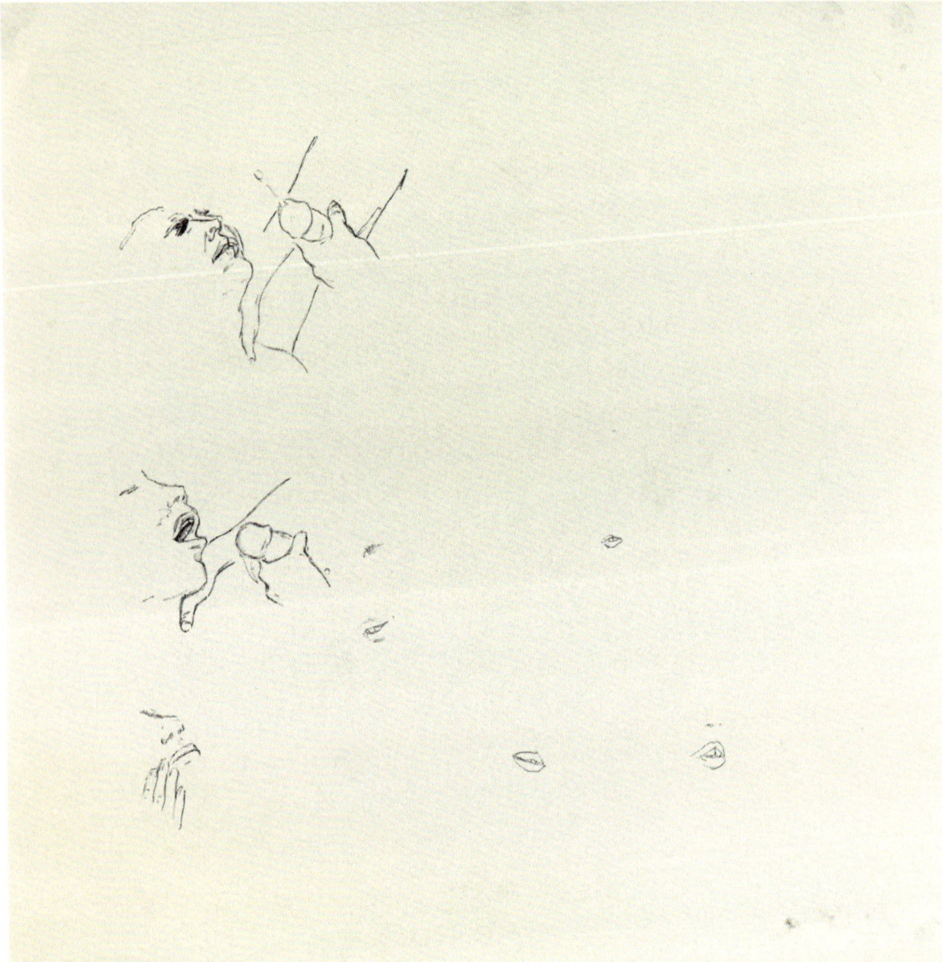

Untitled, 1998

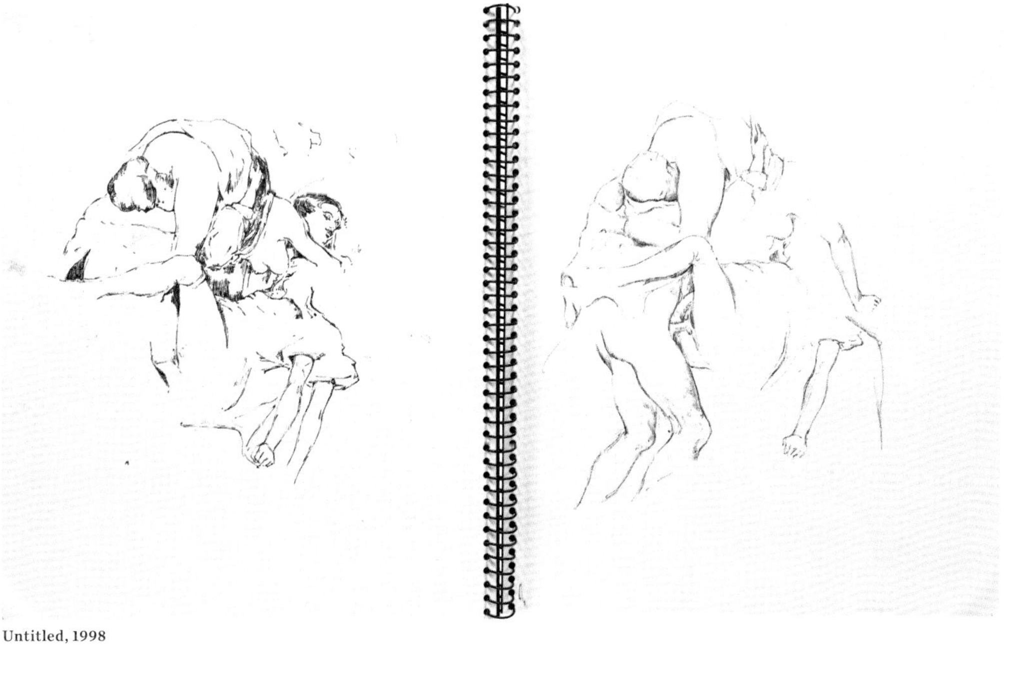

Untitled, 1998

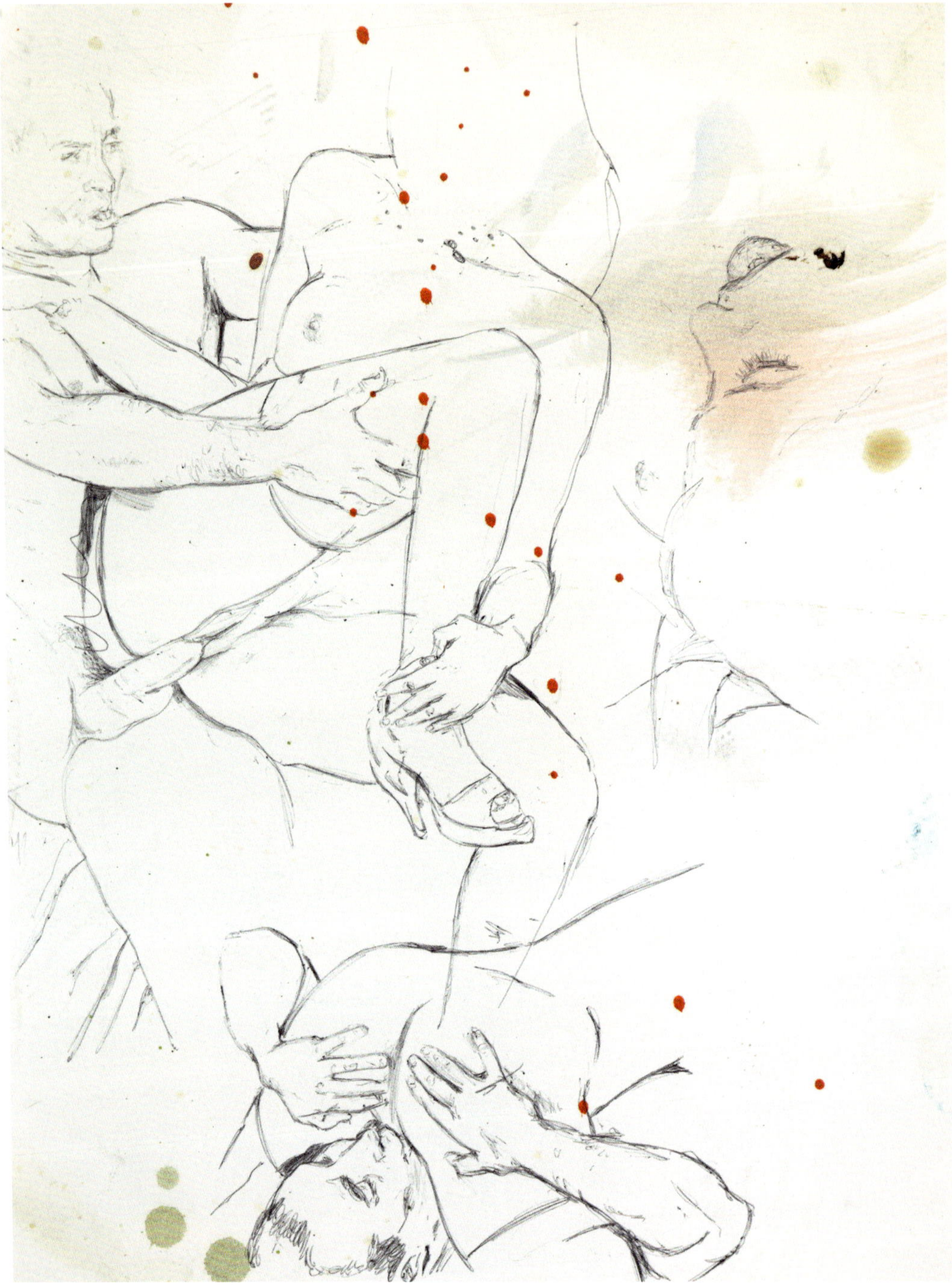

Untitled, 1998

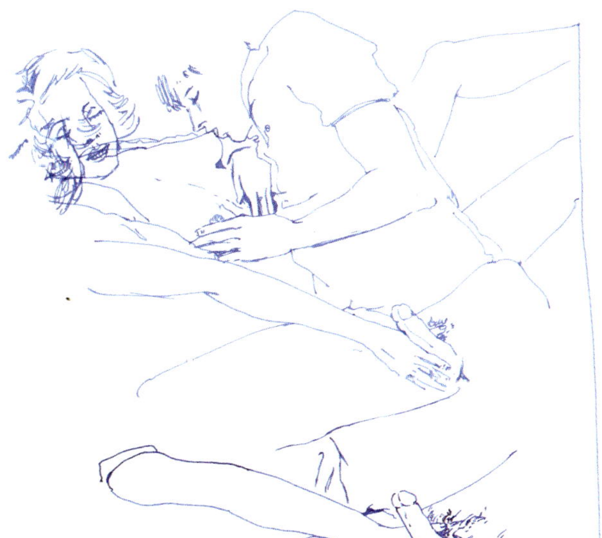

Untitled, 1998

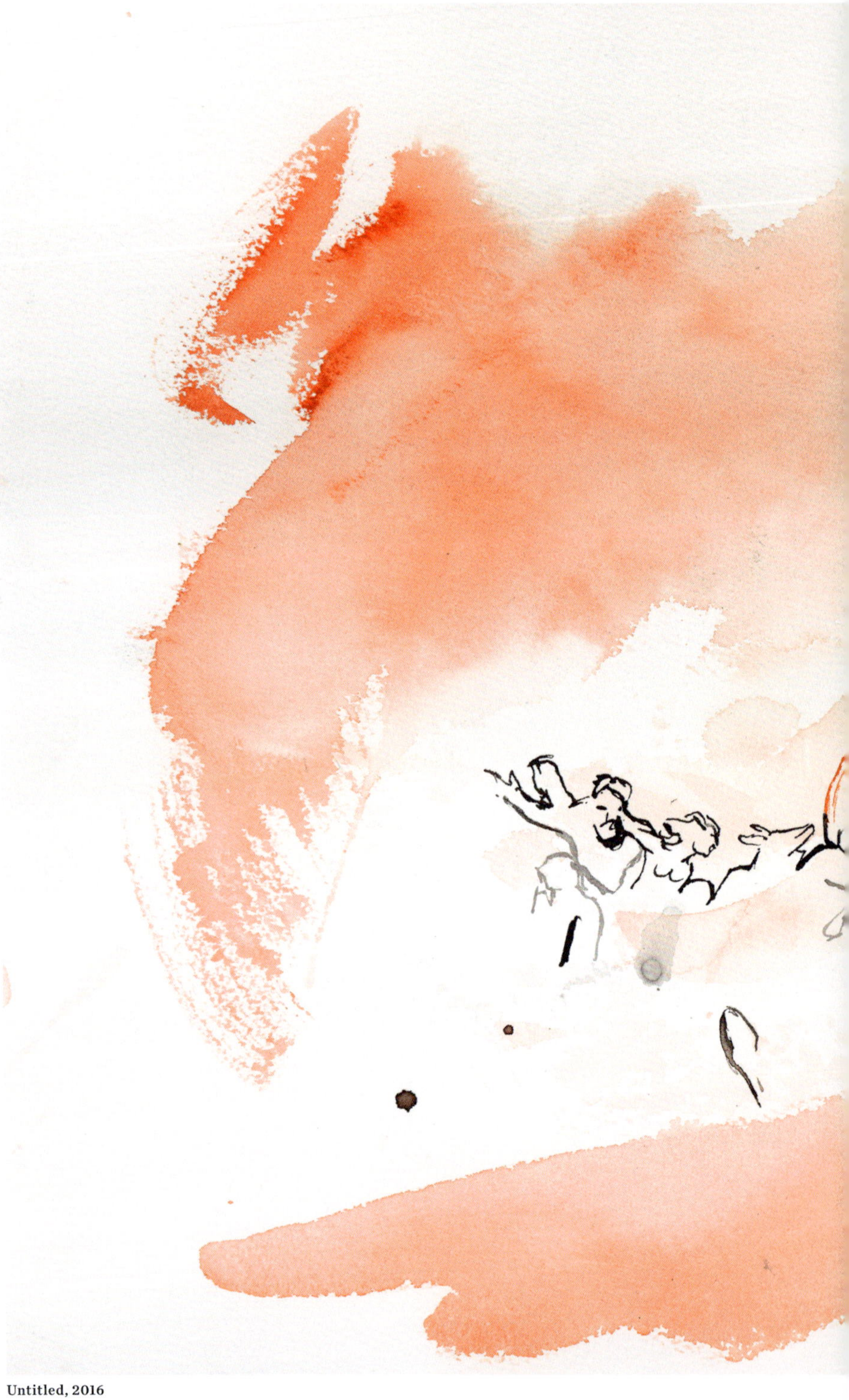

Untitled, 2016

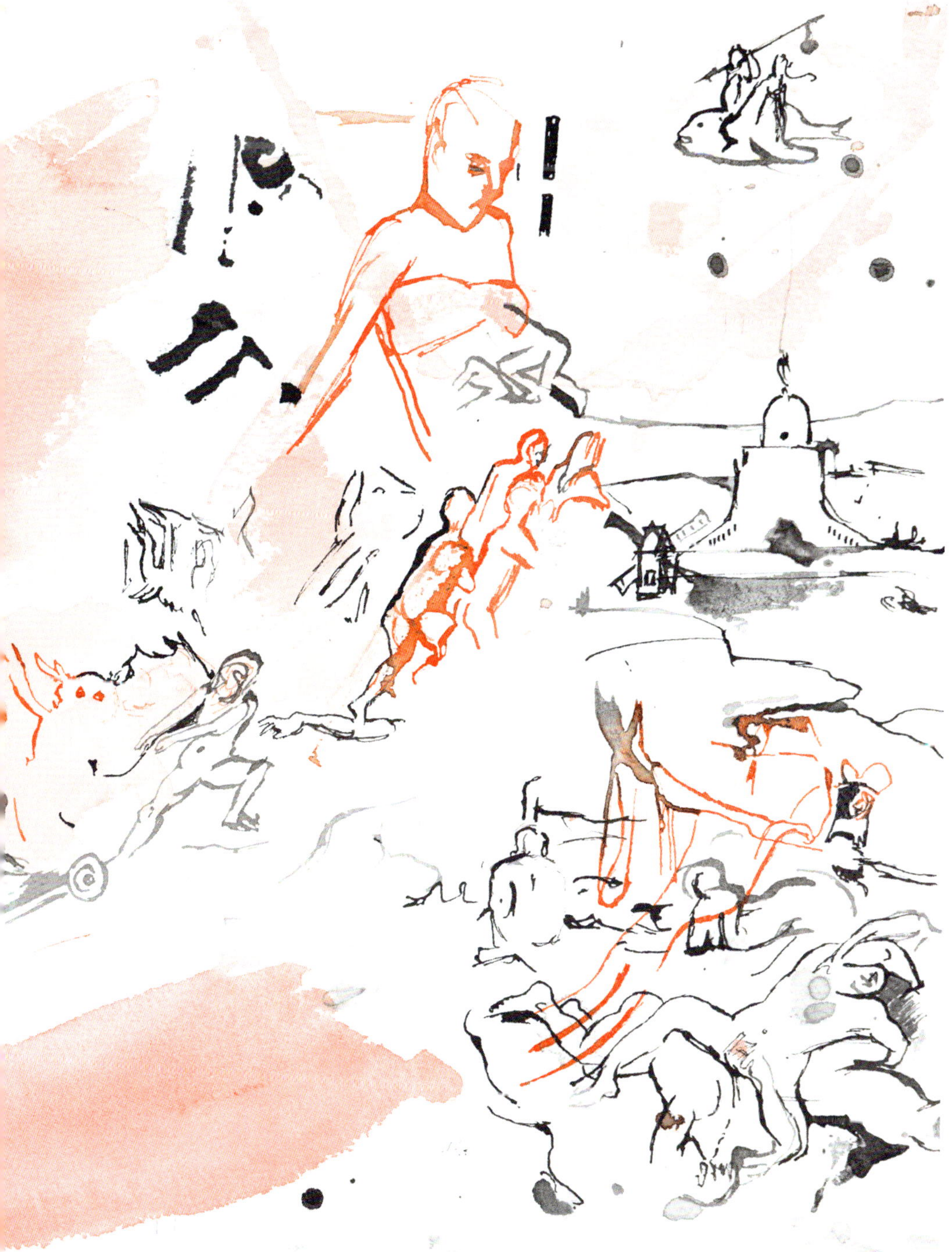

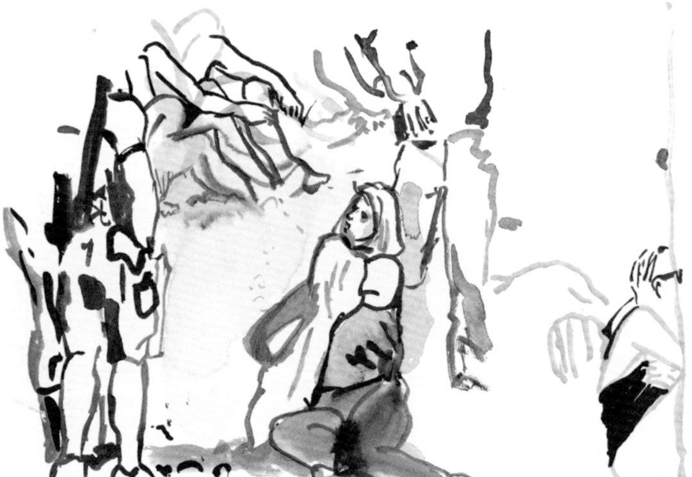

Untitled (Bather with Cops), 2017

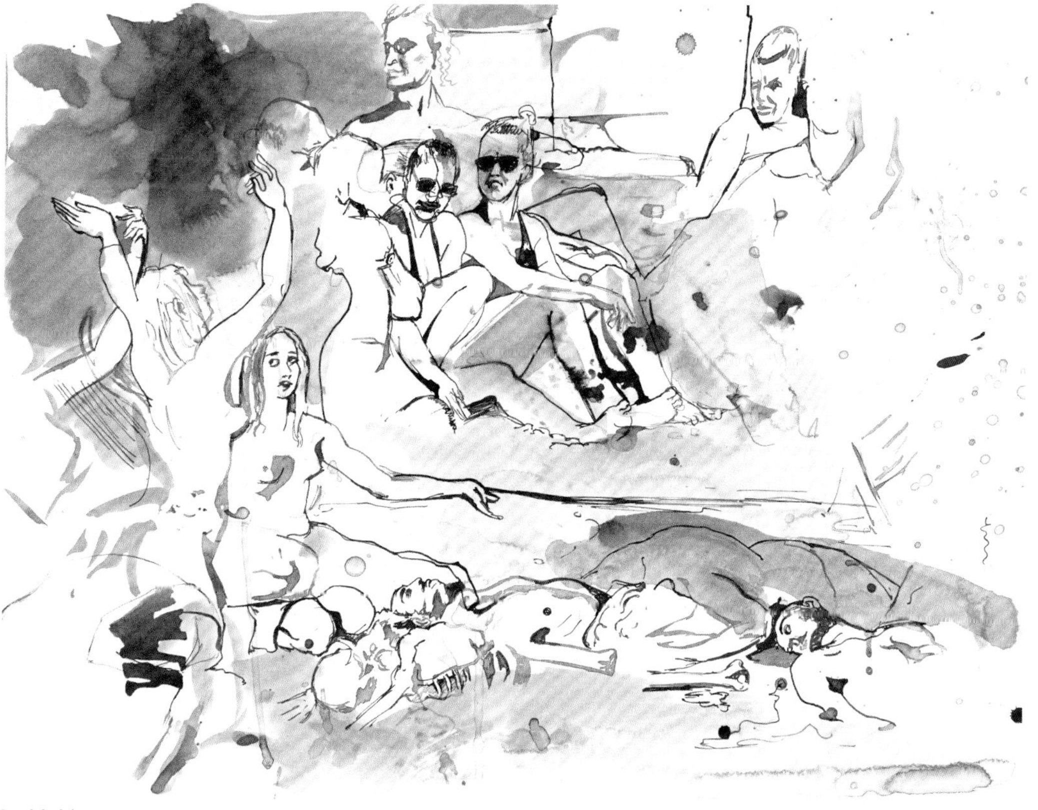

Untitled (Bather with Cops), 2017

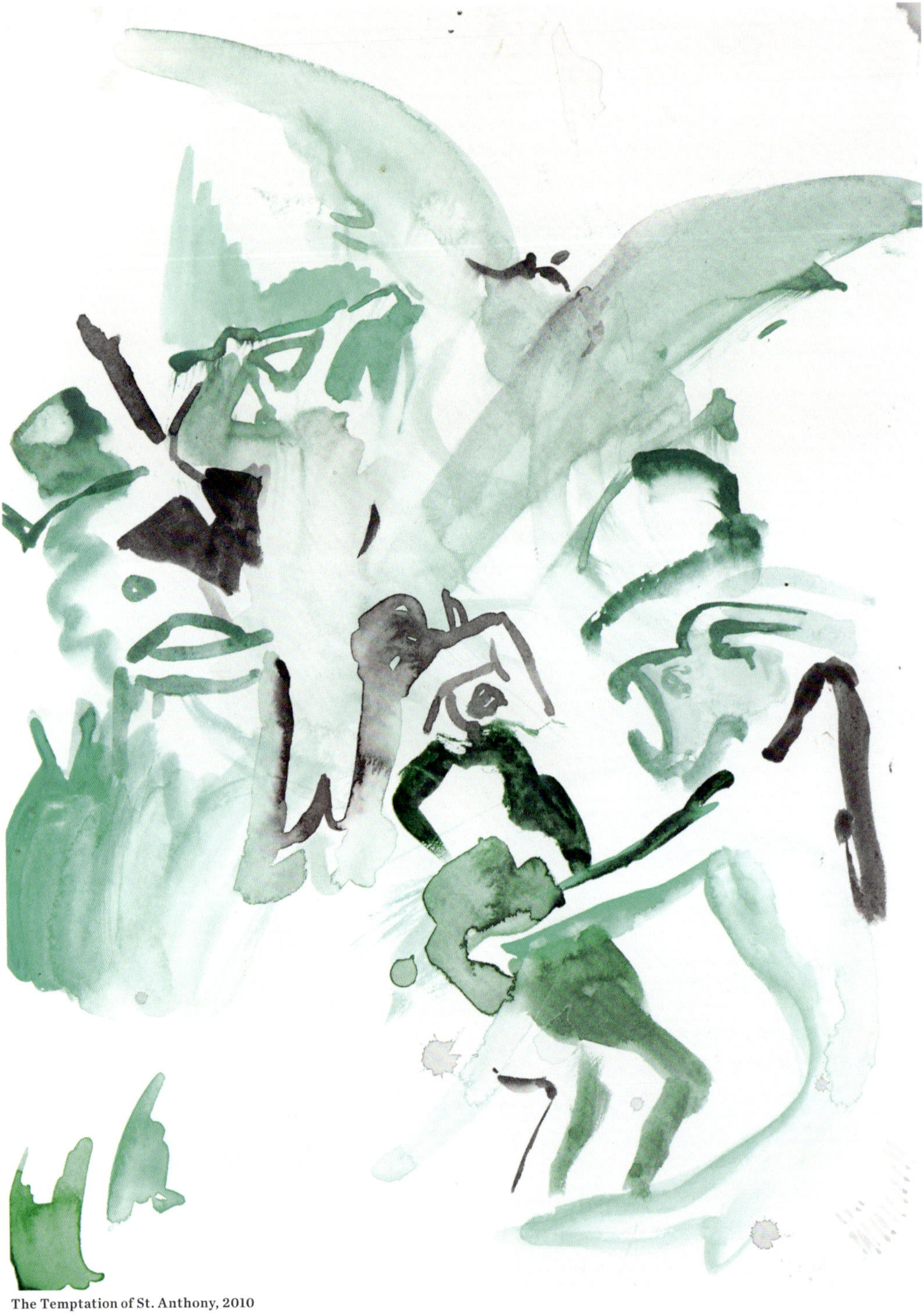

The Temptation of St. Anthony, 2010

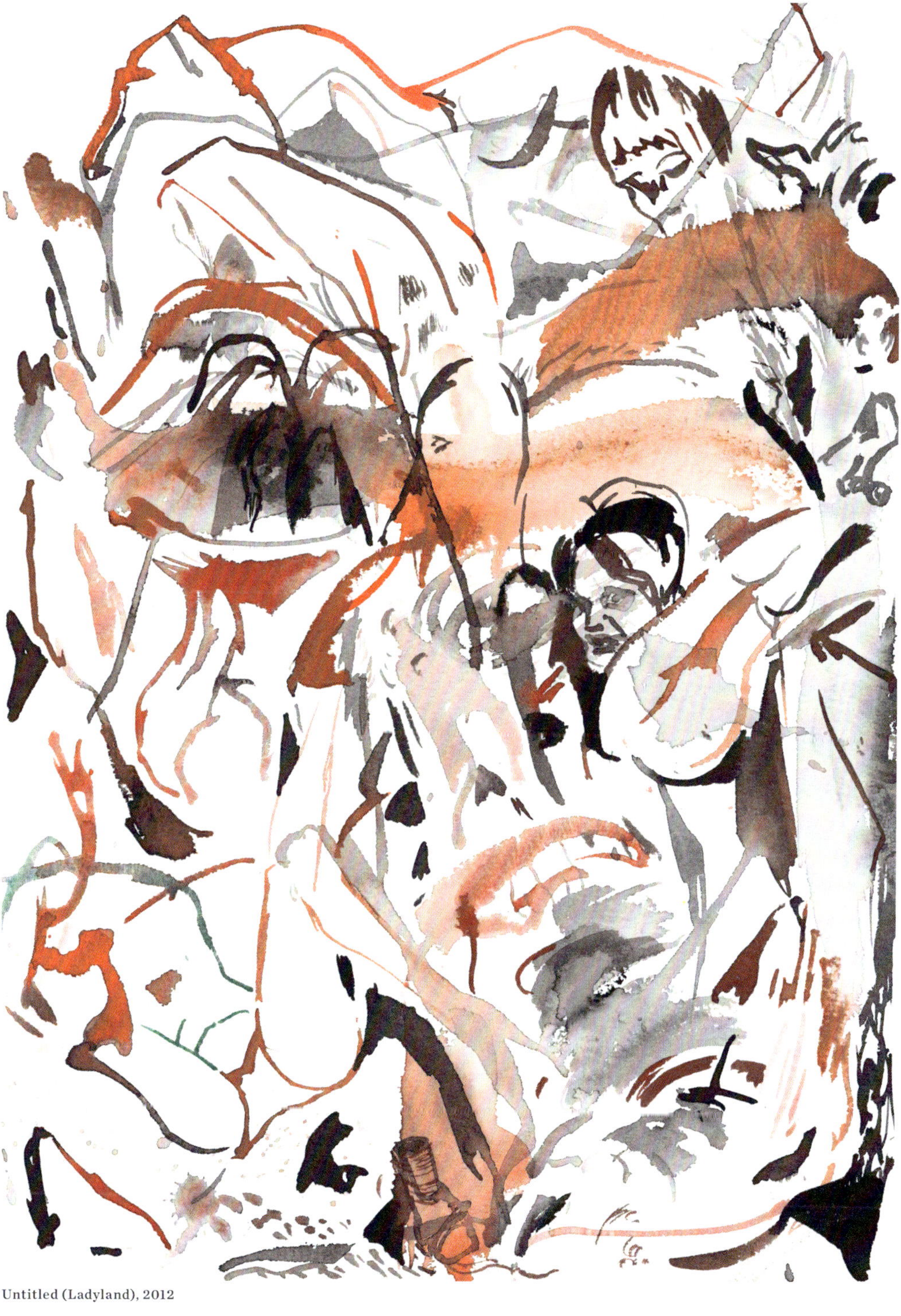

Untitled (Ladyland), 2012

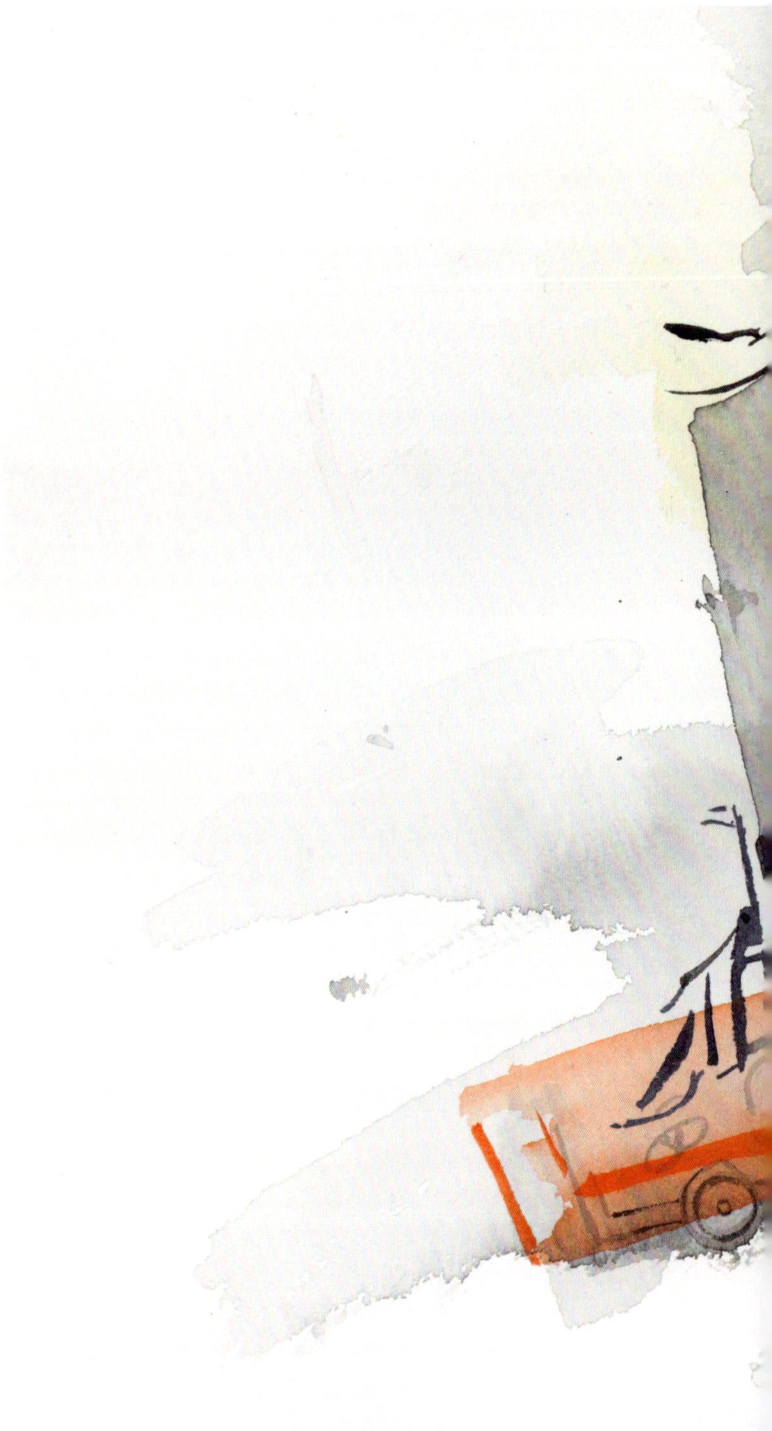

Carnival and Lent (After Bruegel), 2007

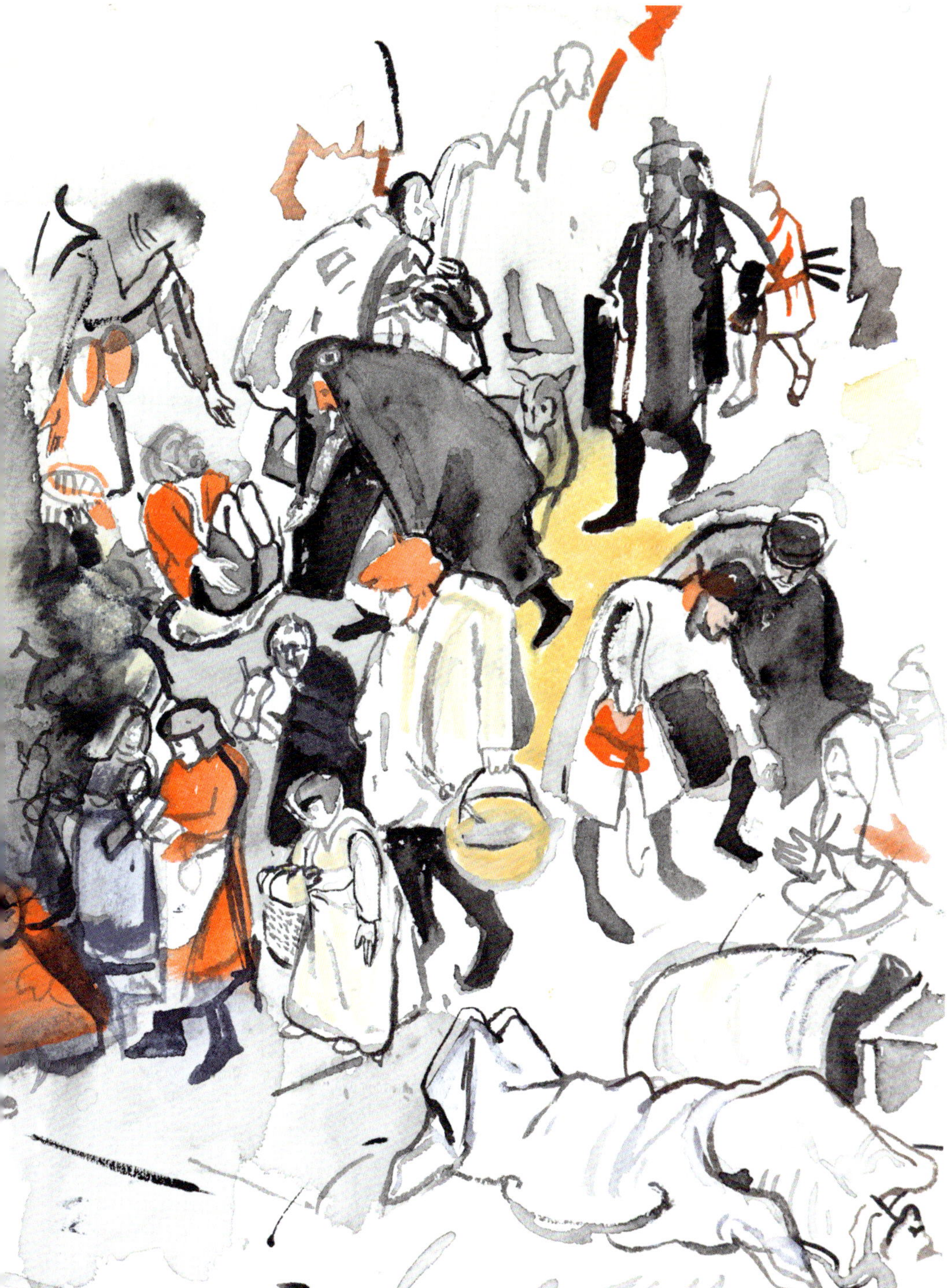

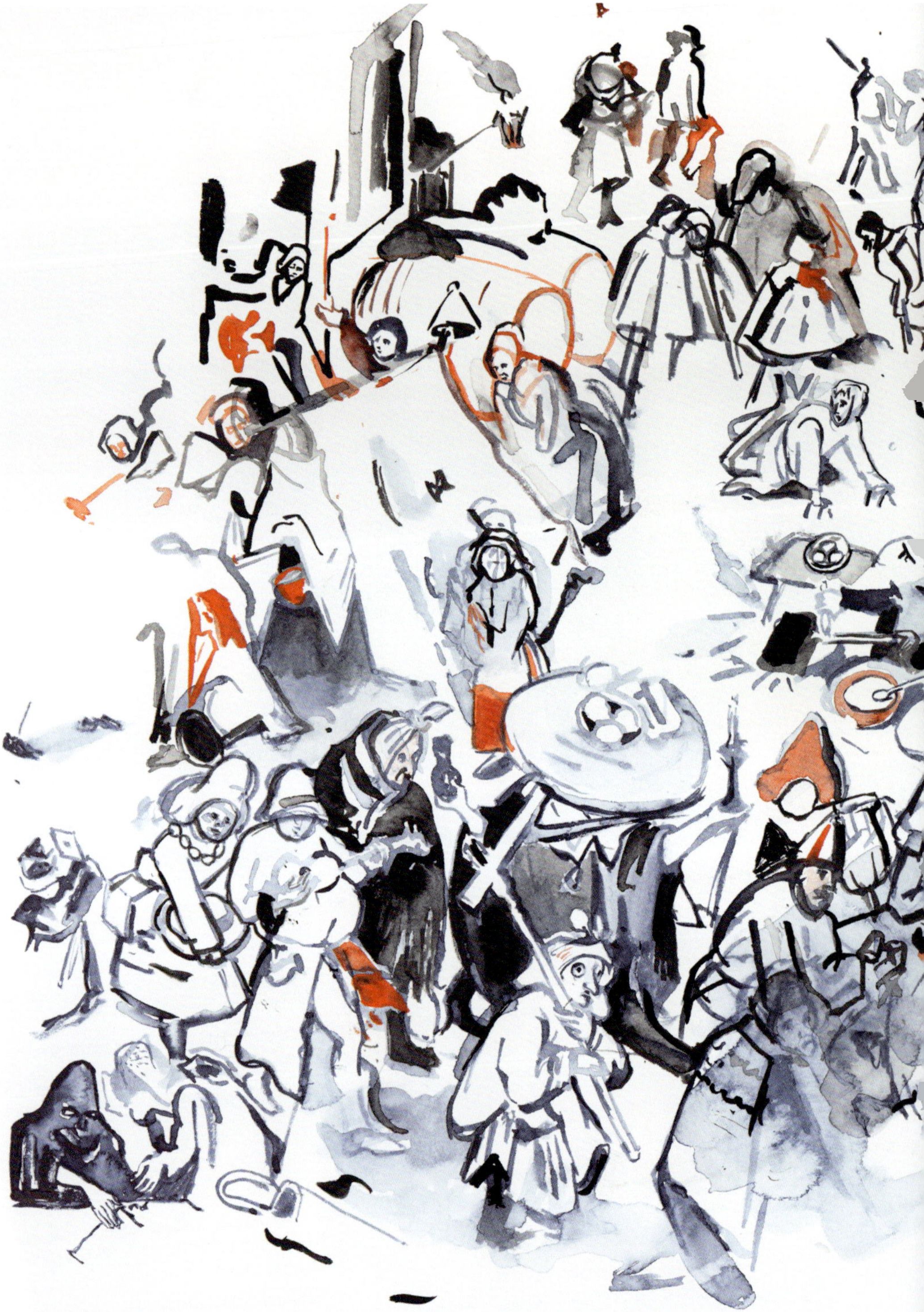

Carnival and Lent (After Bruegel), 2007

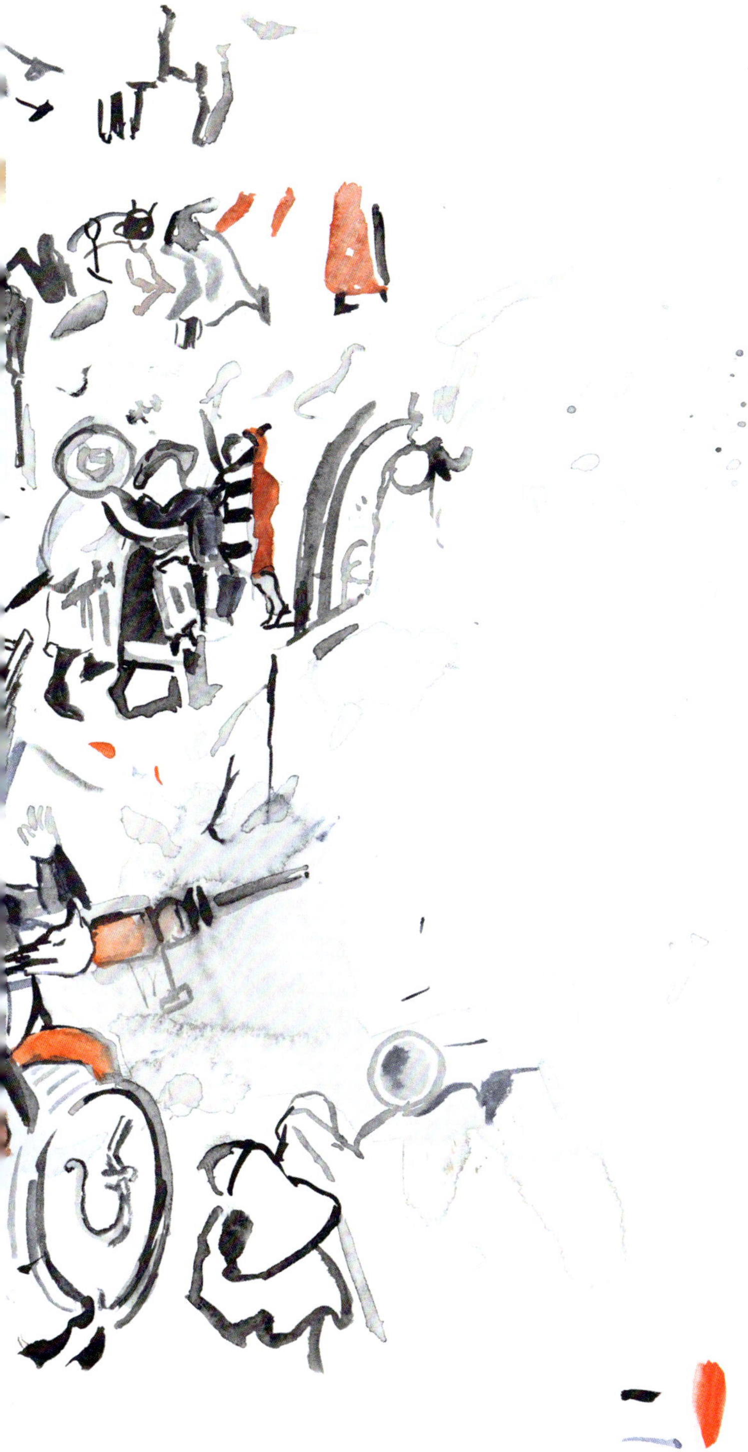

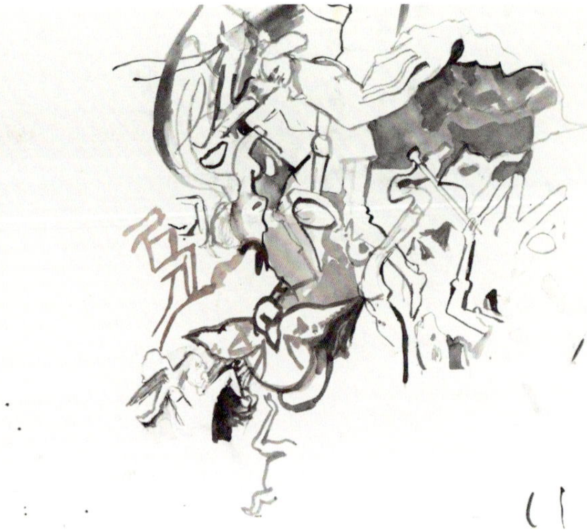

Untitled (After Bruegel), 2007

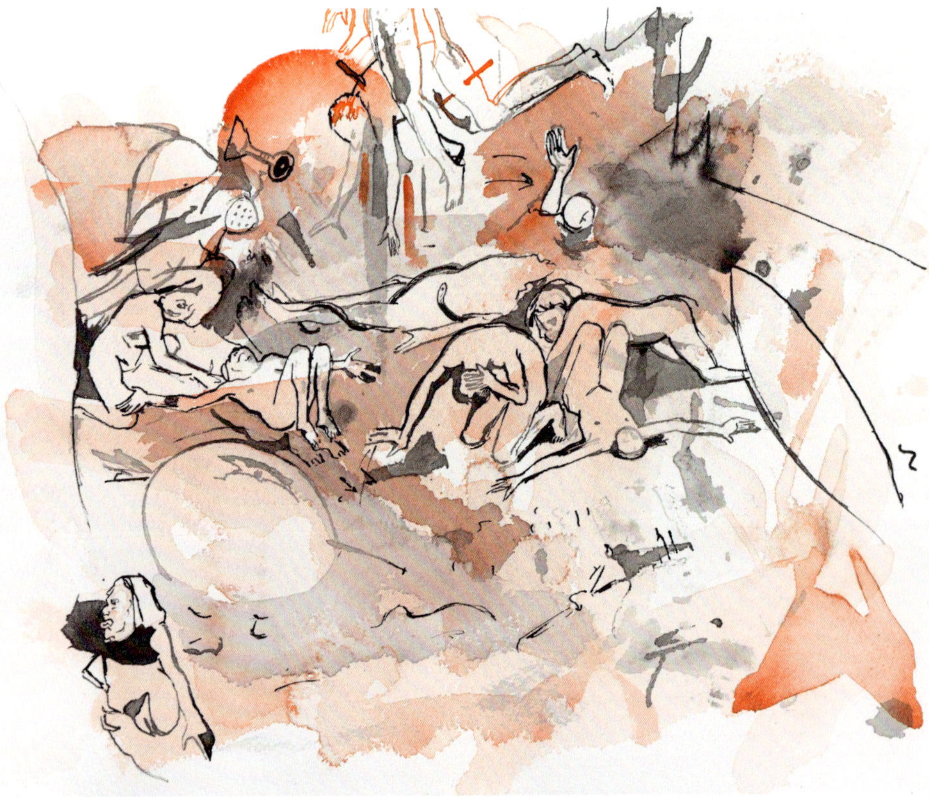

Untitled (After Bruegel), 2007

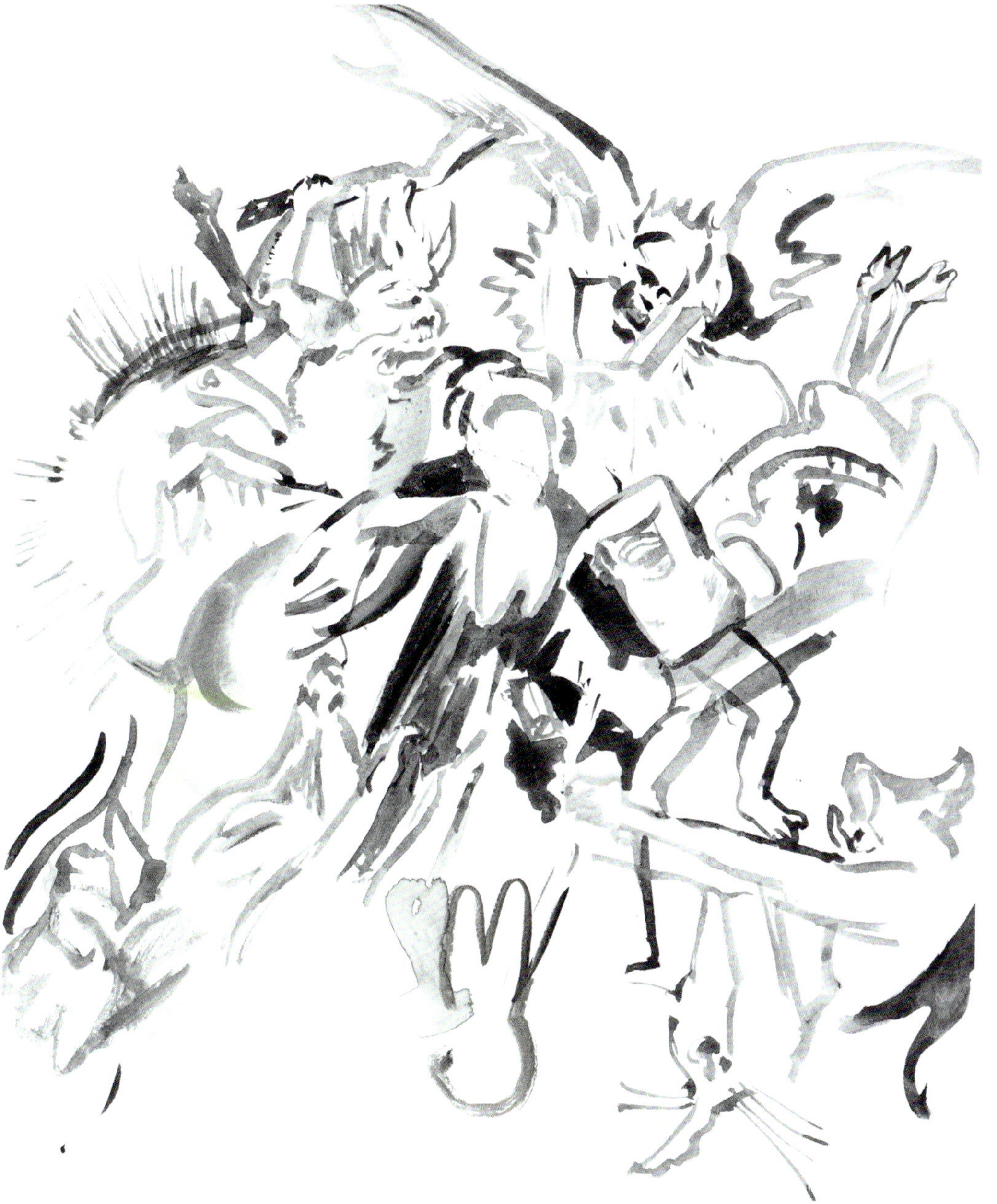

The Temptation of St. Anthony, 2010

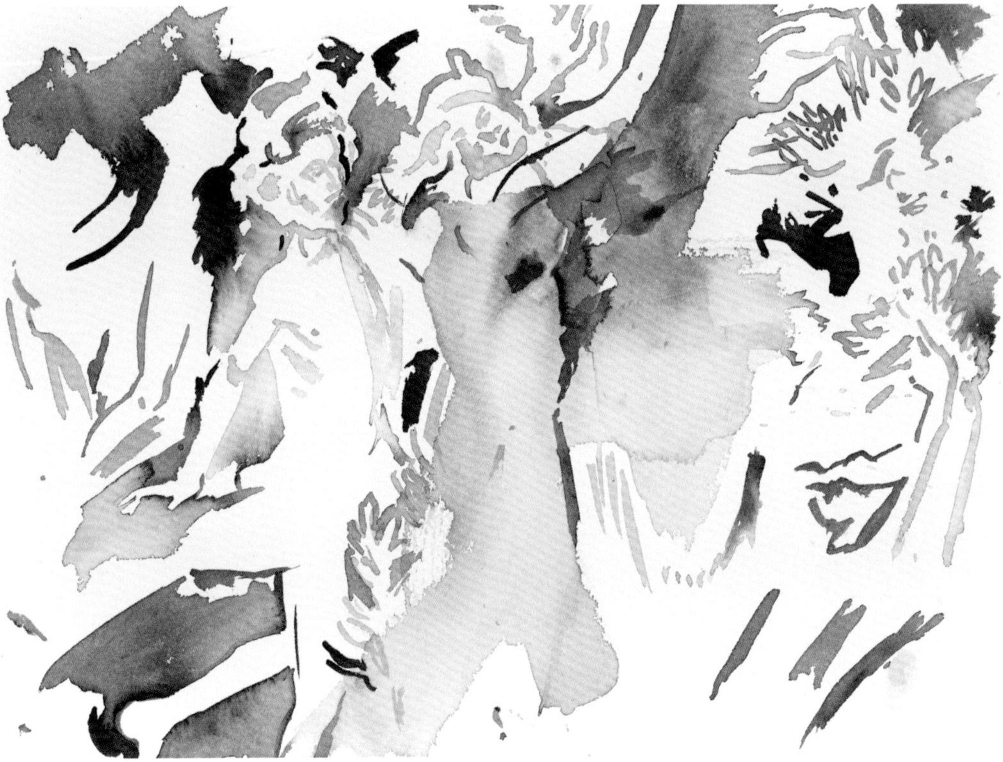

Daphne and Apollo (After Bernini), 2010

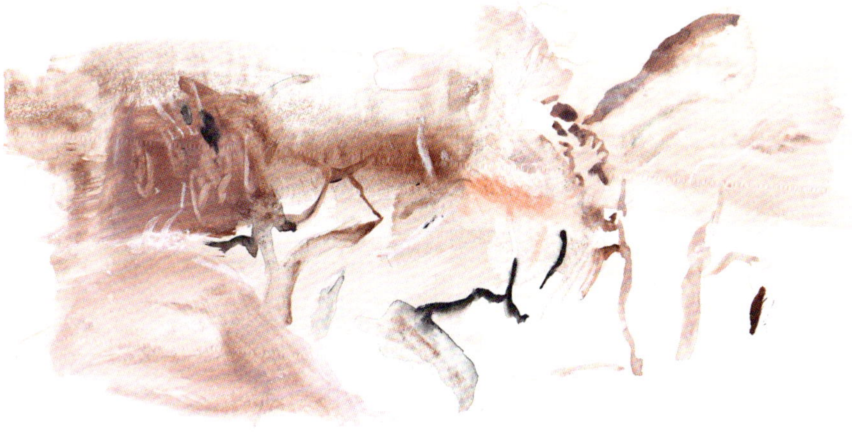

Untitled, 2012

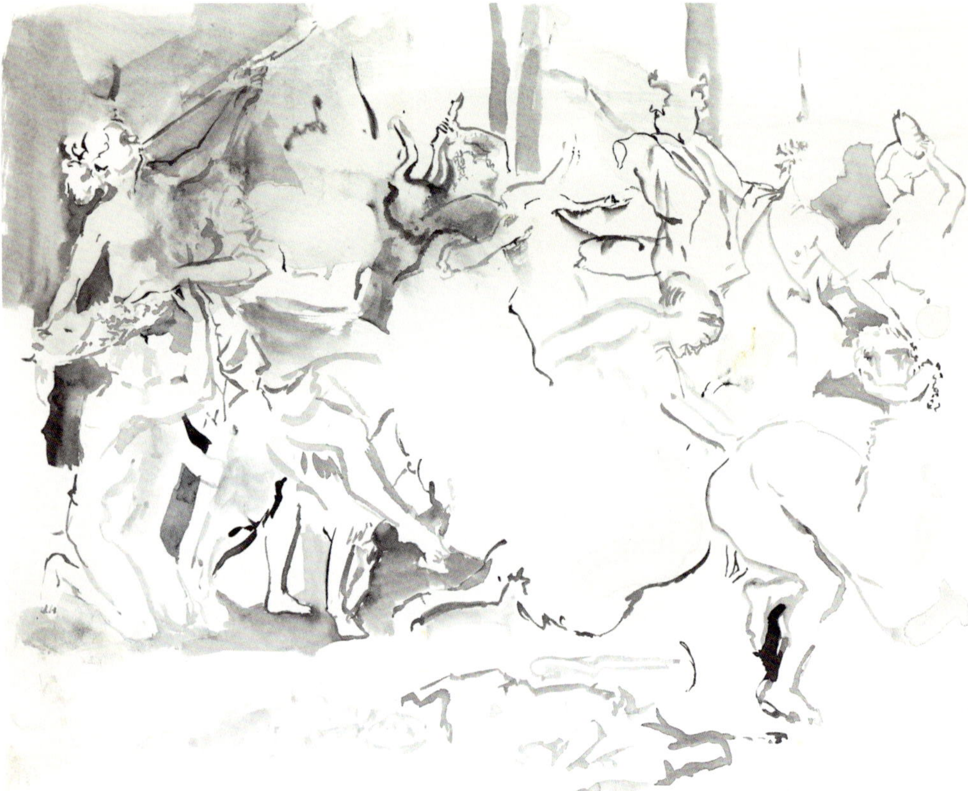

Untitled, 2004

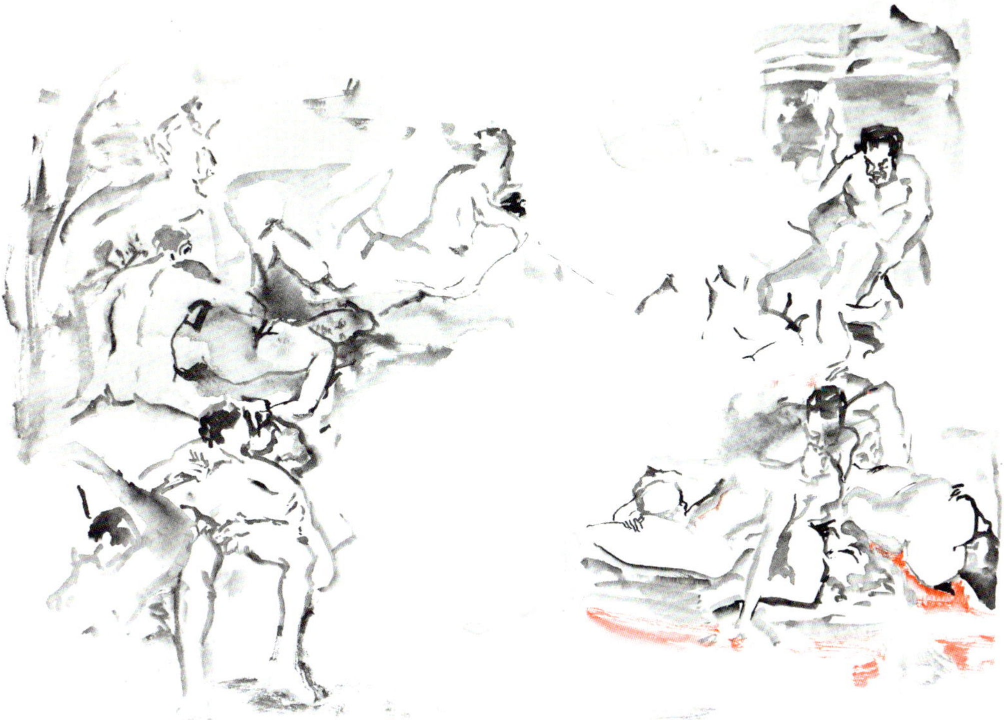

Untitled, 2003

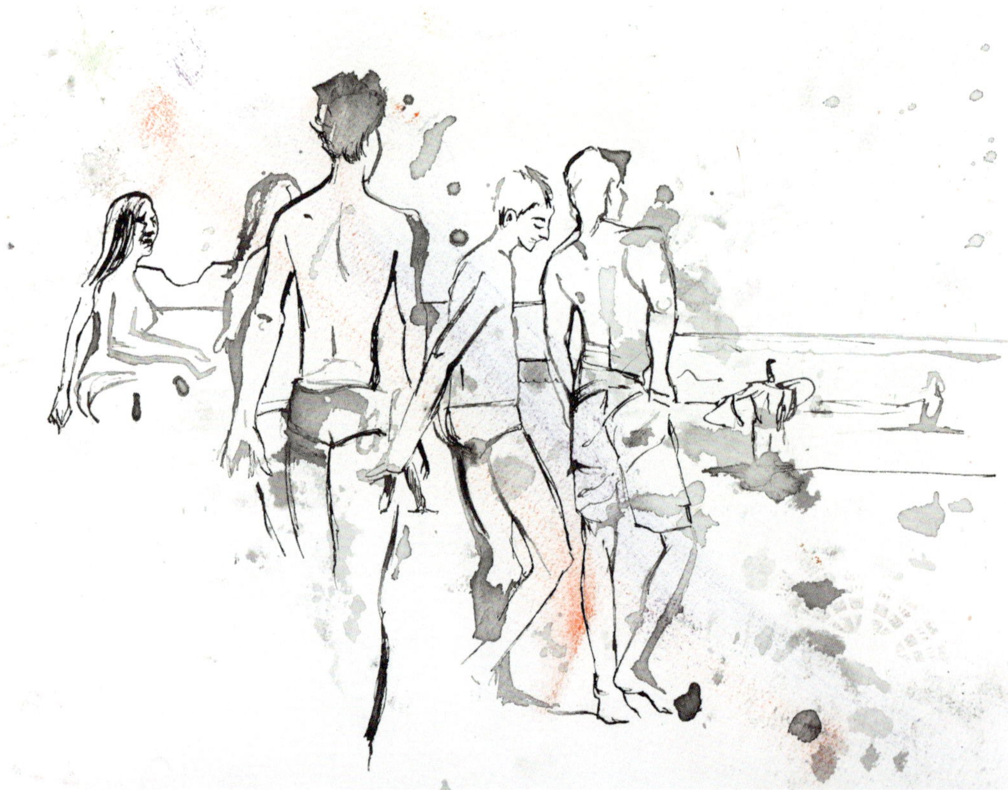

Untitled (Bathers), 2017

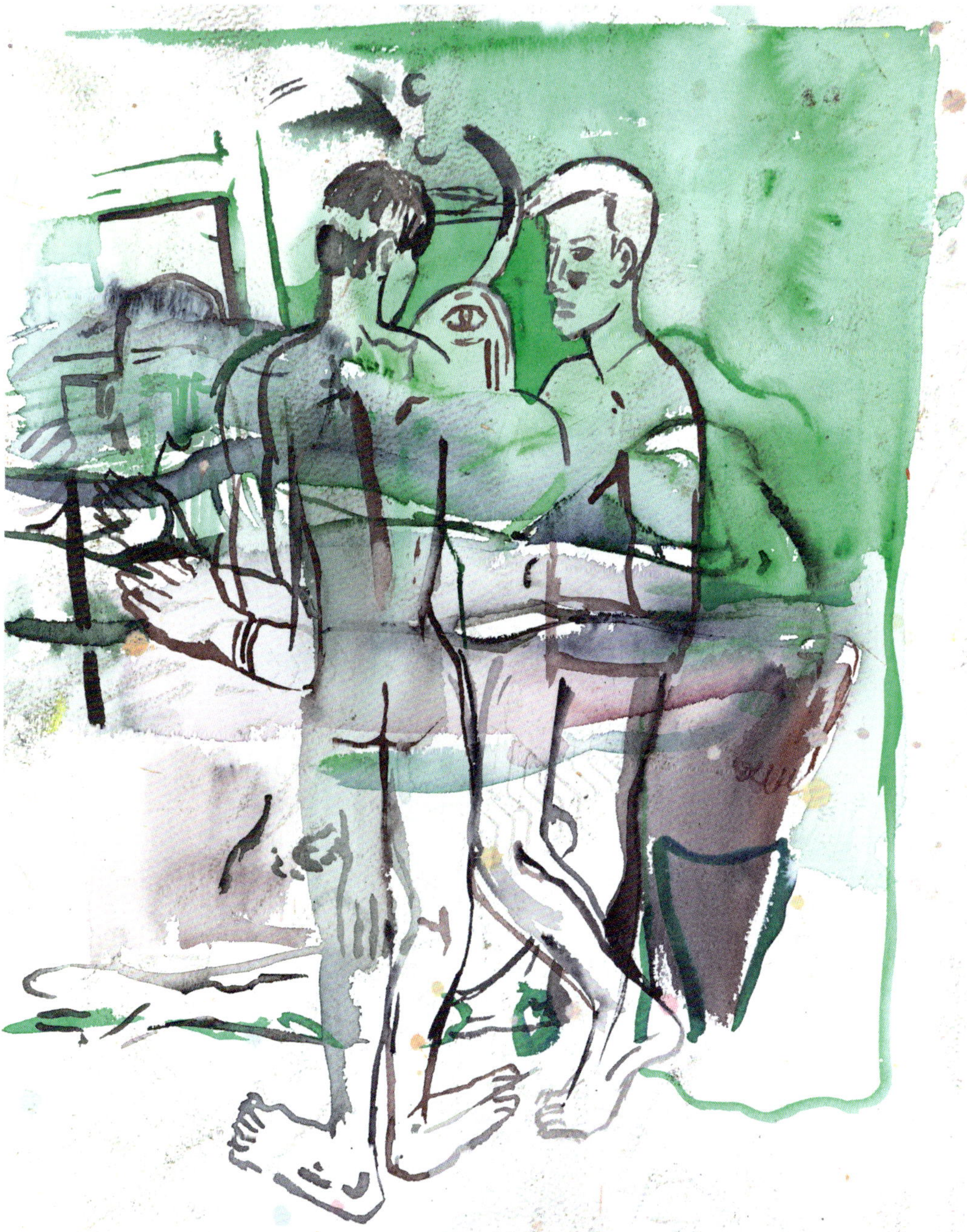

Untitled (After Beckmann), 2012

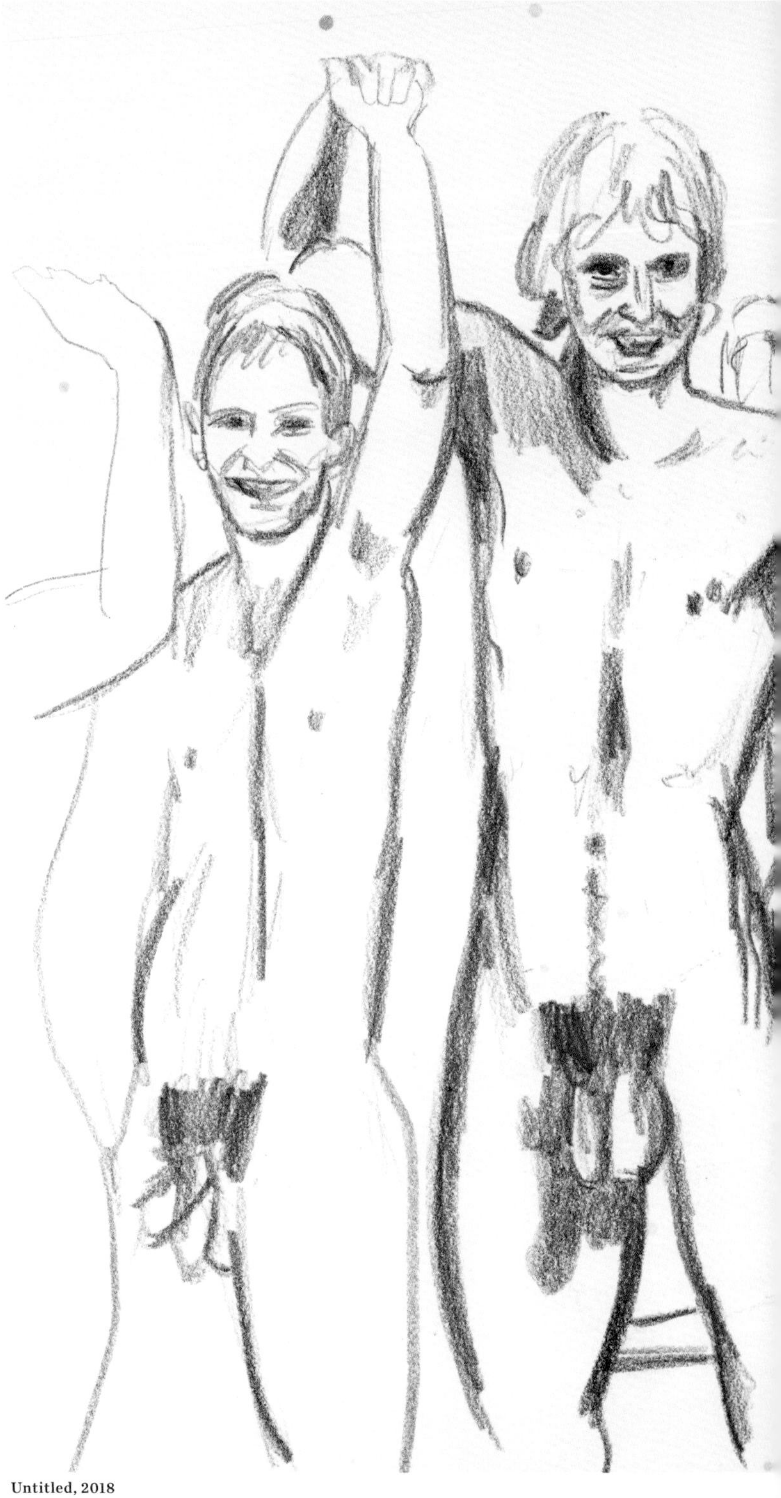

Untitled, 2018

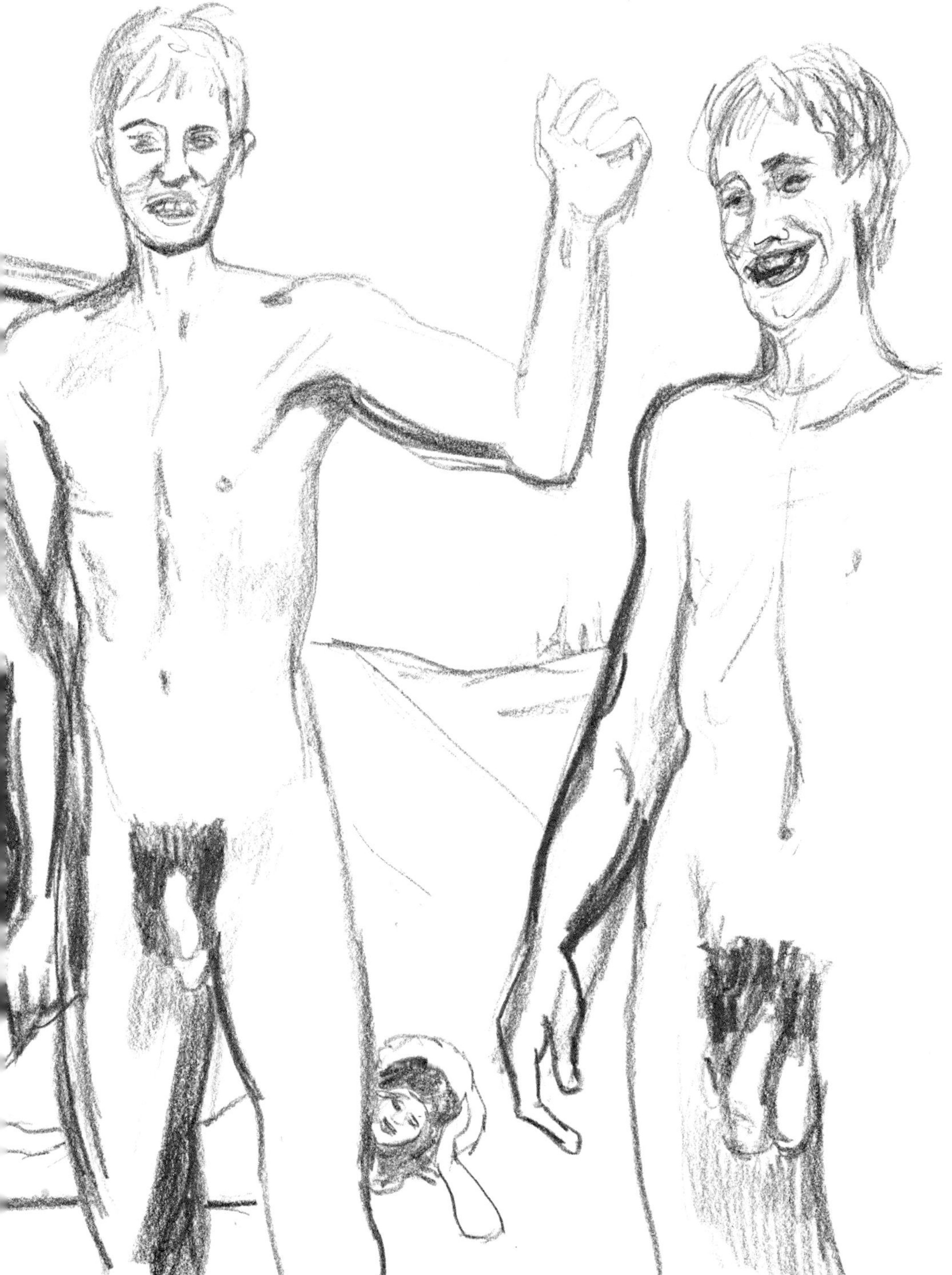

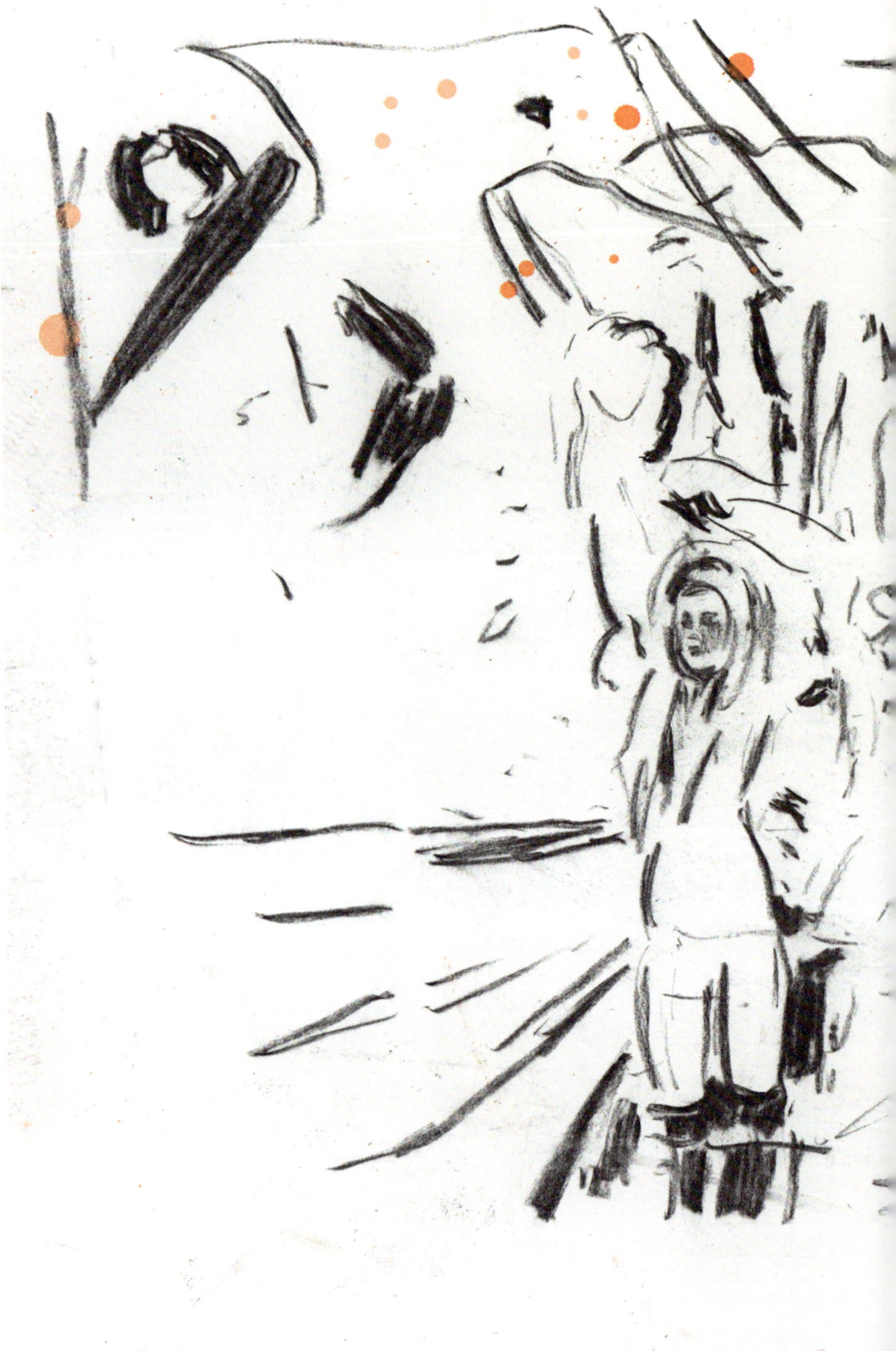

Beach Blanket Babylon, 2016

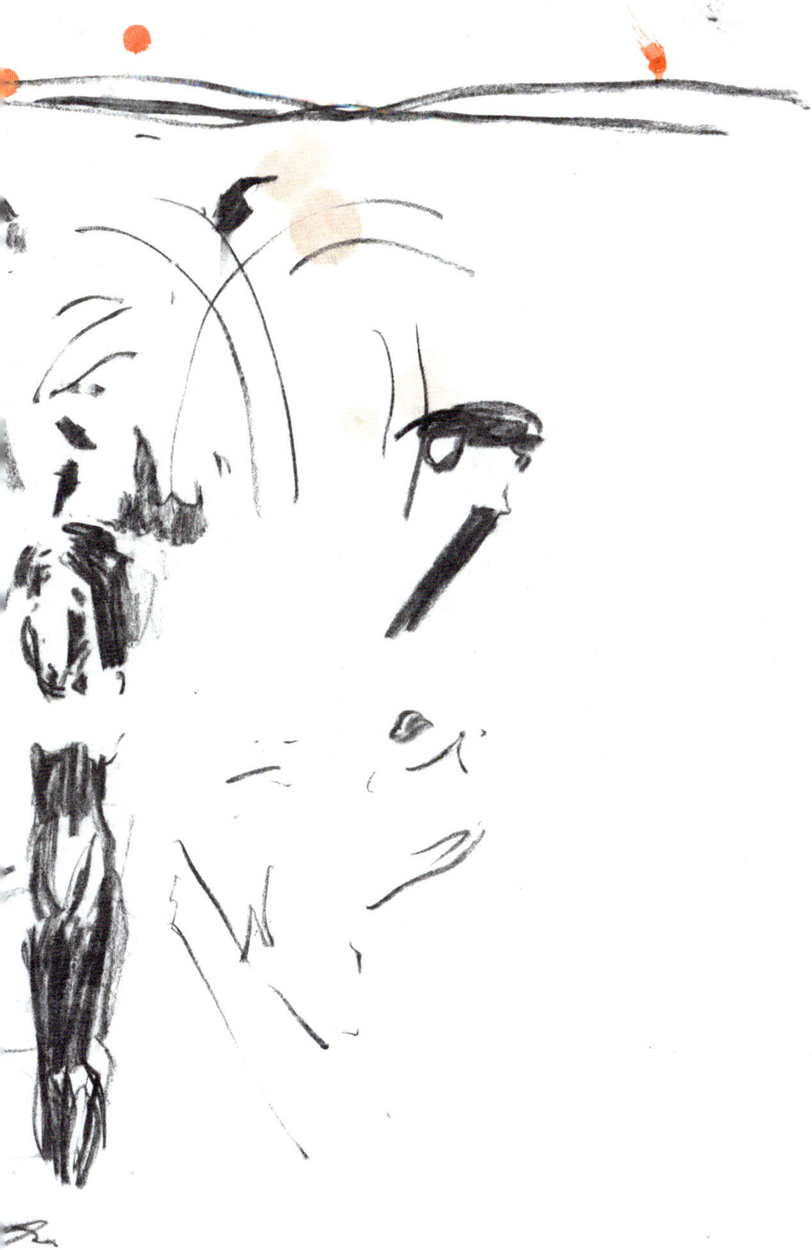

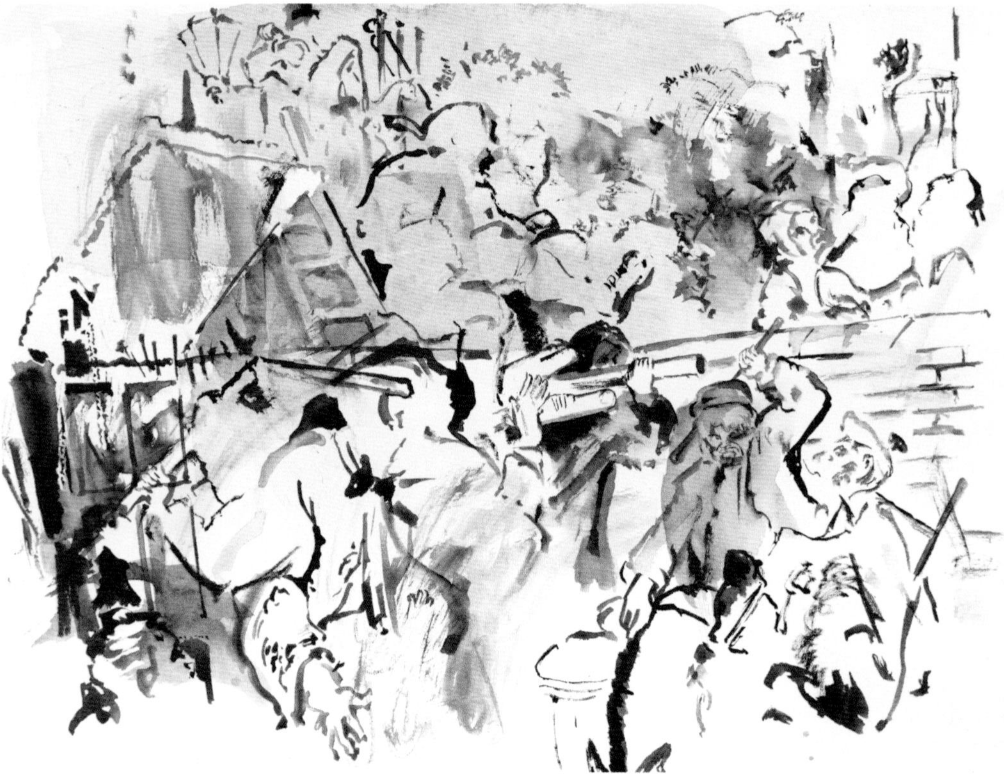

Chairing the Members (After Hogarth), 2004

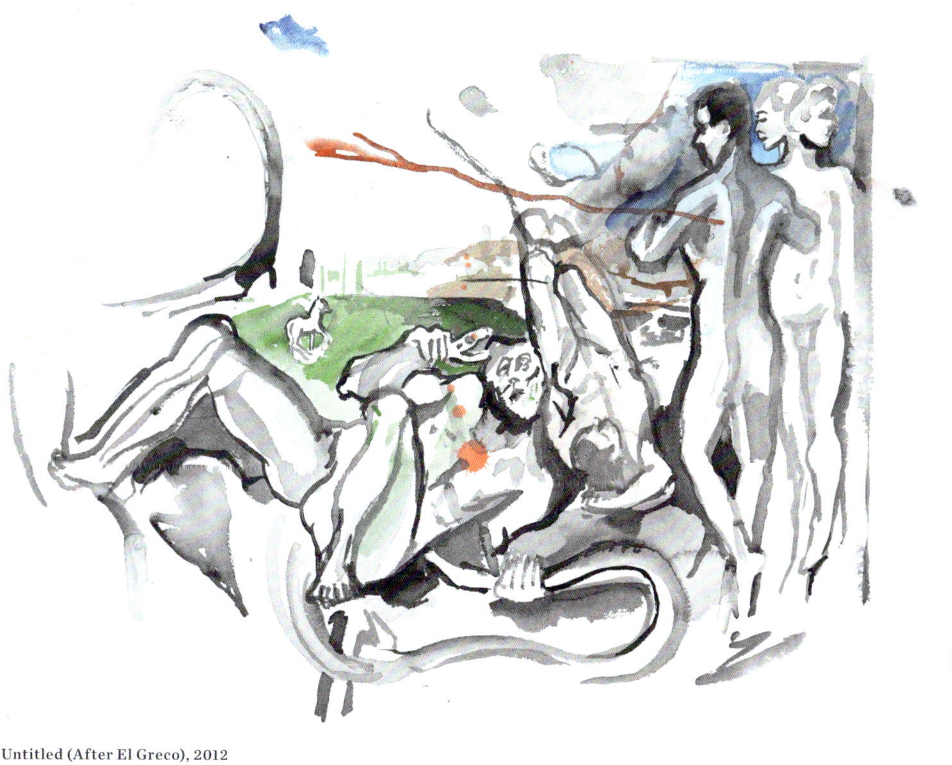

Untitled (After El Greco), 2012

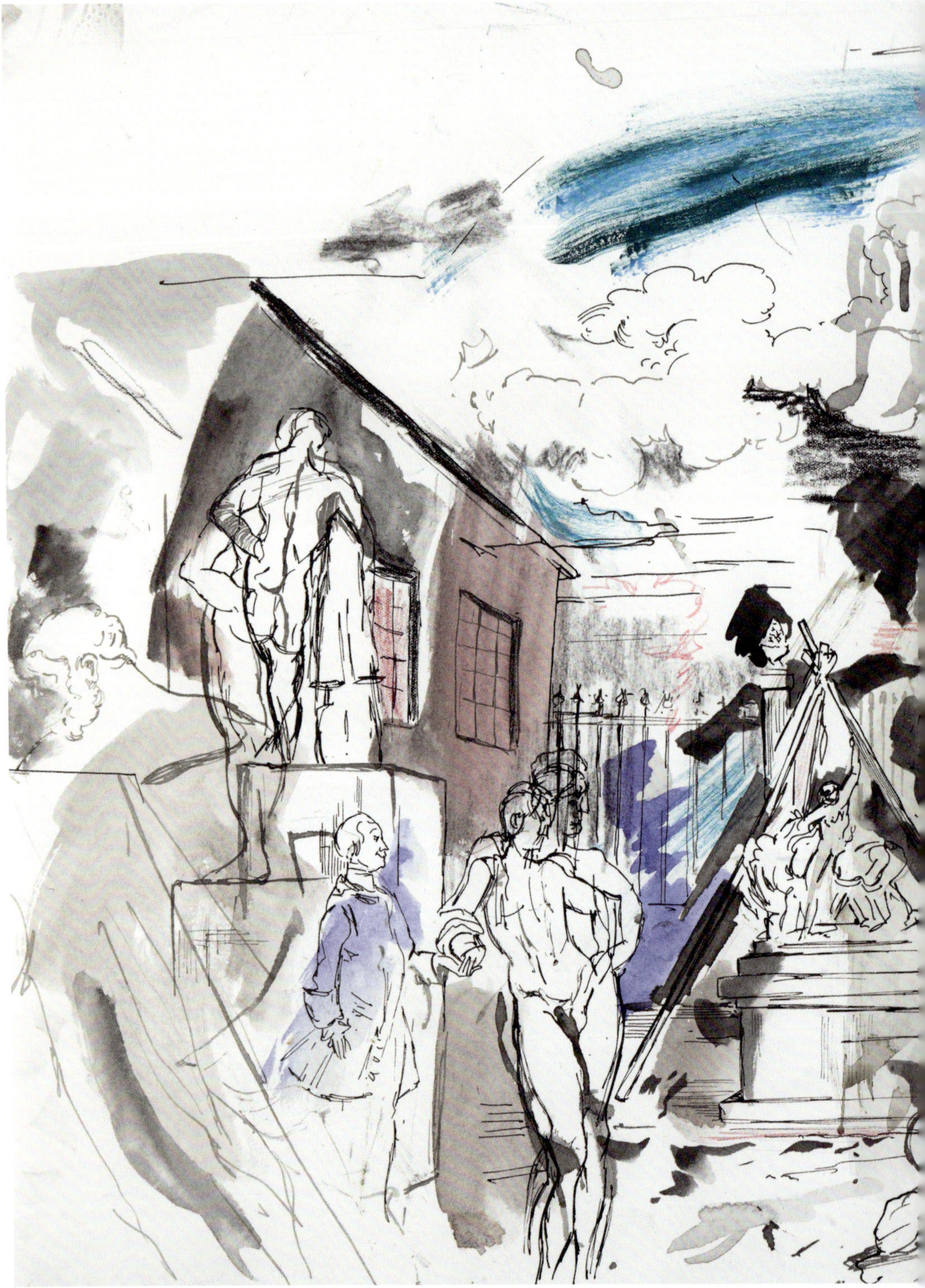

Analysis of Beauty (After Hogarth), 2014

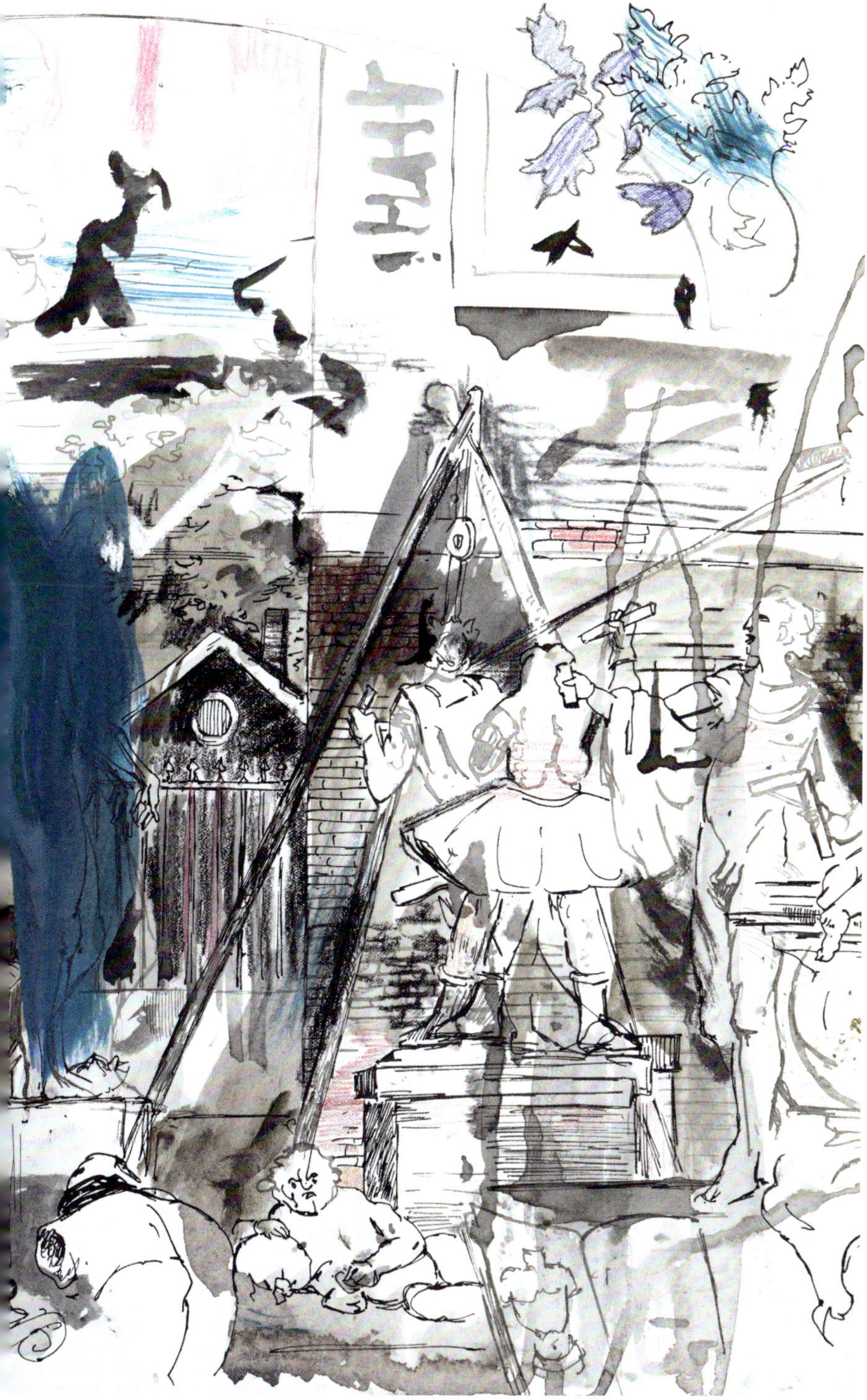

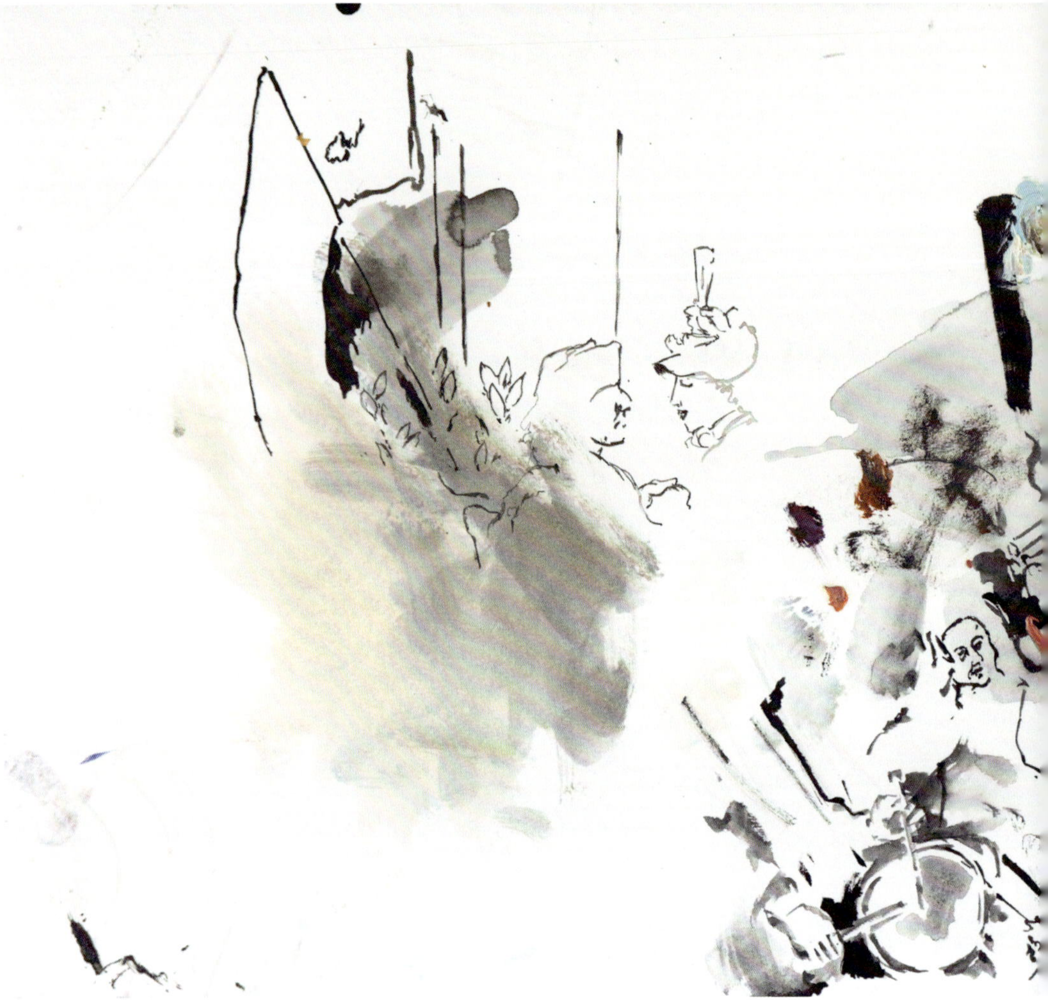

Chairing the Members (After Hogarth), 2004

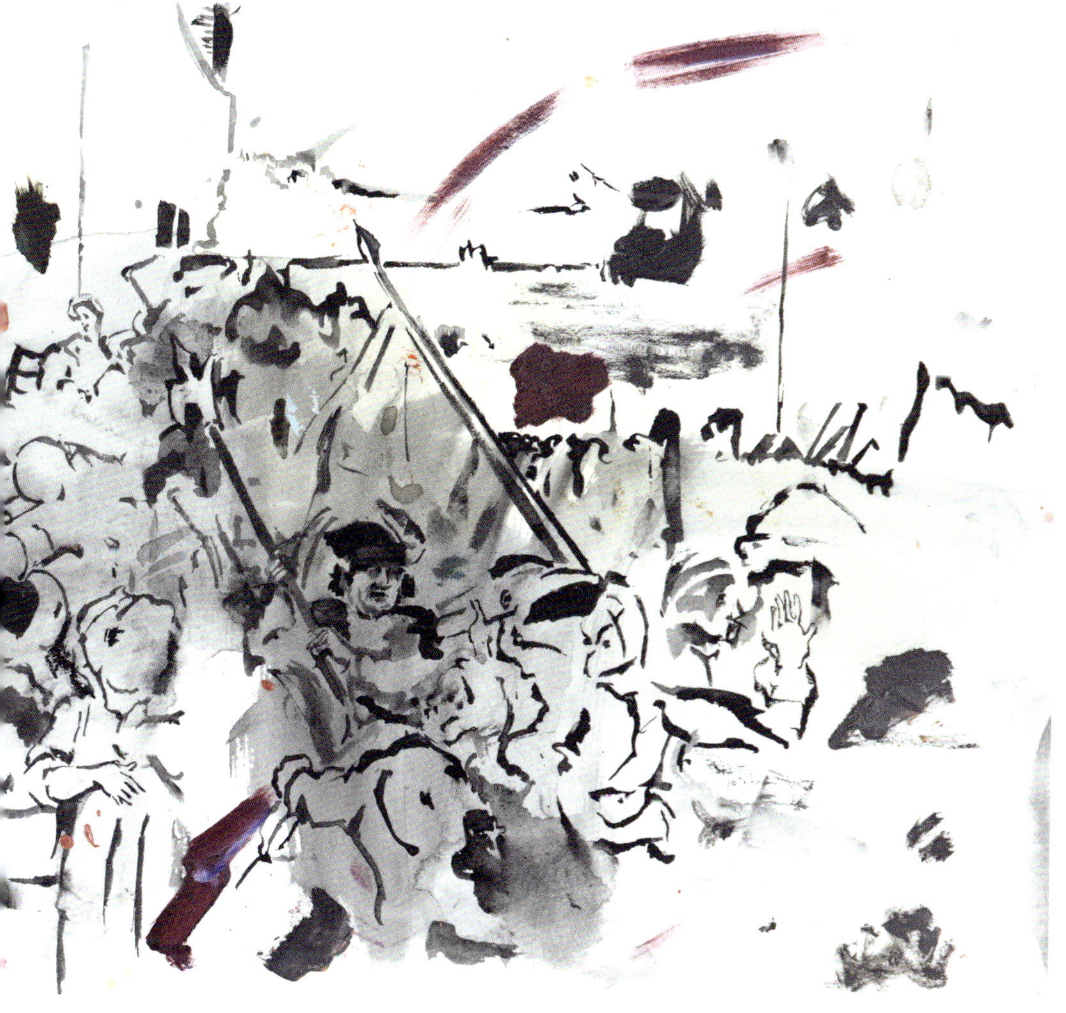

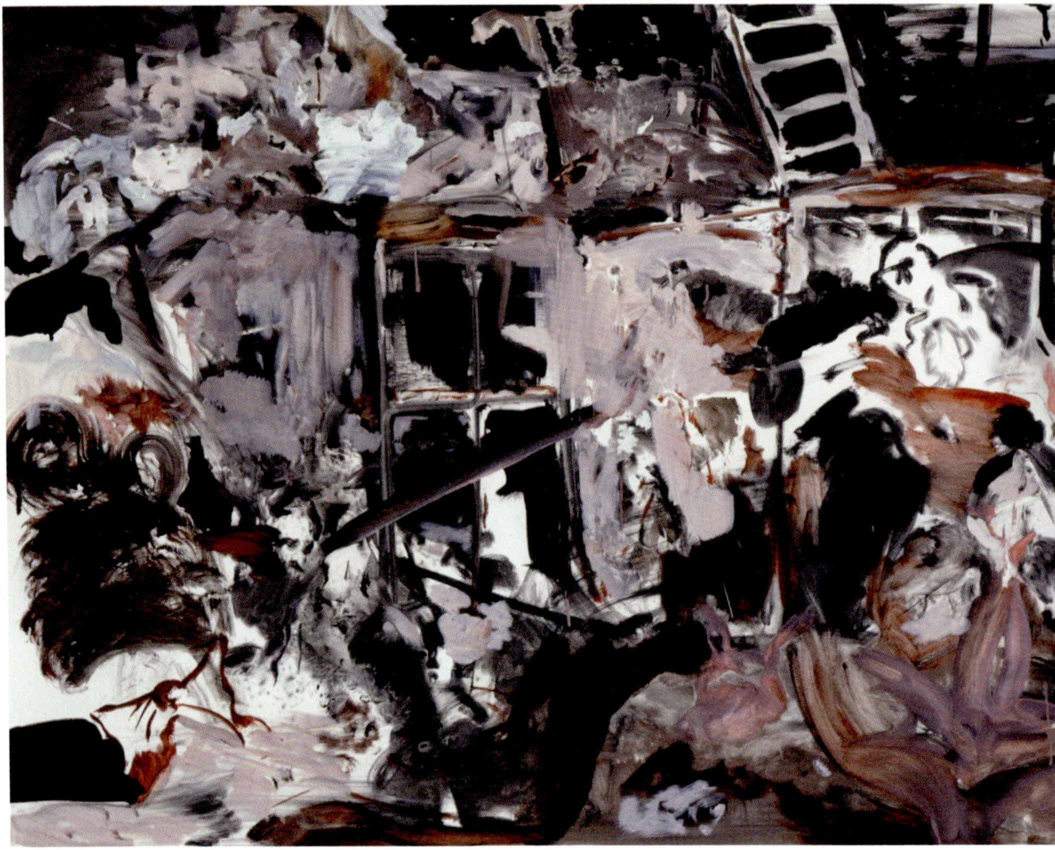
Study after Two Paintings by William Hogarth, 2004

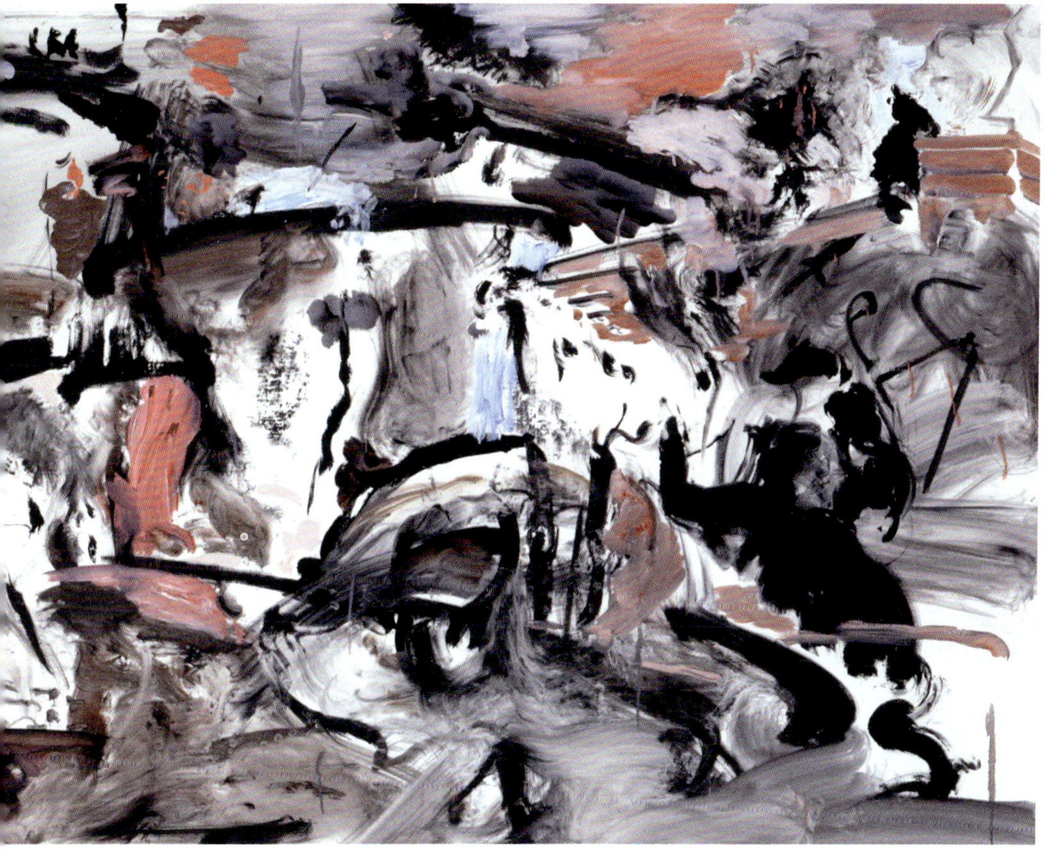

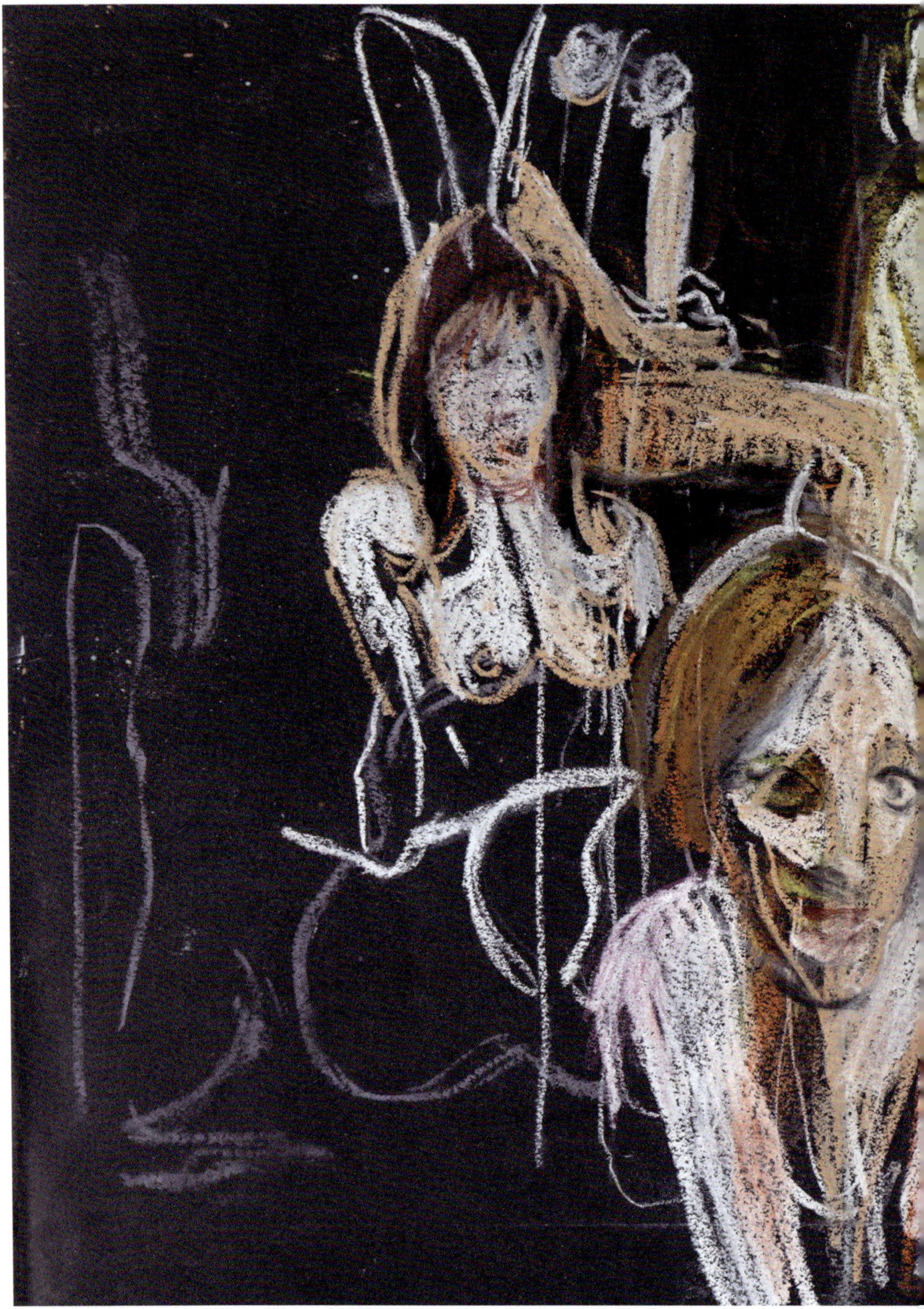

Untitled (Ladyland), 2012

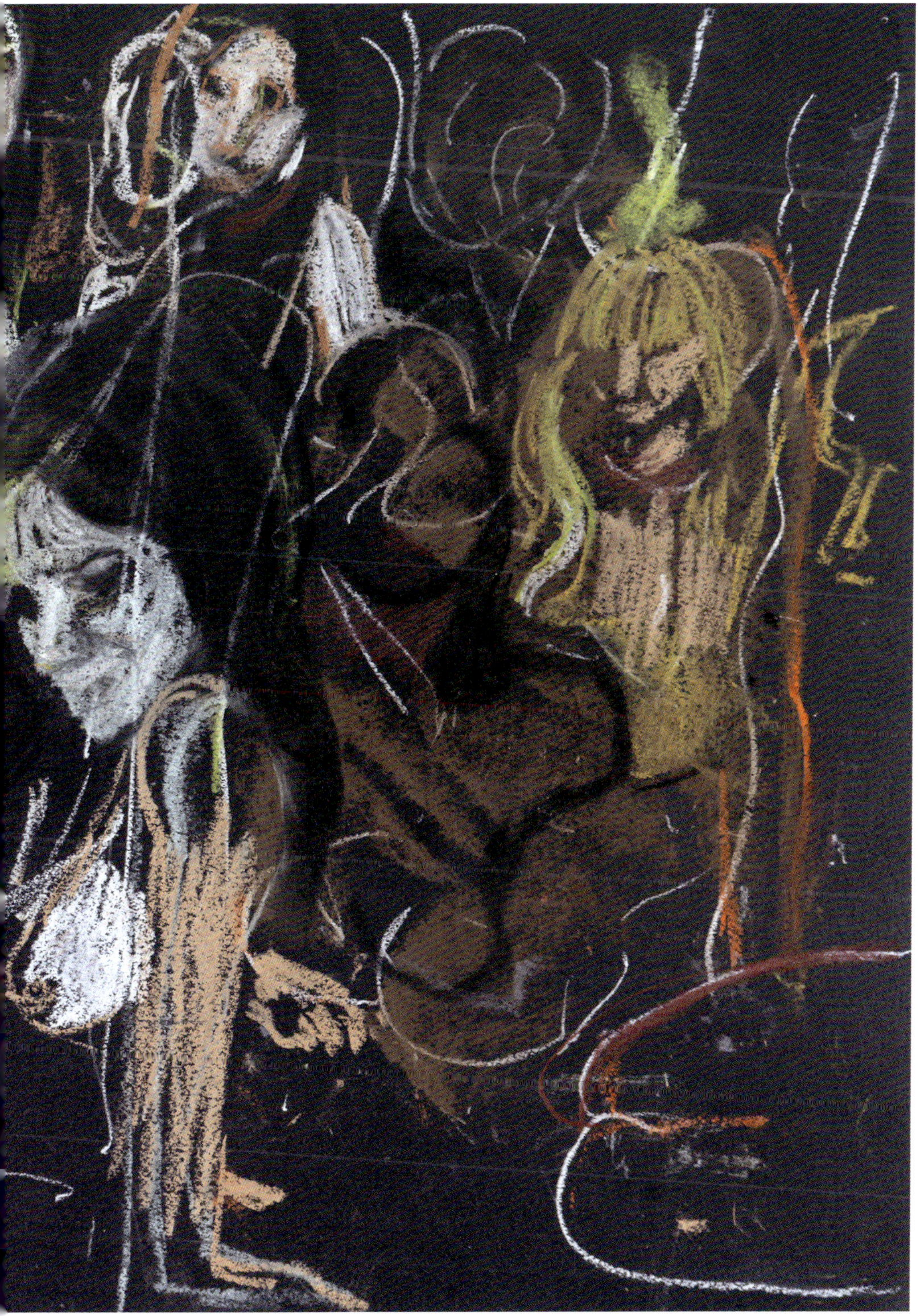

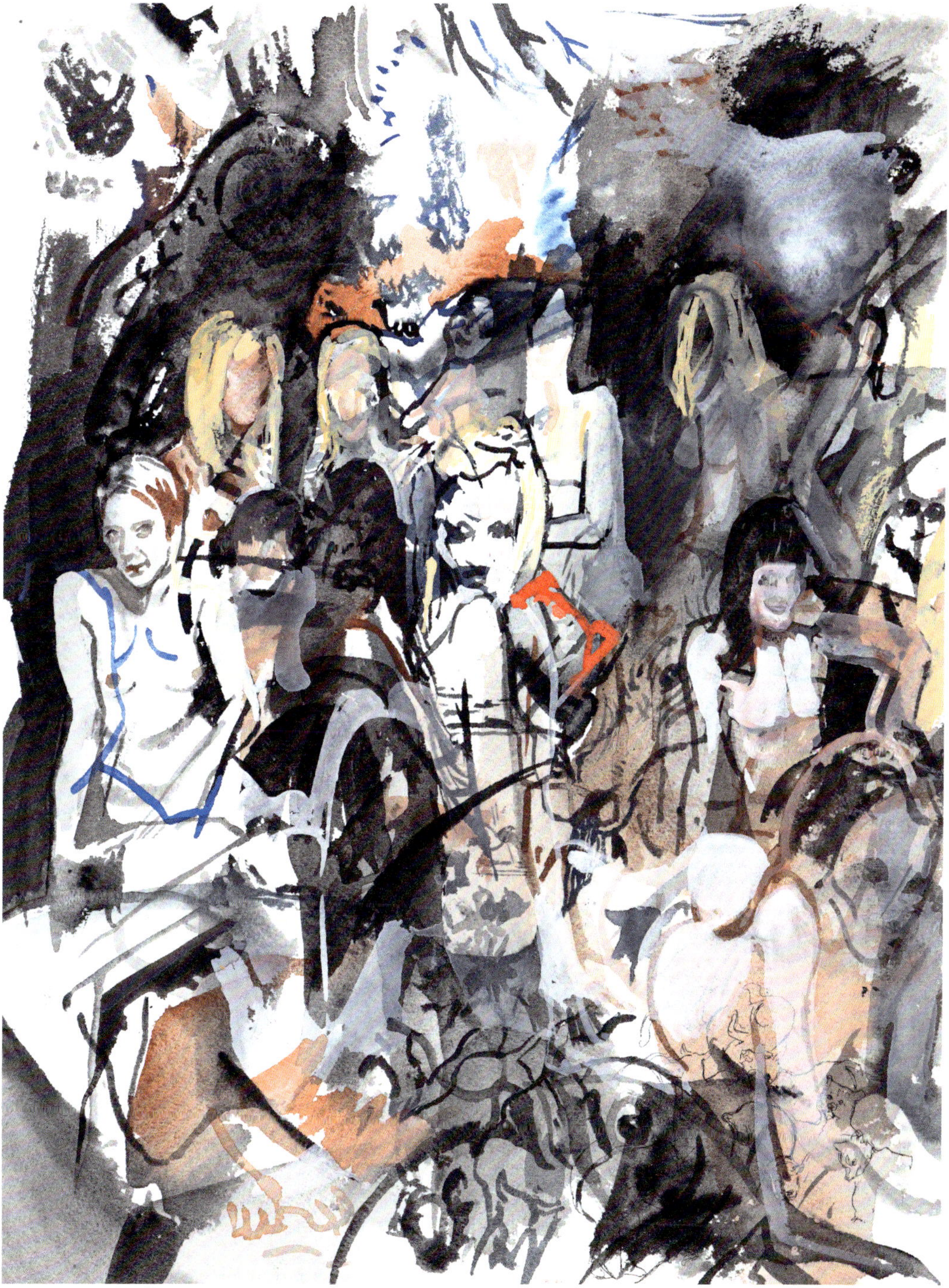

Untitled (Ladyland with Bestiary), 2013

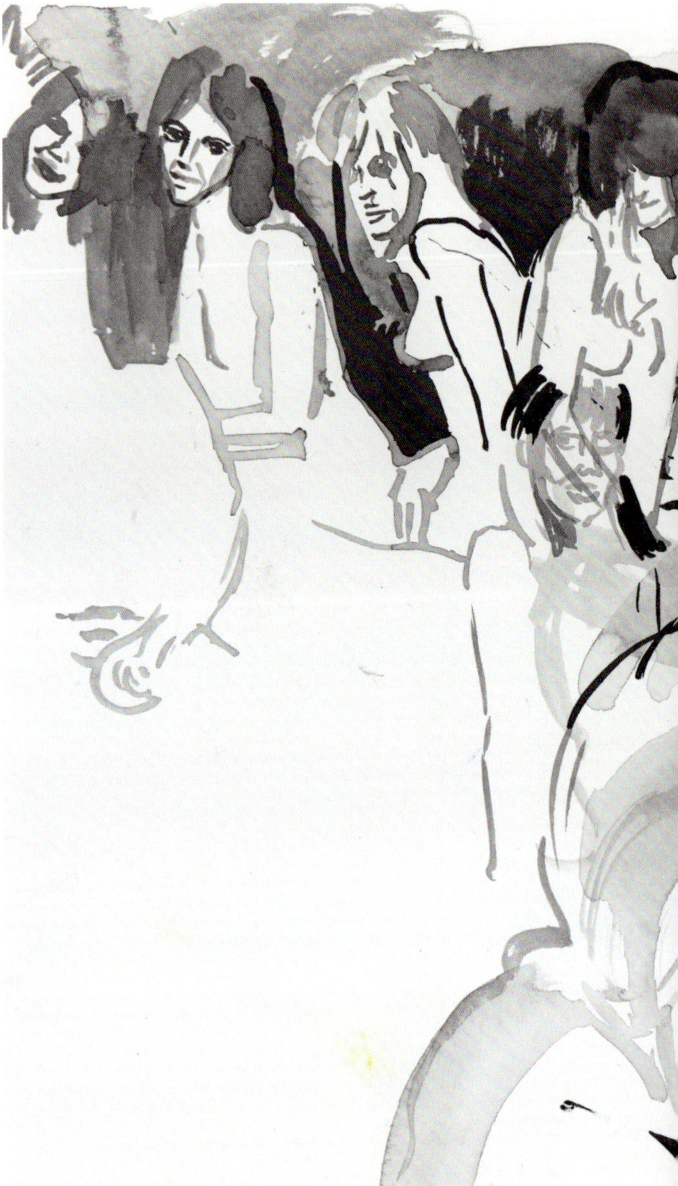

Untitled (Ladyland), 2012

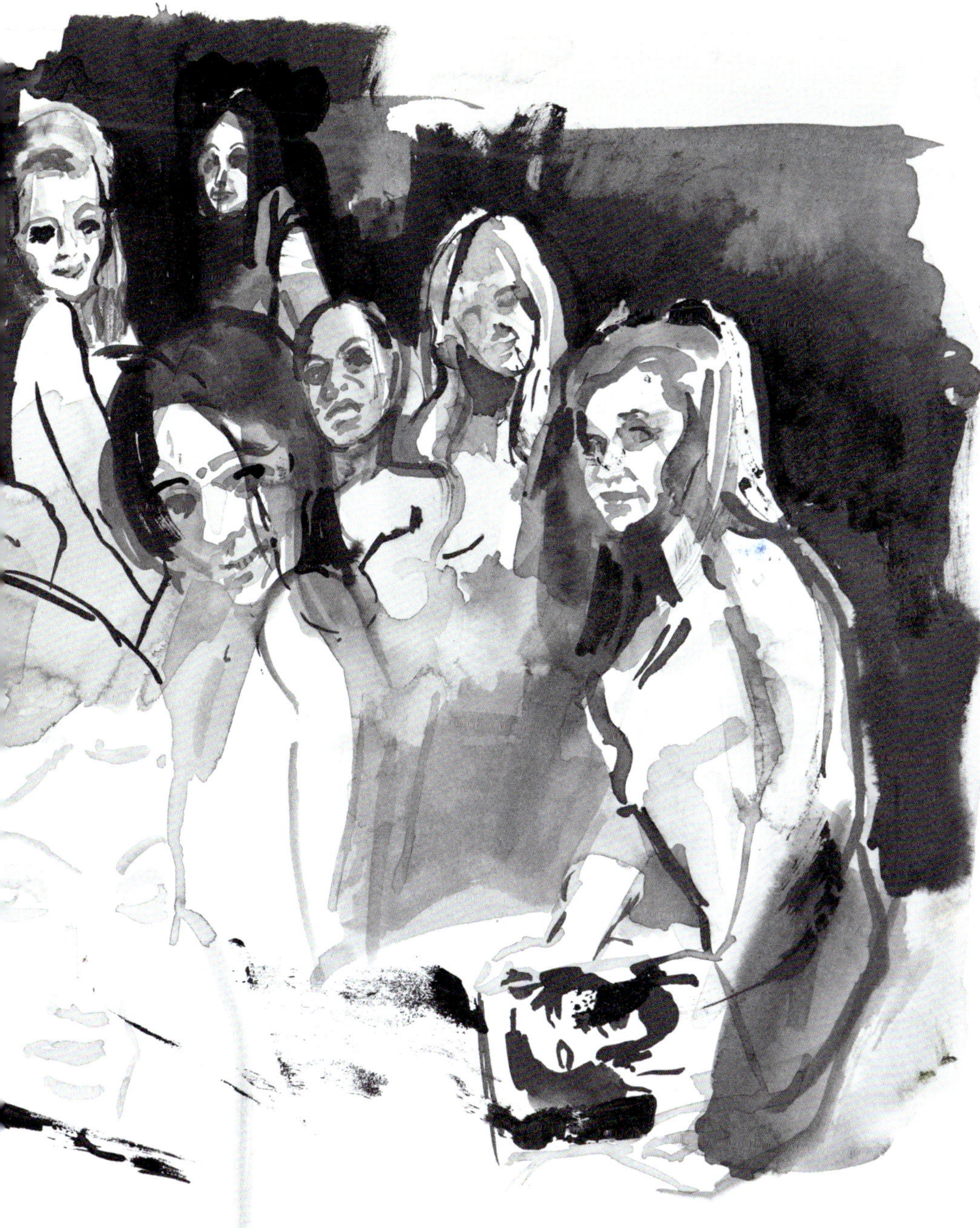

GROUP PORTRAIT

Hilton Als

I don't know if discussing art as an elevating, transformative experience carries much critical weight these days, especially during this era when personality politics and postmodern thinking dominate so much, but when I think about Cecily Brown in the language of our times, language that can most readily be described as abstract, my mind drifts and the memory of looking at her work, paintings that mean as much to me as humans in the flesh, gets reduced to a series of banalities that have little to do with the power of her execution, what painting means to Brown, a born painter, and shouldn't we begin there if we are going to even attempt to talk about what interests her and thus us? I suppose we could begin by saying how Cecily Brown's painting is so specific to paint and not language. And that's the other thing, how language fails to convey even a tenth of the sensory pleasure and joy and "over all" emotional force that her painting inspires in us. No words – "paltry things," as Yeats has it – can compete, really, with the ideas that one sees in Cecily Brown's work, which incorporates so much about women and the body, and sometimes, while looking at the bodies in and on her canvases, one feels as though one were entering the body – a female body – turned inside out, and I sometimes wonder if that turned inside out feeling in her work – the feeling of entering or reentering the first female body one has ever known, maybe, or will ever know – is unfair to the paintings, another act of presumption from a male viewer who as long as he has looked at art has had to unlearn how to categorize, label what he sees according to the privileges of his sex and, historically speaking, the idea that whatever is seen is owned. So, another conundrum: How to let Cecily Brown have her own paintings, the female figures in them, when, to some degree, I want to have them for myself, to be in their flesh as they are (often) in one another's flesh? Cecily Brown is a seer and recorder of female bodies and thus minds and she sees faces as landscapes, as screens on which we project our deepest longings, sometimes, and joys and fears, too. The great artist frequently – often – depicts exteriors with the same existential specificity, a way of being clear and allowing for mystery at the same time, when she looks at the atmosphere to be found in a smile or a grimace, a relaxed foot, the hazards of life and aging. Often, in her numerous masterpieces, places – mises-en-scène – take on the vividness one gleans in Brown's characters' bodies because, as a poet, she does not differentiate between the human form and forms in nature, a glorious confusion that accounts for some of her work's power, too.

Brown's painting, 2012's *All the Nightmares Came Today,* is a shocking work because it illustrates something about aggression and looking, all those young female bodies crammed into a frame, and what's up with that along with the jolt that one feels as a man looking at Brown's painting with all its pink and rose and fleshy browns and what not, colors and scale and immediacy that recall the feeling of what girls looked like to a boy, say, who grew up with girls and their girlfriends, a world where a bit of exposed thigh was not uncommon, this was in the nineteen-sixties and mini skirts and boots were the style, an era filled with memories of clothes and so many memories of sisters' friends crowding into a room as they get dressed for an evening out, stockings off, pilgrim shoes on, hair ironed or sprayed just so: girl armor meant to draw the viewer close while turning him away, their flesh was so far away from me even as I drew close to it, a little boy enthralled by all those girl smells and chatter, how could I be them and live inside them, all at the same time? *All The Nightmares Came Today,* and other works by Brown, is a collision course, one where observation – the painter's, yours – and presence – the various models, history – meet. In *All The Nightmares Came Today,* Brown the painter meets her "source" material and makes it something else. In this case, the source is the painter's memory of an album cover she saw when she was a girl – photographer David Montgomery's 1968 picture of London club kids posing for the British release of musician Jimi Hendrix's album, *Electric Ladyland.* As with so much of Brown's work, the painting is not a literal translation of a pre-existing image so much as it's a painterly and thus psychological rendering of a state – the artist's consciousness as it opens and folds in on the women on an album cover and thus commerce and commodification and male perception as a kind of right or will to ownership. Their nudity is part of a tradition, of course: naked girls for the delectation of a largely male audience, nubile and silent, litter the history of Western art. Now, in Brown's painting, the modes are no longer soundless. In Brown's work they raise their voices and their bodies in gorgeous outrage, smearing the world with their being, and the artist's mind. We know these young women because of Montgomery's picture, of course. How to find them in Brown's field of great whooping smears and lines that run their course here there and everywhere? Brown's delicacy and toughness of line say something about sex as they say something about painting. This painting shimmers with individual trauma and group trauma. The girls have one another and no one at all. What constitutes their trauma? Having a different body? One that a male photographer objectifies and emphasizes in the photograph for its built in pornography of flesh, the "just so" hair and make up that is in stark contrast to all that semi-nudity? The relationship between being "done" by society – that is, looking like what you're supposed to look like based on gender rules and so on – and what Brown feels about that kind of drag contributes to the uneasiness one feels in looking at her work, along with the joy and surprise one feels looking at her art, too: Brown's women are not taking anything lying down, the artist makes them active participants in their own history, has a woman ever taken up as much space as freely and boldly as Brown does because as we all know, so many women are taught the opposite, to make their world tight and small, and I can imagine that Brown's freedom, her expansiveness, is part of the thrill and part of the fear some folks have when they stand in the company of her work, who is this woman who is giving so much of herself and so doing energizes painting and the conversations around painting?

Truth and fiction in Brown's work: They exist side by side. Those girls in the photograph are real and become even more so through Brown's understanding and interpretation years after they made *Ladyland* happen. They are "real" and now historical objects in a work of art. Fiction and non-fiction all at once. This is worth looking at. Let us turn our attention to the question of fiction. And how it stands, presumably, on the other side of truth. And how the waters that separate fact from fiction are muddy, and always have been. And how that muddiness is the result of truth and fantasy living in rather close proximity to one another in our respective minds.

Brown tears at the curtain that separates fact from fiction, history and the now, truth and lies, what makes a man, what makes a woman, what makes an other. This aggression is necessary if we are to rid ourselves of old tropes when it comes to looking not only at Brown's paintings, but at anything real at all. Brown is an avenger against the presumptions of the past – what women are allowed, how they are seen, what makes a painting – by making the questions new. What does it mean to live anything as impossibly fucked and chaotic as life in a "correct" way? Spiritual and actual violence permeates Brown's work, which are documents – documentaries – about real feelings as they exist in the real world for sure, but as metaphors, too: her figures speak for us all. As an artist she is interested in showing us how the illusion – the metaphor – works and how we may enter the tools she uses to create all those metaphors: paint and the eye behind the paint, the scale and spiritual balance she finds in chaos that she doesn't so much control as give shape to, she frightens us with all that she depicts in her landscapes of bodies and landscapes of trees and place, worlds that work on the mind the way the sea works on the mind, making our thinking all the more vast and specific at the same time.

Hilton Als is a staff writer at The New Yorker since 1994 and a theatre critic since 2002. Als edited the catalogue for the 1994-95 Whitney Museum of American Art exhibition *Black Male: Representations of Masculinity in Contemporary American Art,* and is the author of *THE WOMEN* (1996) and *WHITE GIRLS* (2014). He won the Pulitzer Prize for criticism in 2017. Als is also the curator of among other exhibitions the 2017 *Alice Neel, Uptown.* Als is an associate professor of writing at Columbia University's School of the Arts and has taught at Yale University, Wesleyan, and Smith College.

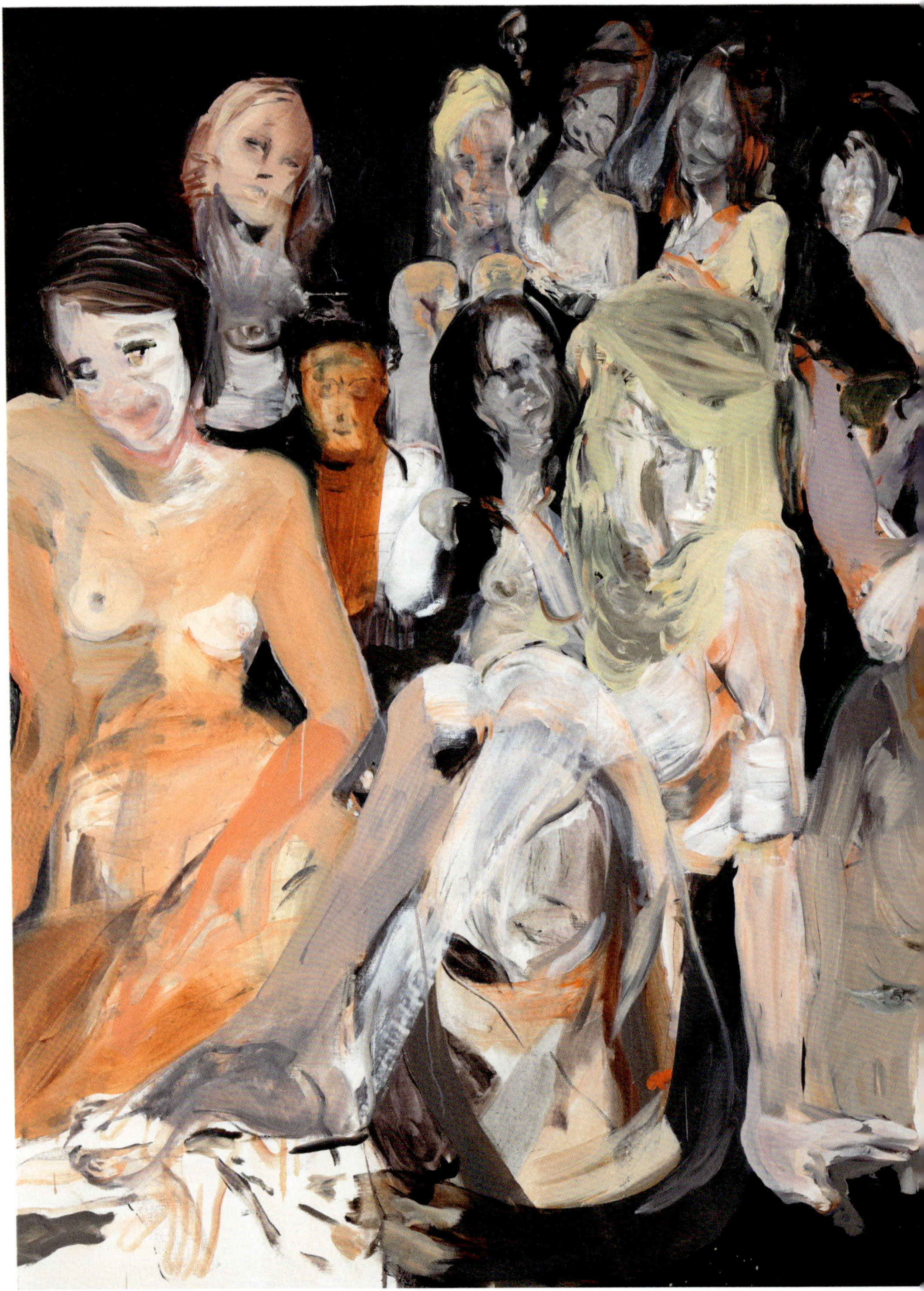

All the Nightmares Came Today, 2012

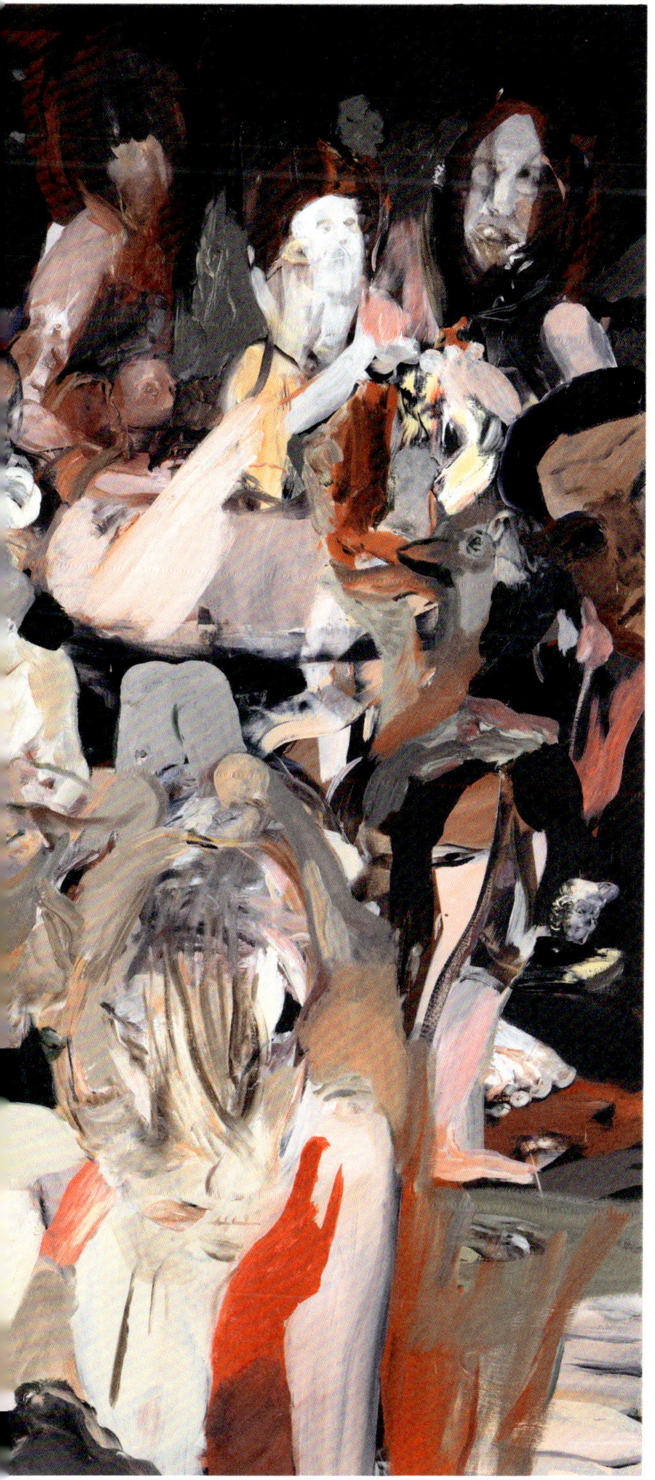

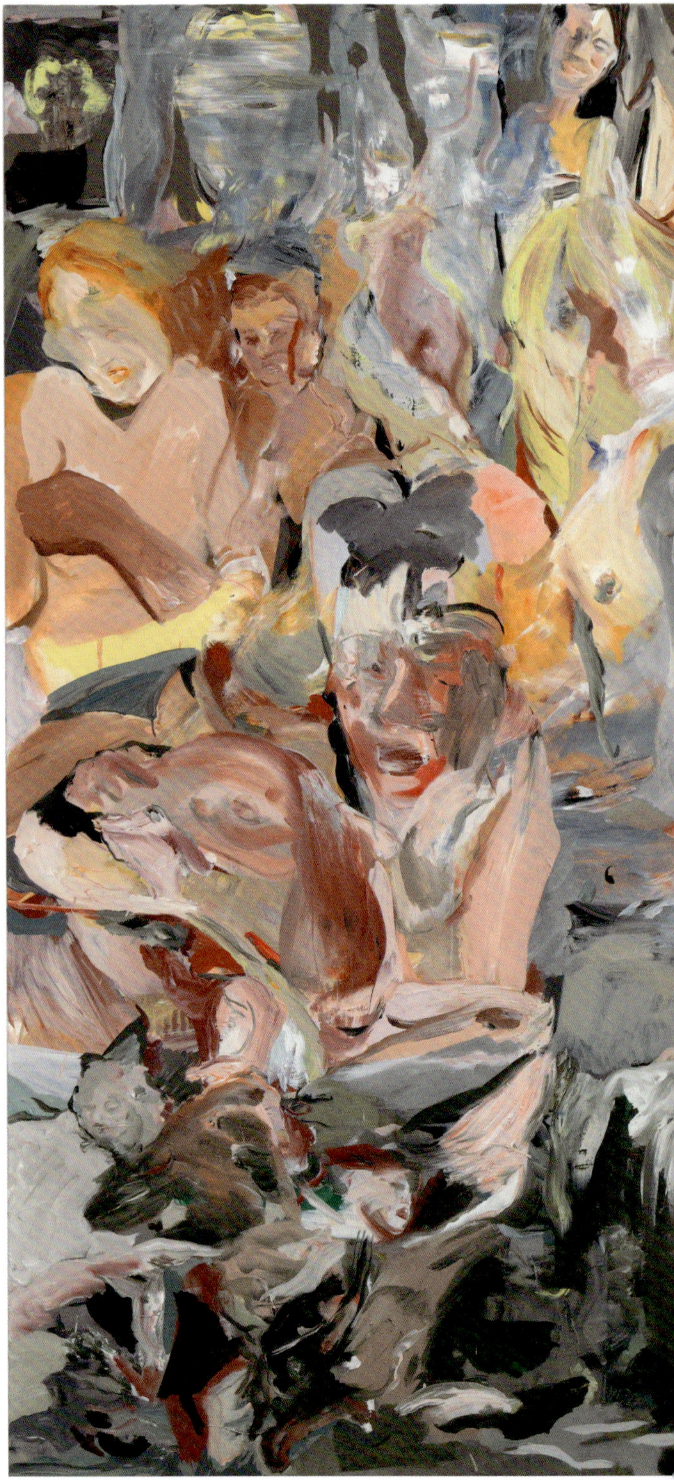

Name That Tune, 2012

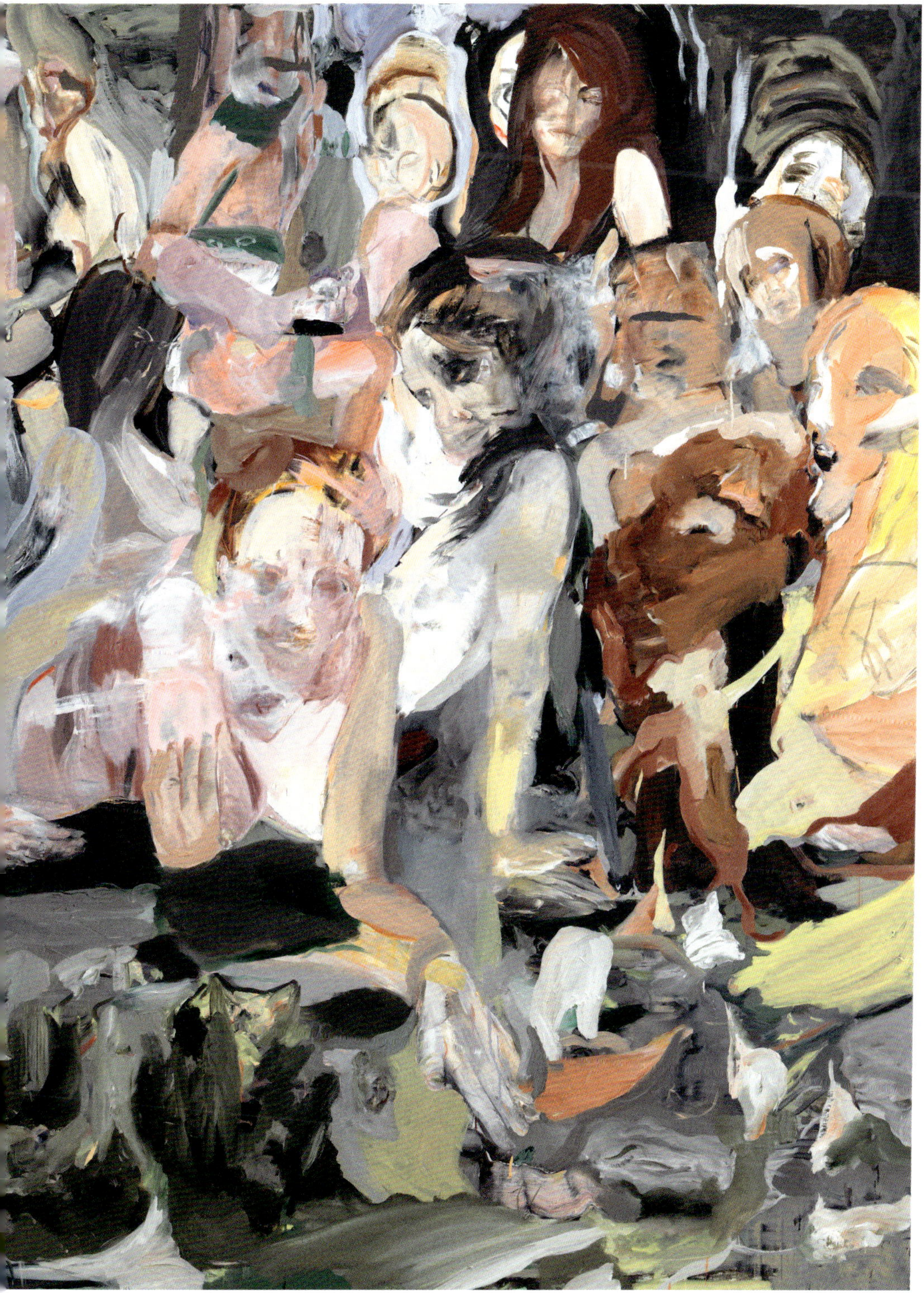

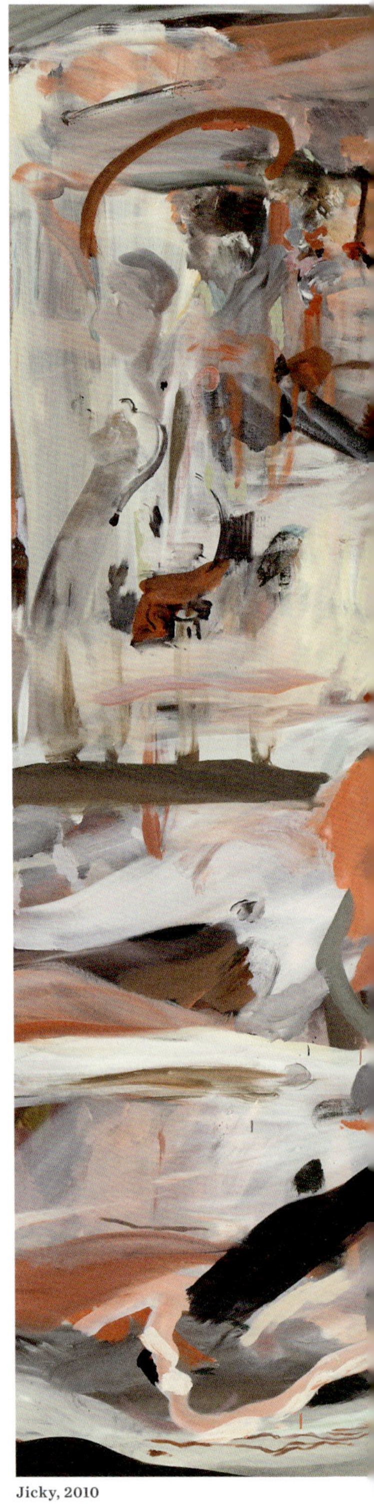

Jicky, 2010

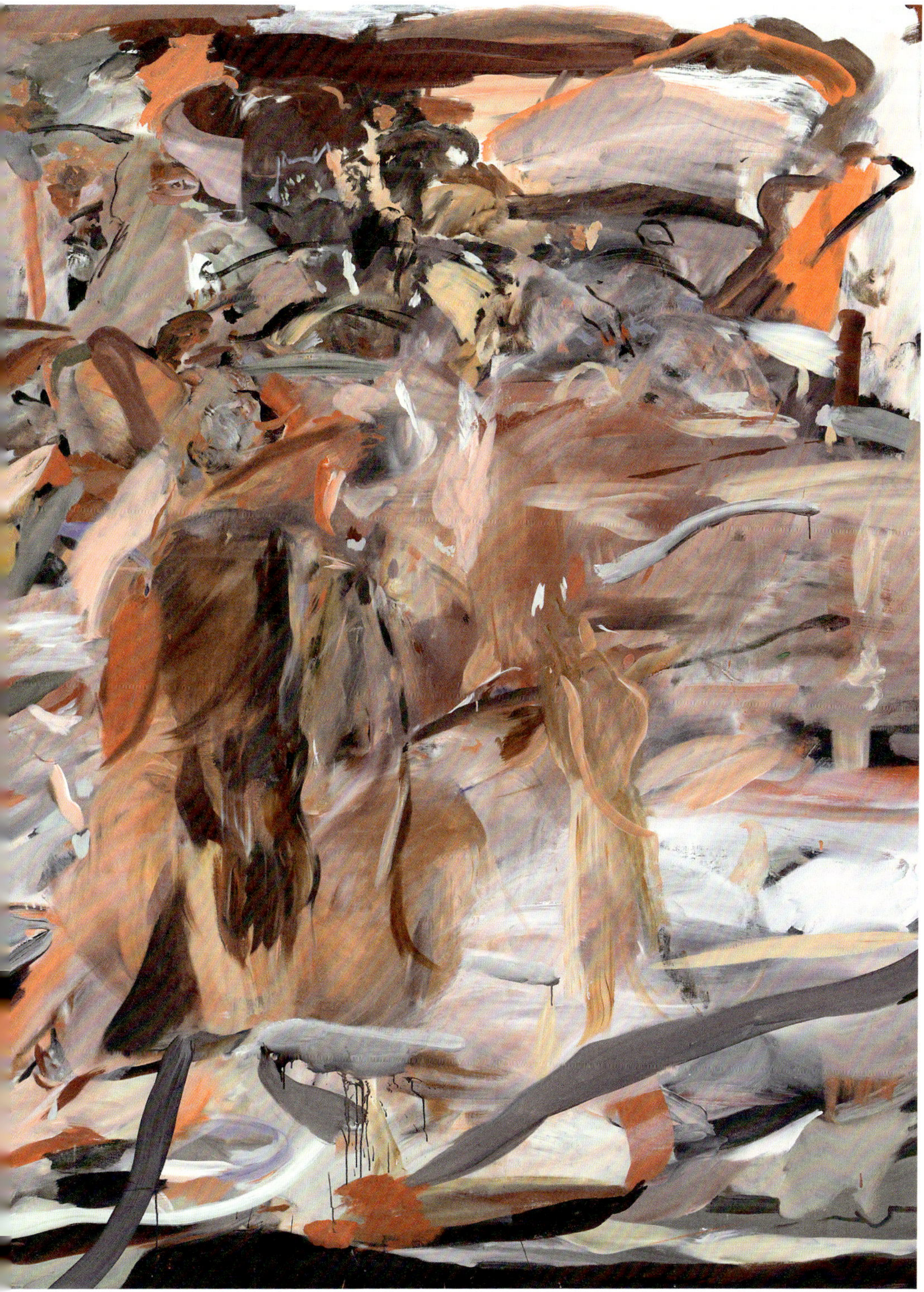

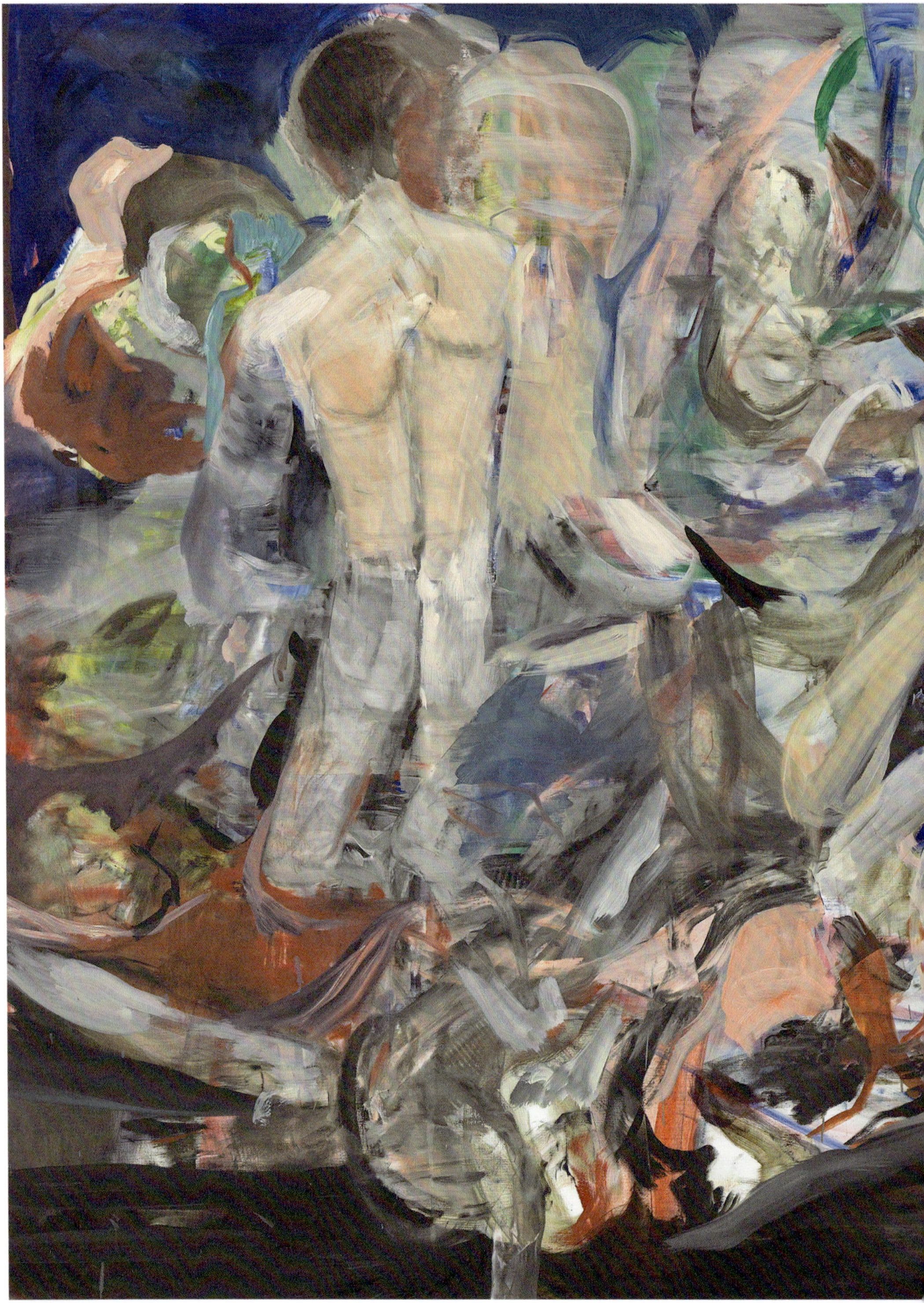

Torch, 2015

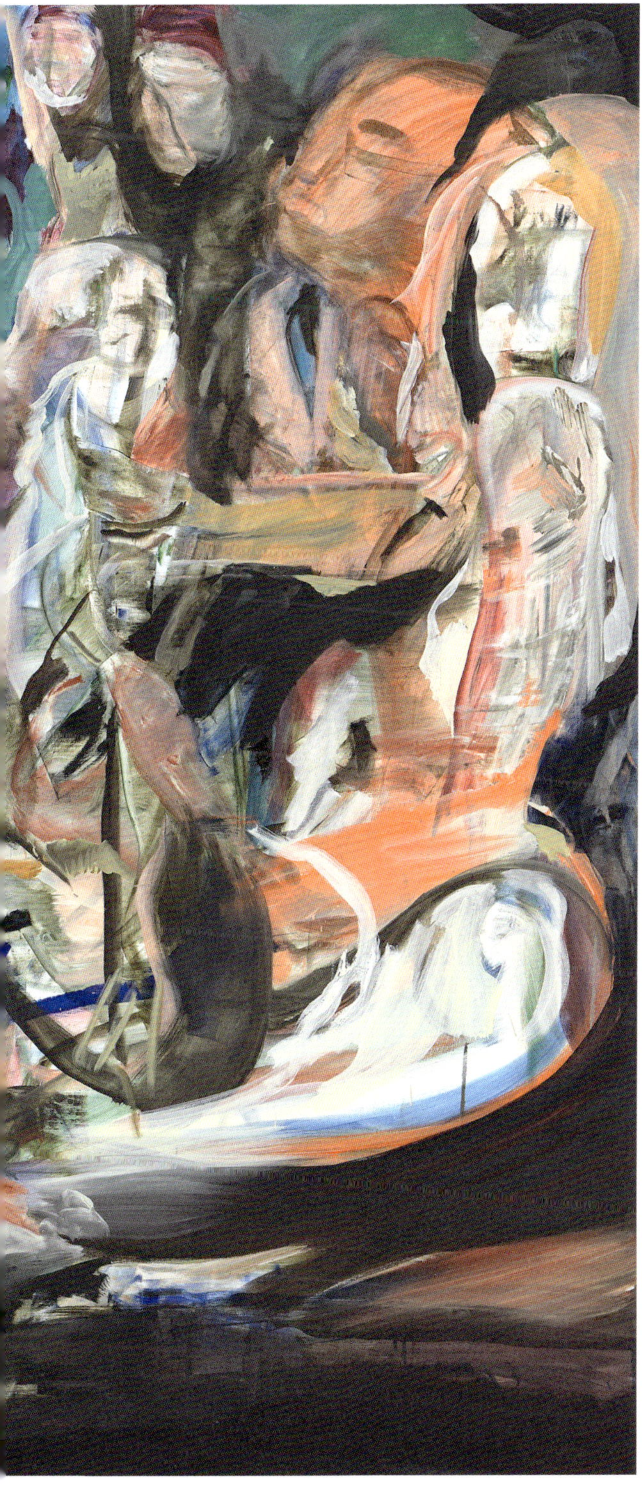

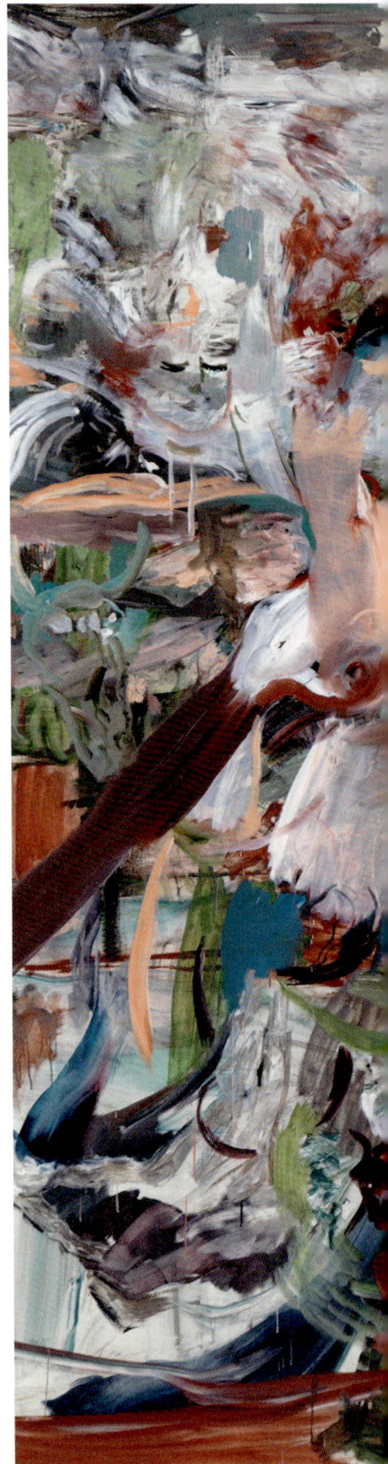

Handsome Stranger, 2010

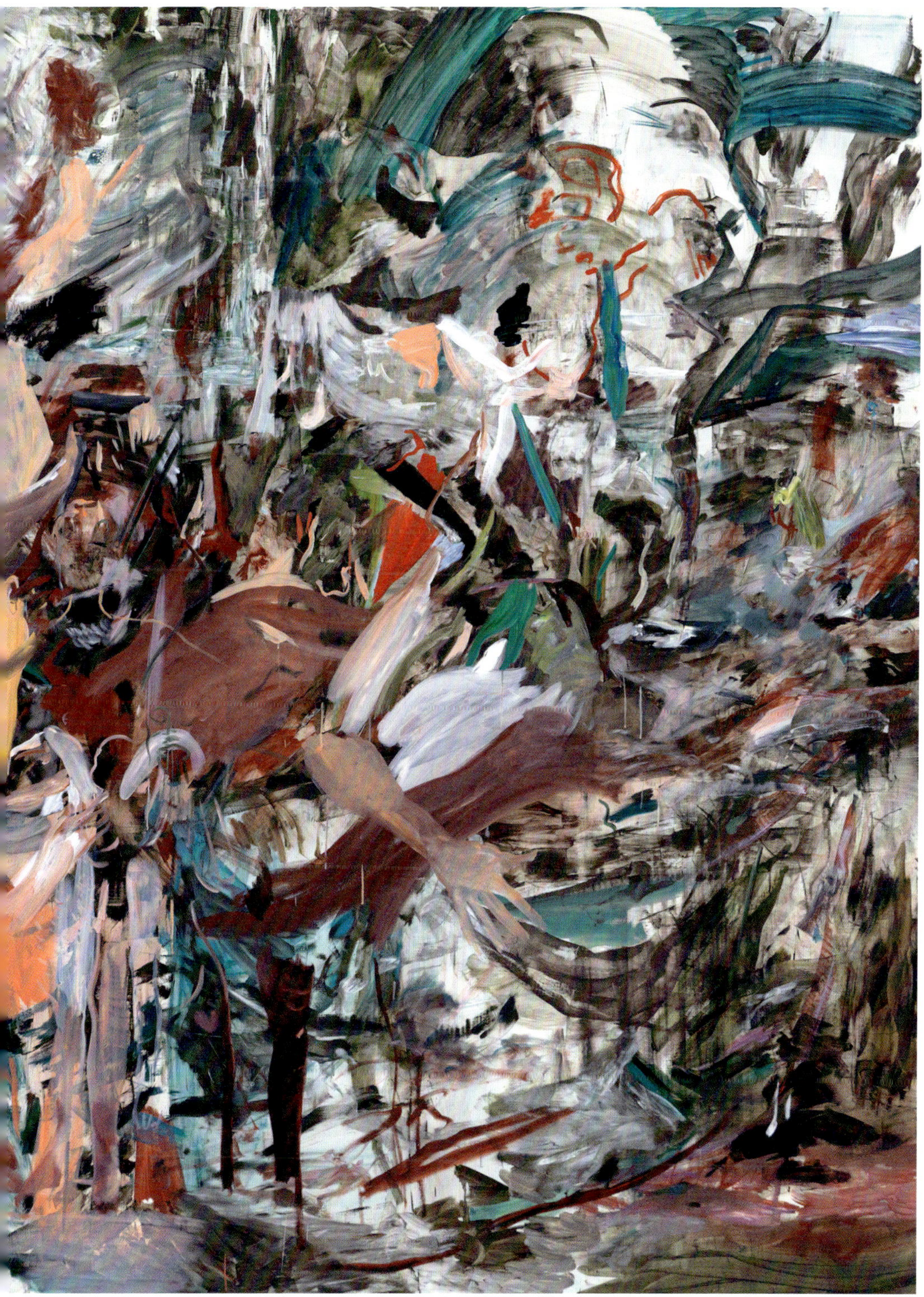

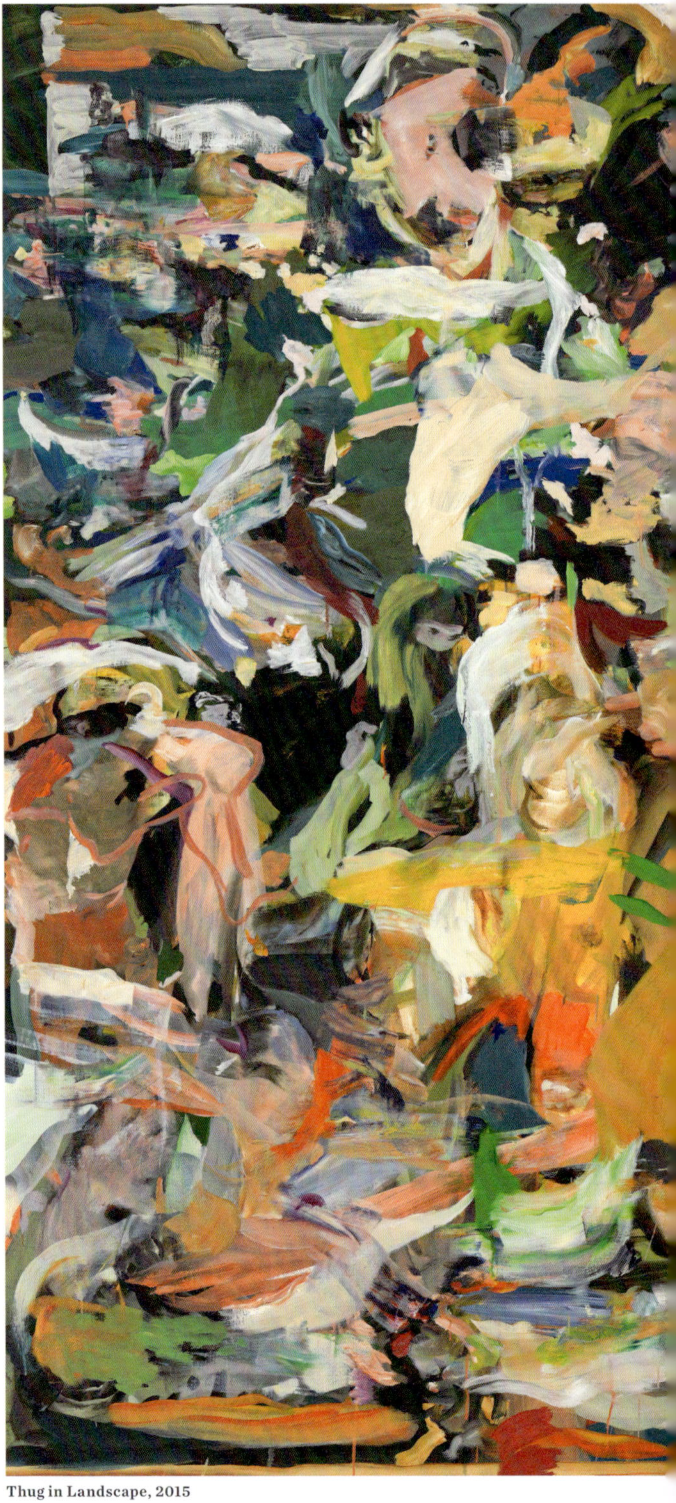

Thug in Landscape, 2015

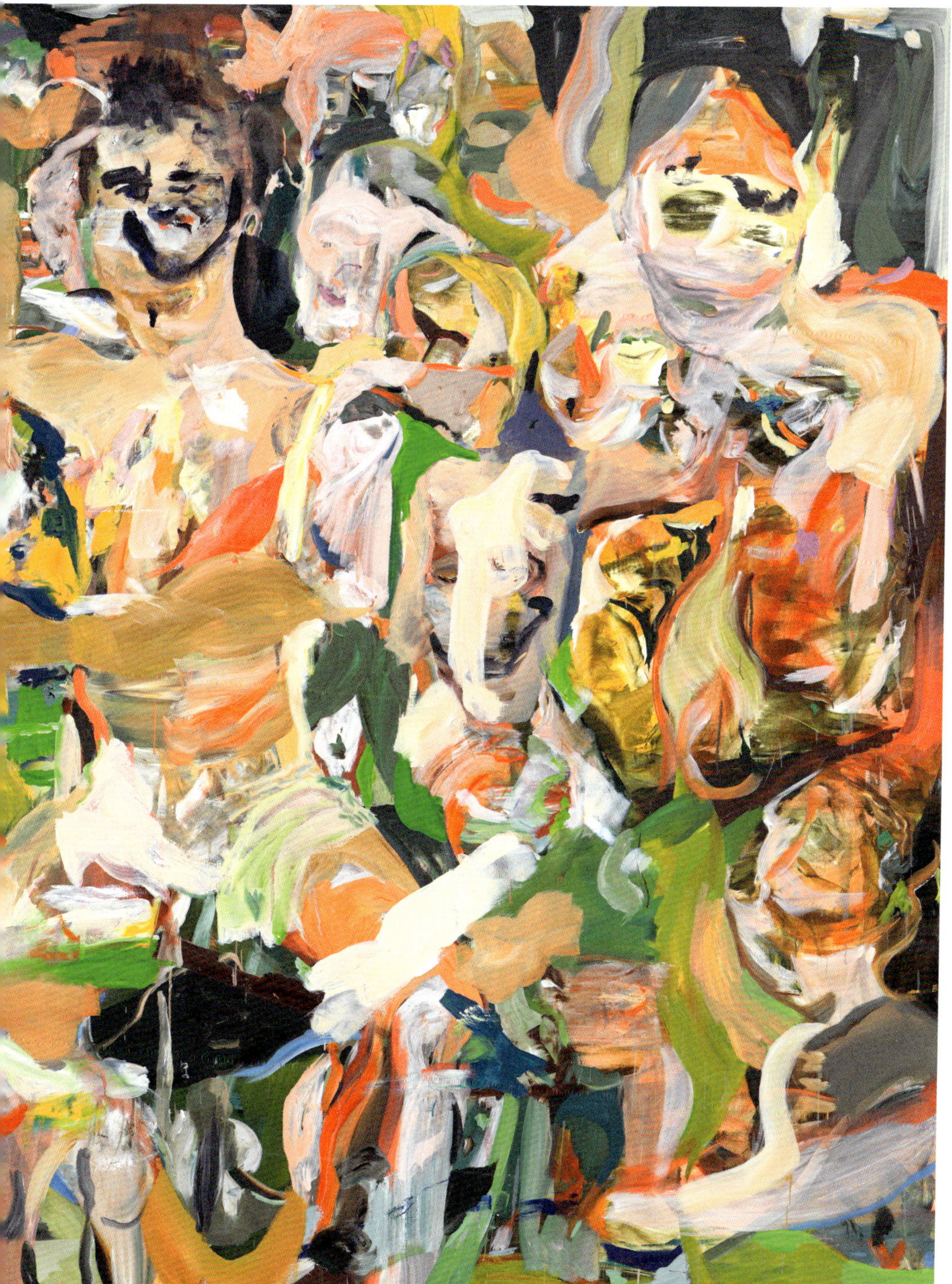

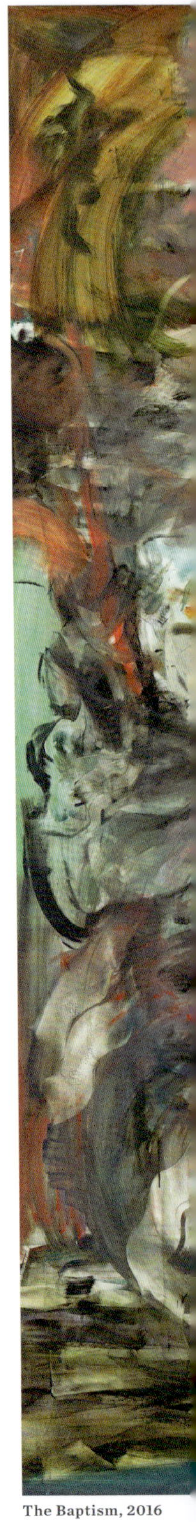

The Baptism, 2016

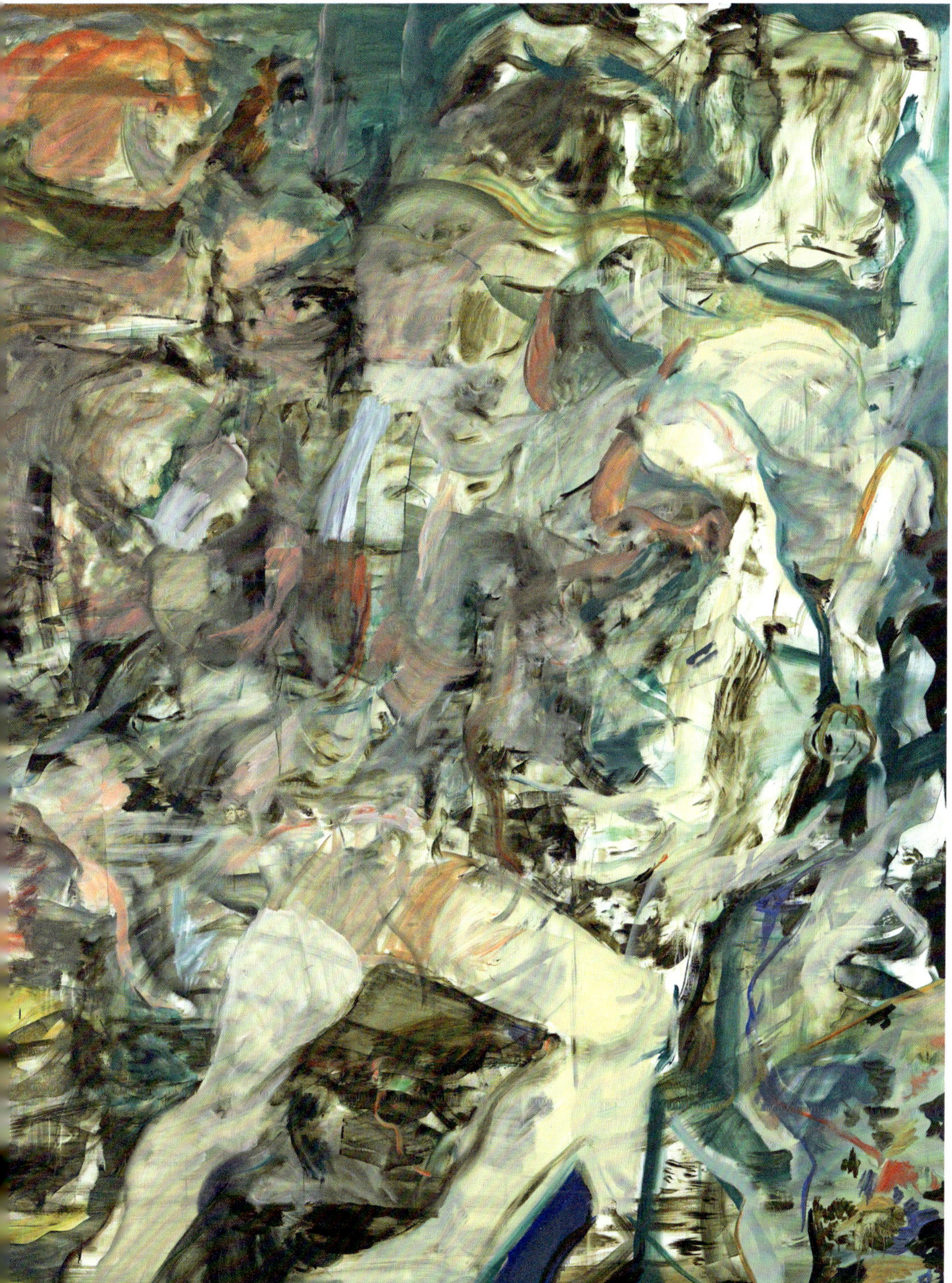

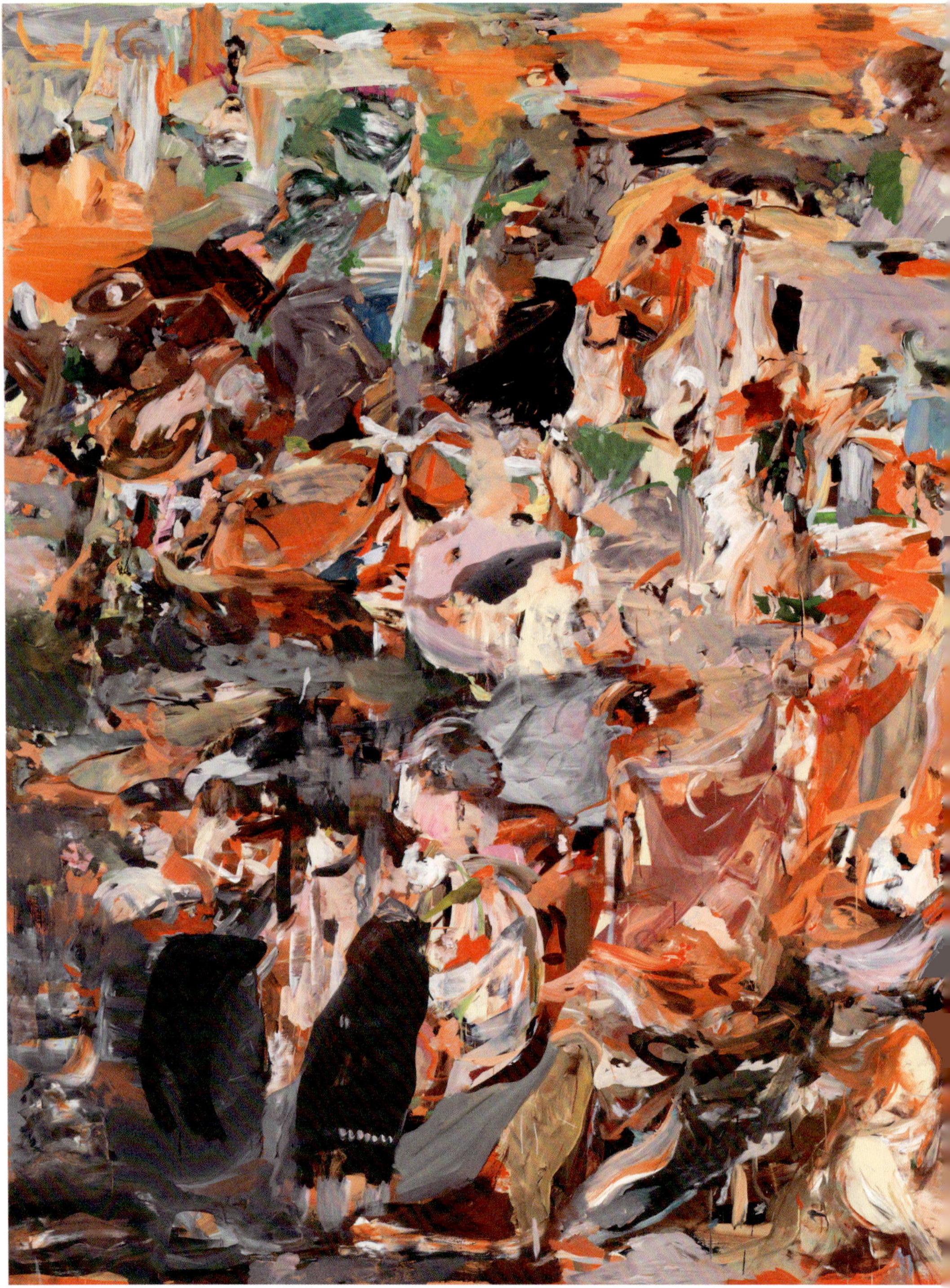

The Green, Green Grass of Home, 2010

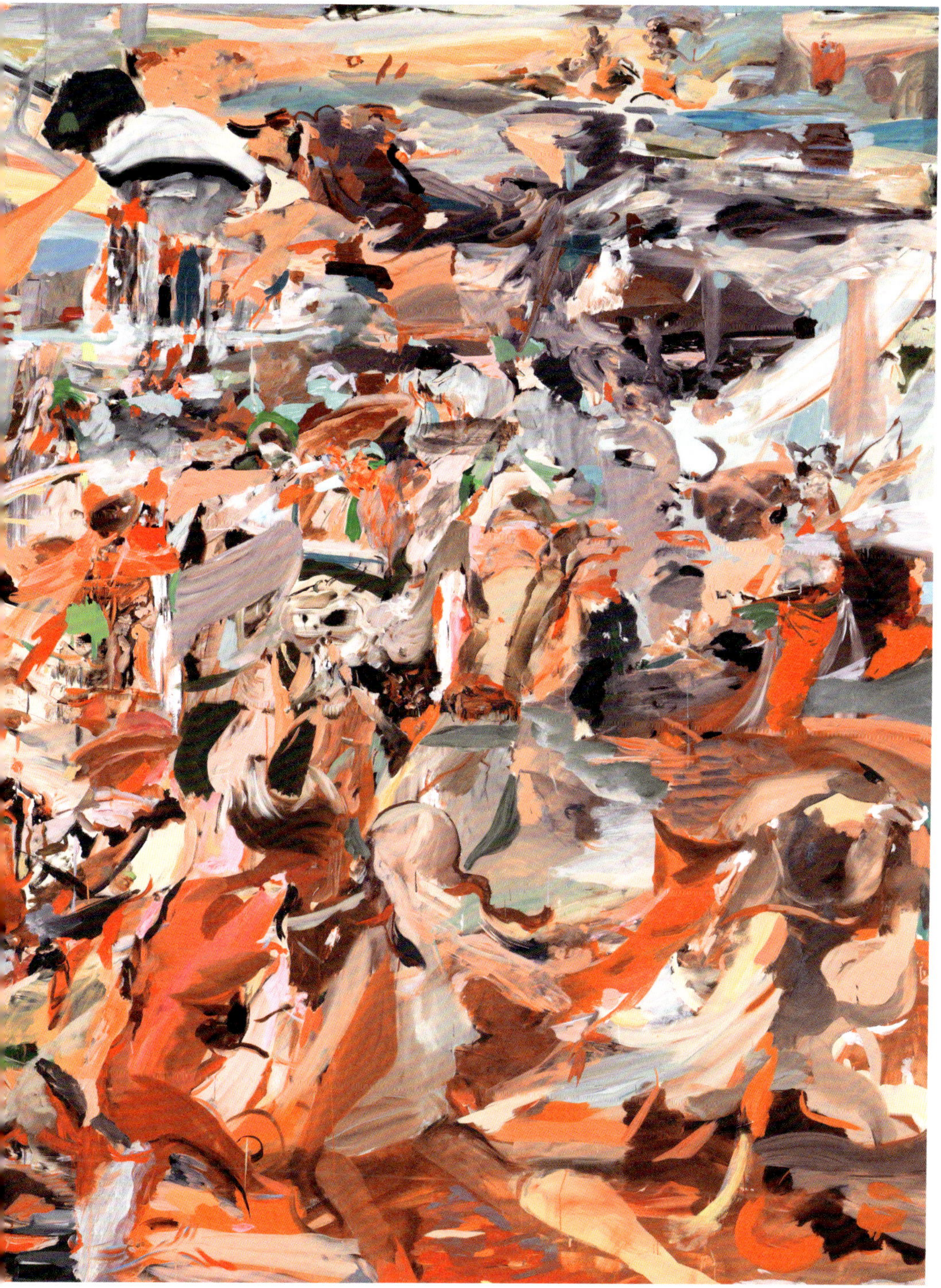

PAINTING AS A MARRIAGE BETWEEN BRAIN AND BODY

An interview with Cecily Brown

Lærke Rydal Jørgensen and Anders Kold
/ Louisiana Museum of Modern Art

Louisiana: ***Let us begin by talking about the painting that gives title to this book*** **– Where, When, How Often and with Whom.** ***What are we looking at?***
Cecily Brown: Shipwrecks. And women – or figures – on a beach. As with all my work, I begin with a specific motif in mind. But during the course of making the painting I can go very far away from that. And if I get lost then I'll go back to that in a very deliberate way. I'm always trying to chase the figure. There will be this struggle to restate the figure, when it tries to disappear entirely. At the same time, I often don't like the figure to be stated too clearly. So it is a battle back and forth. The fun and the excitement is that I don't know where it will end when I start. In this case, with *Where, When, How Often and with Whom,* I knew I wanted something to do with

shipwrecks, which I've been painting a lot of over the last couple years. And I'd also been painting these women that started with a series of drawings and paintings from *Electric Ladyland*. And ever since those *Ladyland* paintings, this group of female figures have haunted the work, but they've almost changed their role. It's a bit like having your actors who in different paintings perform a different role. I steal figures from every moment of art history.

You include other sources in your paintings.
Yes. I draw a lot. Once you've drawn something – say, those boys from Degas' *Spartans* – four or five times they become part of your lexicon. It's as if you internalise the paintings or the images you copy and when you need a figure you can use it as your own. It's not exactly like sampling in music, but similar. Once you've got the cast of characters, they can perform different roles in different paintings. I'd been very struck by a series of photographs of a woman on the beach in Nice being surrounded by cops. It's such a distressing series of images, because you see her just taking a nap on a beach on a beautiful day surrounded by tourists or holidaymakers. Not only is it a very striking series of images, physically, but the story really resonated with me, and of course it is sickening that women are being told what they can and can't wear in the 21st century. The irony being that, there are stories from the 50s where women would get their bikinis measured on the beach to make sure they were covered up enough. And another irony, for me, being that with most of the people around her, who are wearing almost nothing, the Western tourists, in most cases, you think: Well, they're not so pleasant to look at, perhaps they should cover up a bit more.

Is it the human conflict that interested you?
Yes, exactly. I think one of my main subjects has always been conflict. Also the dichotomy of good and evil existing in the same place at the same time. Whether it's bunnies being gang-raped in the most beautiful bucolic landscape on a day with scudding clouds and sunshine or something like this. And I was really struck by the hardness of the figures around her that were just watching. I've almost always included watching figures in my paintings, from the year dot.

Where did you get the idea to work in this large triptych format?

I always work on many things at once. I change the scale all the time, working from very large to very small. I think every young artist wants to work as big as they can as soon as they have a decent sized studio. I feel like my work's just gradually got bigger and bigger, until I realised a couple of years ago that it's probably much harder to work on a smaller scale, so I went very small. I find it more conducive to making paintings that work if many things are going on at the same time. *Where, When, How Often and with Whom* was the second I made on this scale, which are the largest paintings of my life, and actually the biggest that I can fit into my studio. The first is called *A Day! Help! Help! Another Day!*, which is taken from an Emily Dickinson title. When working on a large scale like this, I'm very free to go with the momentum of the painting – the painting has to tell me what to do. The painting is

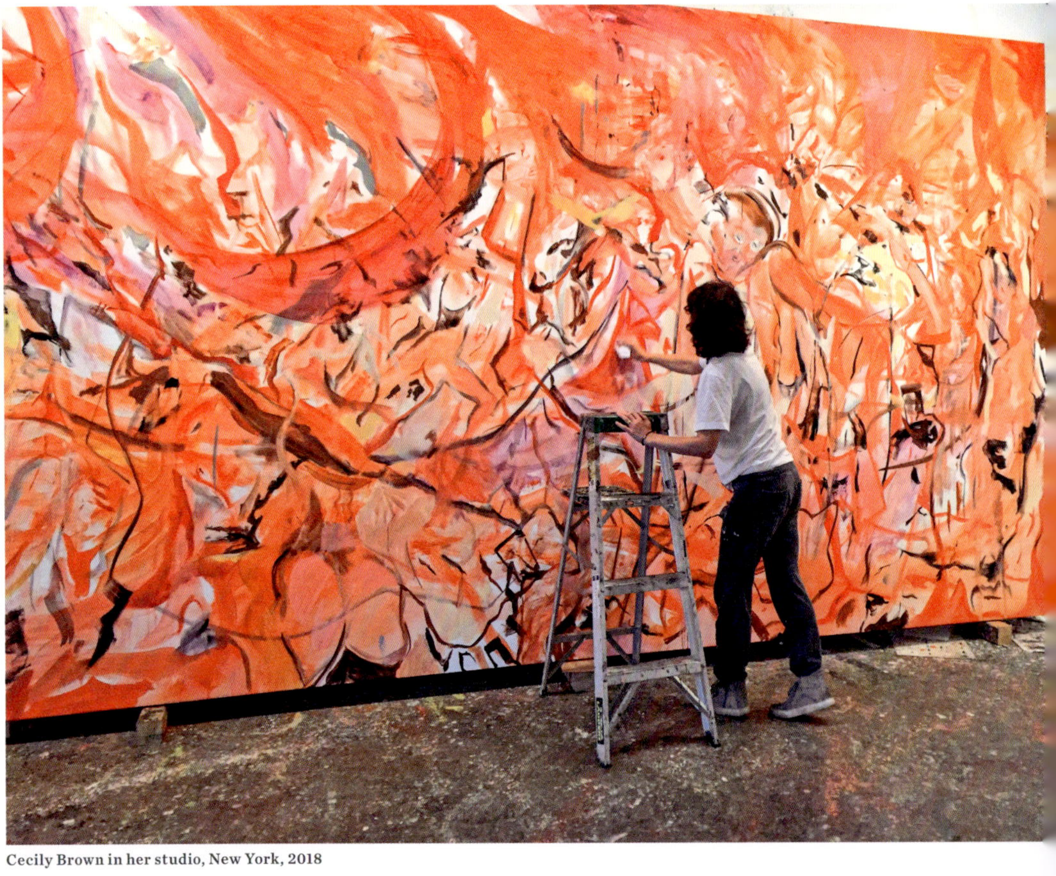

Cecily Brown in her studio, New York, 2018

more or less in charge. It's always a back and forth, as most painters know – putting something down and then not just going along in a linear way and pursuing what you thought you wanted to do but seeing what the painting throws back at you. I paint quite fast. Not that I finish a painting fast, but the physical act is fast. I make decisions on the fly and most of my painting decisions are made while I'm physically moving paint around. I found that working on this scale was incredibly exciting. One was involved in the painting in a performative way, far more than with any other scale. You really had to be up and down the ladder, and back and forth. It was a very physical activity. People forget how physical painting is, even medium-sized and small ones. But it's this marriage of your brain and your body. When you go into the studio in the morning, you have to feel that you've got the physical energy to take it on. And if you haven't, then you should do something else. You have to be very present, physically. Over the years, I've thought more and more that painting is closest to both dance and poetry.

How did you come up with the title,* Where, When, How Often and with Whom*?
I have lists of titles going back years of things that I think I might want to use at some point. I've had *Where, When, How Often and with Whom* written down for a little while. And it seemed appropriate. But one reason I liked it very much for this painting was the Gauguin association, not a physical resemblance to his painting, but I'd always loved that Gauguin title, *Where Do We Come From? What Are We? Where Are We Going?* I didn't want to steal the title altogether, but I like the fact that it's a series of questions. In a way, it's nonsensical, which I also go towards a lot with titles. They're very rarely descriptive, and I try to avoid descriptive titles. I like being light with the titles, especially if the paintings sometimes get overly morbid.

It's a very open title, beginning with what sounds like questions. Only there's no question mark – and no answers.
Obviously paintings are always asking questions, and each painting asks its own set of questions. Every few moves you make, you've set up a whole set of new problems that you then have to answer and deal with. I want to leave

that openness. The whole nature of my work is that there's this openness and that the questions are unanswered.

So you aim for the openness both with regard to titles and the painting?
Yes. I've always preferred starting a painting to the dreadful state of trying to finish it. There's a flow and an ease at the beginning, where everything is kind of thrilling. Every avenue is new, and you don't know what's about to happen. I don't want anything to be too resolved. That's probably my main formal issue, that balancing of having something there but not too there, but there enough. I started saying a couple of years ago, "I don't finish, I just stop," because it's a moment where you say: I'm going to stop now. It's not that it's finished. The compelling thing is that it's not at all predetermined. Apart from the colour. I pick the colour very deliberately. I try to be very slow and decisive about the palette, otherwise, every colour in the world enters in within the first days. So, I try to be very disciplined about when I allow a colour to enter.

In an interview with the Louisiana Channel from a couple of years ago you mentioned that you like the point between figuration and abstraction and that you try to avoid explaining to people what happens in your pictures.
Sometimes I go further into abstraction than either I mean to, or I realise, and I think it's very different if you're the person painting it – you know all the figural things that you put in there. With every stroke, I always feel like I'm making something figurative. If I feel I'm getting lost in a painting, I'll make myself think of the form again. It's almost like trying to remember someone's face and then letting your mind drift. Painting is very much about how much you drift and how much you come back to the form. And the concentration disperses and then it's diffused, and maybe something else starts going on. I have to feel like I'm pursuing something when I paint. The minute I'm not thinking of something specific, whether it's someone's arm or leg, or a church in the distance, or a ladder, or a pair of glasses, it becomes masturbatory paint that's only about itself.

You mention your lists of titles, and you call your titles "light". Could you explain how you work with titles?

Nearly every title is taken from something existing. The very first time I titled paintings was for an exhibition in the late 90s, where I named all the paintings after movie musicals like *High Society, The Pyjama Game,* and *Seven Brides for Seven Brothers*. I liked the idea that they were gaudy and bawdy. It was really right for the body of work because they were very bright and chaotic, very much like a Busby Berkeley song and dance routine, maybe with a hand grenade thrown into it. My paintings were very broken up and fractured but they had this sense of being too loud, with too much action – too theatrical – all things which I thought belonged in a painting. I liked the idea that a painting could contain all these things at once. This is the strength of a painting – it never has to be one note, it can be a drama, a comedy, a tragedy, hilarious and ridiculous all at once. It really is a great stage. It's this fixed object, but it can be read in many ways, and have many moods or atmospheres – you can gauge many possible meanings from different readings of the imagery. I never wanted to use any film titles after about 1950. I didn't really want my peers to know the movie well, because I wanted it to be suggestive rather than descriptive. It wasn't as if I'd find a title of a musical then watch the musical and see if it had anything to do with the painting. It was very much finding something that already existed, that belonged in a parallel world. For example the painting titled *Can-Can,* it doesn't mean that there are girls with their legs in the air. It was more the sensation of a can-can. Of course it was like a can-can as well. So *Can-Can* was the beginning, and it was so freeing. After that I went to just song titles, and for the next few years, everything was named either after a film, a play or a song. Those early years were the best in a way, because I used up most of the best titles in the first five years, and after that it became harder and harder. I've used names of perfumes, nonsense spam, pub names. Now, I've had to resort to poetry and the Bible! It's not that I was having a religious moment. It was more that I was desperate, that I felt I'd used up all the outside sources I possibly could. I'd come to the end of my title list that I had kept for so many years. And I can't remember what made me stumble on thinking of using the Bible, but it worked well for a while. For years, I wanted to avoid poetry as well. When I

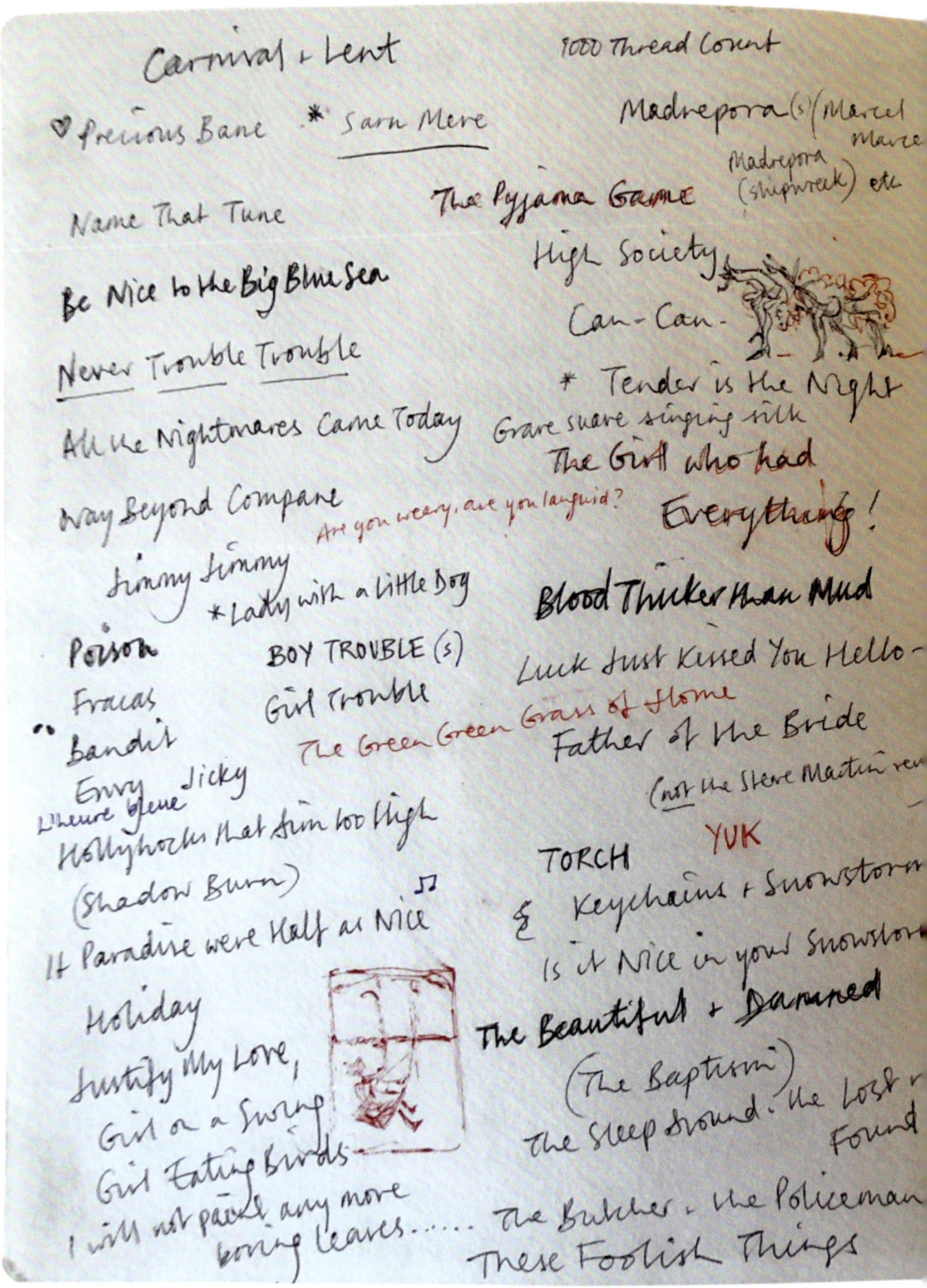

Carnival + Lent

♡ Precious Bane * Sarn Mere

Name That Tune

Be Nice to the Big Blue Sea

Never Trouble Trouble

All the Nightmares Came Today

Way Beyond Compare

Are you weary, are you languid?

Jimmy Jimmy

* Lady with a Little Dog

Poison

BOY TROUBLE (s)

Fracas

Girl Trouble

Bandit

The Green Green Grass of Home

Envy Jicky

L'heure Bleue

Hollyhocks that Aim too High

(Shadow Burn)

If Paradise were Half as Nice ♫

Holiday

Justify My Love,

Girl on a Swing

Girl Eating Birds

I will not paint any more boring leaves.....

1000 Thread Count

Madrepora(s) (Marcel Marcé

Madrepora (shipwreck) etc

The Pyjama Game

High Society

Can-Can

* Tender is the Night

Grave snare singing silk

The Girl who had Everything!

Blood Thicker than Mud

Luck Just Kissed You Hello

Father of the Bride

(not the Steve Martin ver

YUK

TORCH

& Keychains + Snowstorm

Is it Nice in your Snowstor

The Beautiful + Damned

(The Baptism)

The Sleep Around. The Lost + Found

The Butcher + the Policeman

These Foolish Things

Spread from Cecily Brown's notebook

We Think the Same Things at the Same Time

New Face in Hell

~~Daydream Believer~~

There's no right way to do me wrong.

Carnival Traffic

No You for Me

British People in Hot Weather

Candy

New ~~Kicks~~ Louboutin Pumps

Shipwrecks

Sweetie

Combing the Hair(s)

~~Beach~~ ~~Boys~~

FUNNY CRY HAPPY

Suddenly Last Summer

(Cote d'azur, Miami, in the garden)

HA HA FRESH

Black Friday

The Girl and Goat

Banquet

No Room for the Groom

The Fox + Geese

Picnic

Cruel Frederick

Armed + Fearless

Make it Rain

Serenade

Looking very good vermeil concierge

The Quick One

Spree

This is fun fun

Frenchy

Dodgy

Park

Name That Tune

Song + Sugar + Fire

B.F.F.

Unfurl the Flag

When Time Ran Out

A Yankee in King Arthur's Court

Rush the Night Prowlers

Canopy

Where Every Season Smiles

Summer Storm

Couple

Skulldiver(s) Unbent by wind, Unchilled by snows.

Performance

An Exhortation

ODE to the WEST WIND

The Sick Leaves

Sick Mood at Sunset · A Day! Help! Help! Another Day!

Love me till Tuesday

The Sea + the Mirror

Beach Blanket Babylon

The Year of the Scavenger

A Sublime Misadventure (J.S.)

Lady Luck

Thanks Roody Hooster

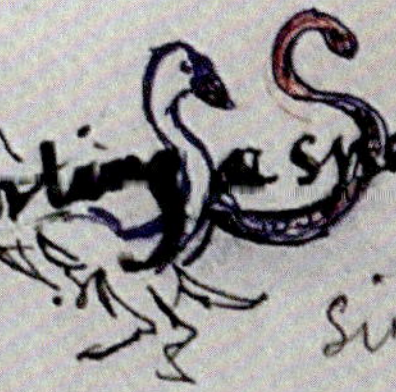

A Swan Comforting a Snake

Tripe with Lemons

Sirens + Shipwrecks + Bathers + the Band

S.A.P.

In the Midst of Wild Quietness

L.C.V.

Cold walls, hot spaces (wild mouths)

Black Painting(s)

Red Painting(s)

was younger I thought that was much too corny and romantic. I think now I have embraced that I am just a romantic painter. I've now almost used every title I possibly can from Emily Dickinson.

You could also have taken the easy modernist way out by just naming your paintings 'Untitled'?

Titles are basically for other people and for identifying the paintings. At the very beginning, I never titled anything. I title because I'm lucky enough to have things that go into the world, and one wants to be able to talk about them, "this one versus that one." I'd made dozens of small paintings over the years that I'd never thought of titling as I went along, they were just things I'd made and put in the corner of the studio. Then I did a show of them in New York about three years ago and wanted to title the ones that would be in the book. Now when I see half of them are untitled and half of them have

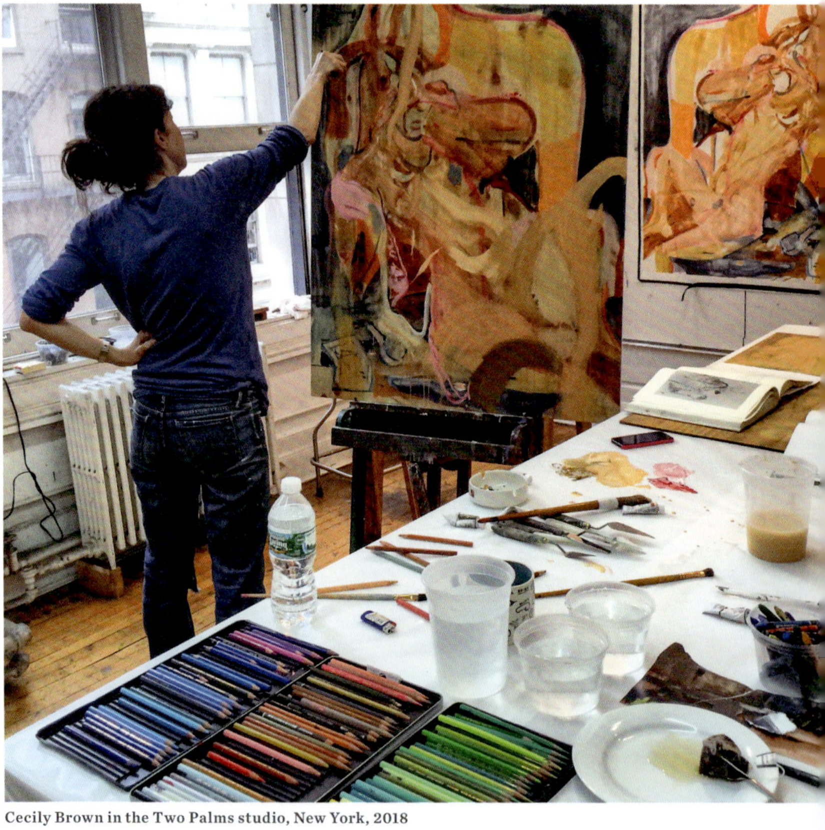

Cecily Brown in the Two Palms studio, New York, 2018

these very sweet titles, I do feel guilty – I feel I should go back and name the others. By the '90s 'Untitled' seemed pretentious, overused, and also hinting too much at the sublime. "This work is so … I can't possibly attempt to describe it." And many paintings back then were not really untitled – they would be 'Untitled' and then have some great, long, poetic title in brackets. In a way, my frivolous titles were a reaction to that. It was the same as when I started writing just my first name on my canvases, with this sort of girlish flourish of "Cecily." You could have added underneath "age nine and three quarters." I needed the frivolity in order not to be overly portentous, as I was working in this sort of macho tradition – and in order to give myself permission to make this kind of painting. After having been a painter in the early '90s in London, it took me years and years to let go of layers of shame and guilt for all the different things that I was doing wrong. Like painting a figure, painting in oils, painting on rectangles – the painters I liked being too emotional, being too highly-charged. Someone once said to my dad: "Oh, I know why your daughter doesn't really fit with the YBAs, they're cool and she's hot." With the titles I wanted to show that the paintings weren't expressionist – I hate the word in the way it implies that it's expressive of a certain mood, and that mood is probably dark and angry. You can make a gesture or a mark in many kinds of mood. I always wanted to avoid the reading that these gestural marks were expressive of the "dark night of the soul." I wanted to have the dark night of the soul, but along with something like a singing, dancing, 42nd Street.

You call painting "a macho tradition." In what way have you experienced that as a female artist?

I've often been asked these autobiographical questions, like "Who are you in this painting?" With the *Ladyland* women, I didn't really feel I was any of the figures. I felt very much that I was looking at them as much as any man or any person would have been. I'm not trying to make a case for the female gaze. Of course this is told from the point of view of a female, but, as I've said before, I don't feel that I'm painting as a woman, any more than I feel like I'm painting as an English person or painting as a … When I'm painting, I'm just a painter. It's also been said, quite often, that I paint in the tradition of these males. I can understand why people want to say that, but from a female point of view I think it's slightly absurd. That I'm taking on the mantle of male painting. That's not why I get up in the morning. I even had a review once that said, "Cecily was on top in this painting," which was really offensive. But, I think one tries to be both and one tries to be everything in the painting.

In our time, though, it may seem difficult just to adopt a general 'human perspective', because the zeitgeist very much is that we have to acknowledge that we are men and women, the different races and so on. How do you relate to that as a painter?
I've always thought painting is something that most humans can relate to, and it's very relatable and easy to understand. I know from experience that any person from any background – for example a person who might come to read your electric meter – might walk into my studio in New York (you know what buildings in New York are like, there's different things on every floor)

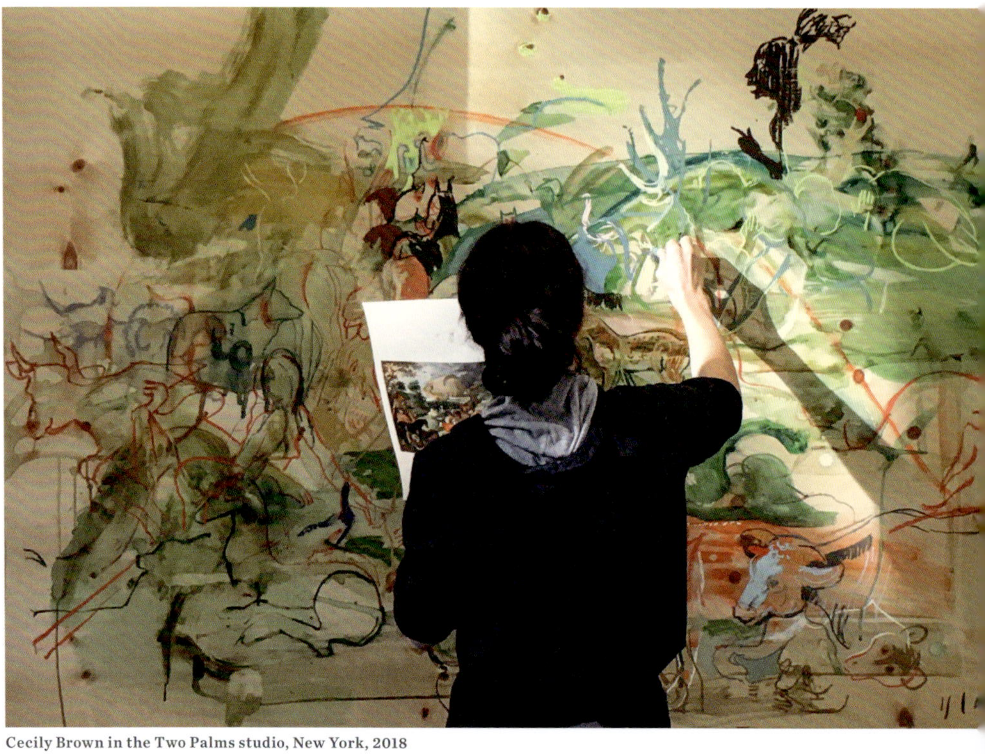

Cecily Brown in the Two Palms studio, New York, 2018

bu wouldn't be expecting to walk into a big studio and see all this stuff. It's very gratifying that people who are obviously not from an art background or are not used to looking at art, stand there and look at it, and get something from it. I'm not saying everyone responds, but I think painting is the least elite of all the visual arts anyway. You stick most kids in front of a painting and they'll find they have something to say and something to look at.
I think it's a huge problem in the world that a lot of people – certainly in America – don't realise that museums are for them. That they might not have access, except maybe on school trips. But there's a feeling that museums are for rich people, or white people. Not that this is something that everyone can come and see and get something from. They may not always find themselves represented. I just read a line last night by Steinbeck about not finding yourself represented. When someone feels they're not being spoken to, if they aren't represented, it might be harder to find a way in for them. If you're black and you go to the Louvre and the only black people in there are servants. It's a bit like Hollywood. You don't want to only be shown as an extra in the background.

You've talked about the morbidity in your work. Where does all the morbidity or the darkness of your paintings come from – is it from somewhere inside you or from outside?
The world's in a worse state right now than it has been in my lifetime. In a way, it has only heightened things that were already there. It's not that they were in my character, but all that's going on at the moment, which is horrifying, in politics, and the way people are treating each other around the world, unfortunately, is nothing really new. It's never been as close to me as it is at the moment because of where I live. I have very rarely let current events enter my work before. And even in the triptych we just discussed, it's not there in an overt way. I did try to paint the burkini woman in an overt way also. But I want it to be more general – not tied to one specific event. I certainly use subjects that are about humans' vileness to one another, and the atrocities people can commit. The horror of the world, I think, has been there in my work from the beginning. Part of my attraction to older paintings is that the most terrible subjects on earth are depicted. I love paintings

of Hell. I always liked the expression "the Devil has all the best tunes." I always find that I go to a depiction of Hell and look at it for an hour and then look at Heaven for 30 seconds.

You are very often generous in terms of citing your sources. Some of your drawings are titled 'after Bosch' or 'after Hogarth' and so on.
The whole point of it is that I'm figuring something out and, by copying a work, you internalise it and get to know it so well. It will be useful to me later on. You just learn so much from copying a Hogarth or a Bruegel. And it's also very challenging technically – just keeping your eye and hand and mind very precise, because you have to get those things in the right place, and they're very complex. They're great for teaching you about complexity and composition.

Is that a way of saying that the grand narratives and the great tales of man are still relevant today?
That's what art is for, isn't it? To not just talk about them, but to process them, to show there's a continuum for hundreds of years of people going through similar things. There's a solace in feeling that we're going through similar things. It's perhaps reassuring to know this has happened before. Everything old is new again.

And an artist in a studio is a very solitary figure. There's something completely archaic about the artist in the studio. Géricault, Bosch and Hogarth were also just standing in front of a canvas.
This is one of the things I've always thought – that my problems really aren't so different from Bosch's. The day-to-day, the making of the image. To go back to what you said before about the whole taking-on of these old guys: it's more of a conversation with them than a competition, though I am very competitive with the dead artists, and that's why I'll never be satisfied. And, of course, I'm going to take from everyone who I go and look at, and use them. I need to respond to the art that I look at. So in a way my paintings are my reply. To go back to painting being a question, and art being a question, I want to talk back.

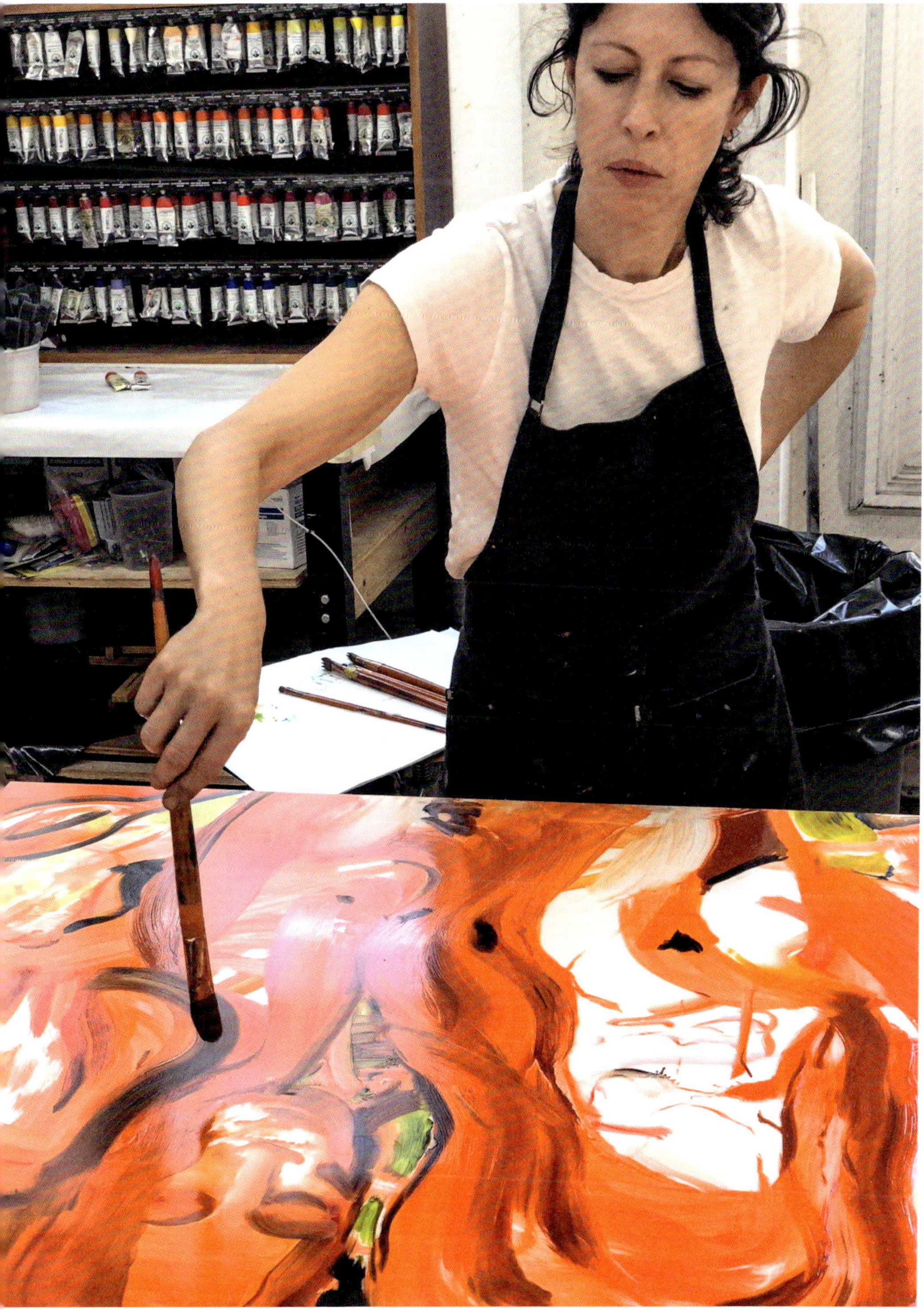

Cecily Brown in the Two Palms studio, New York, 2018

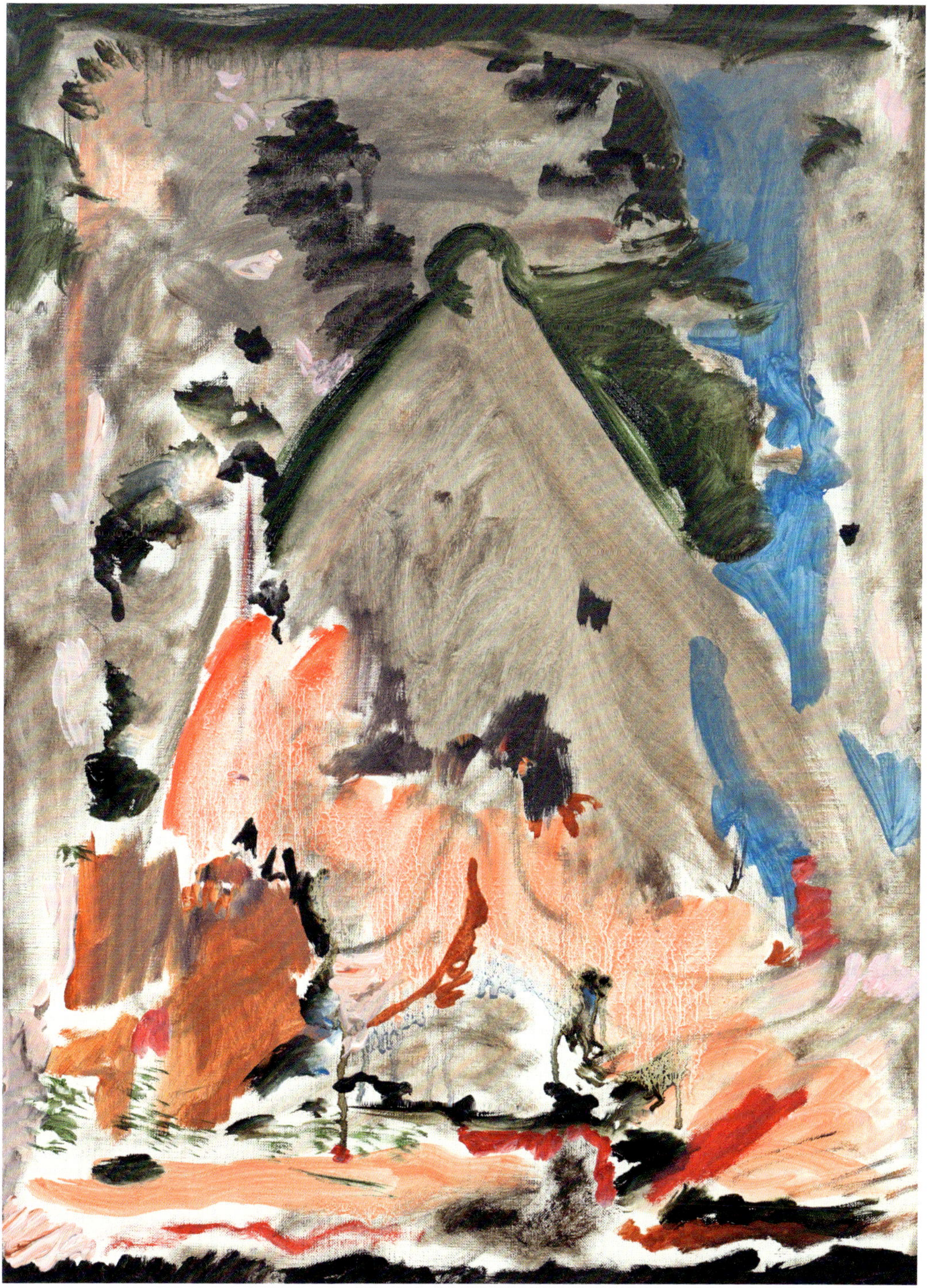

Imaginary Calamities, 2016

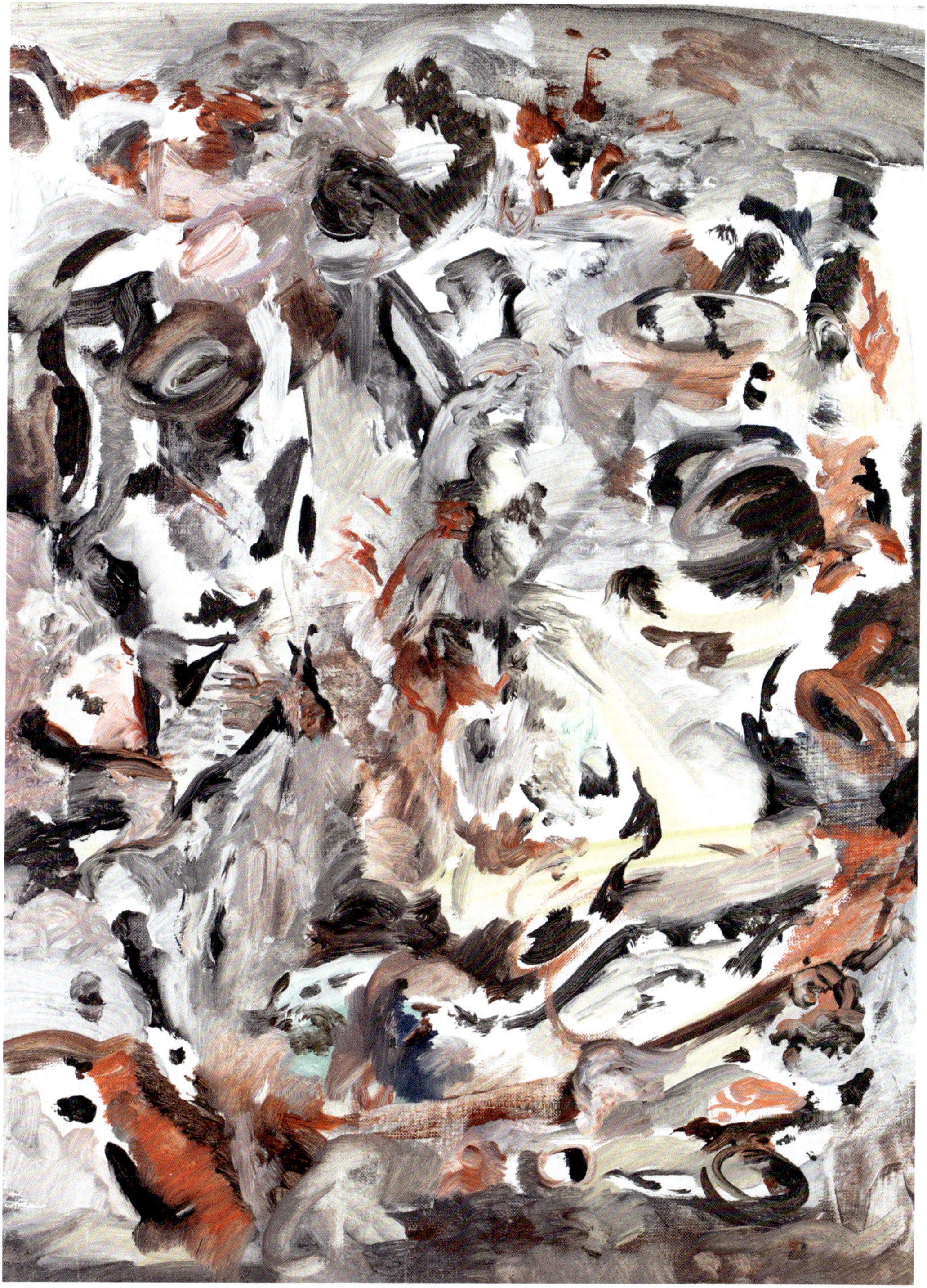

Untitled, 2009

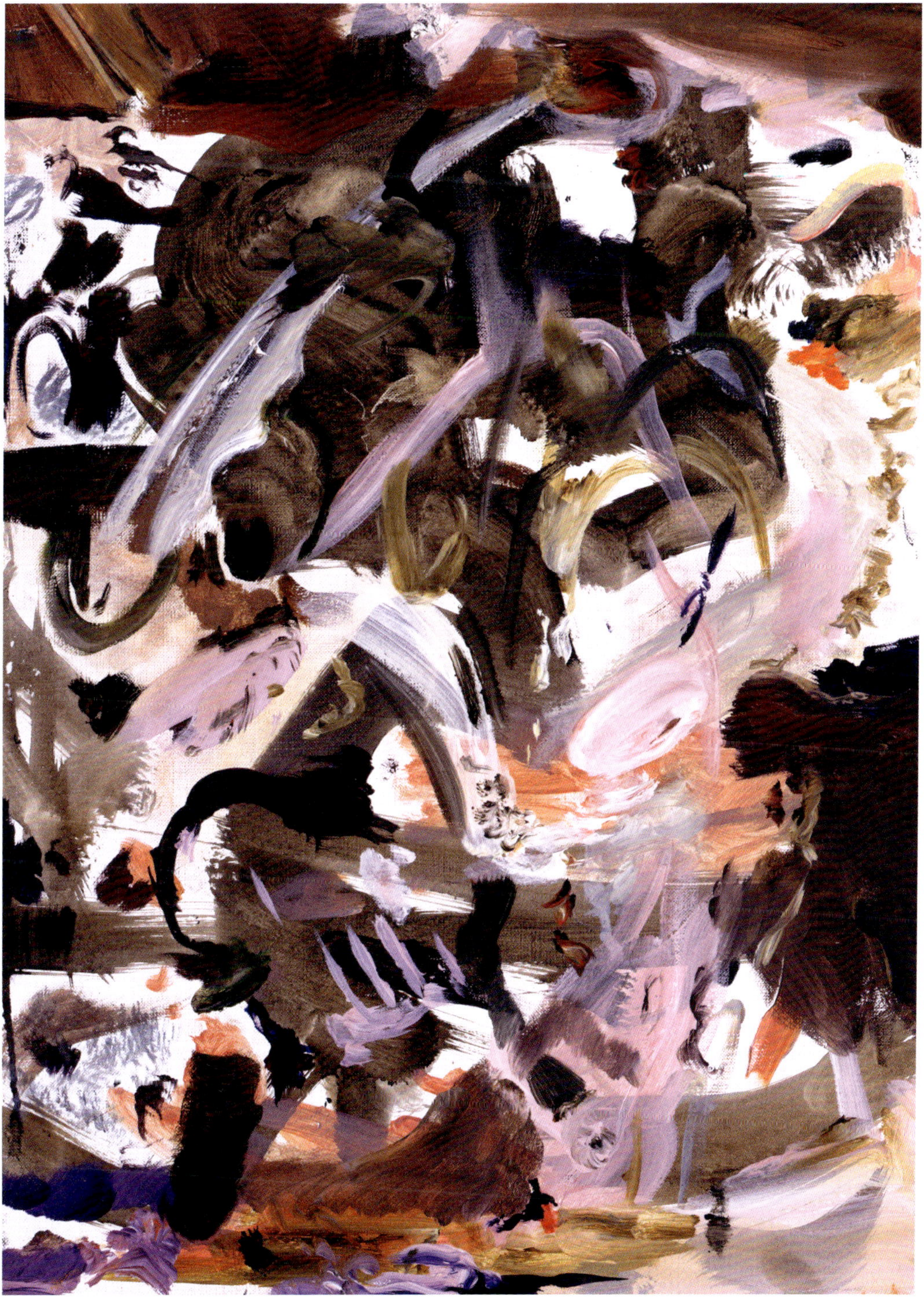
Untitled (#102), 2010

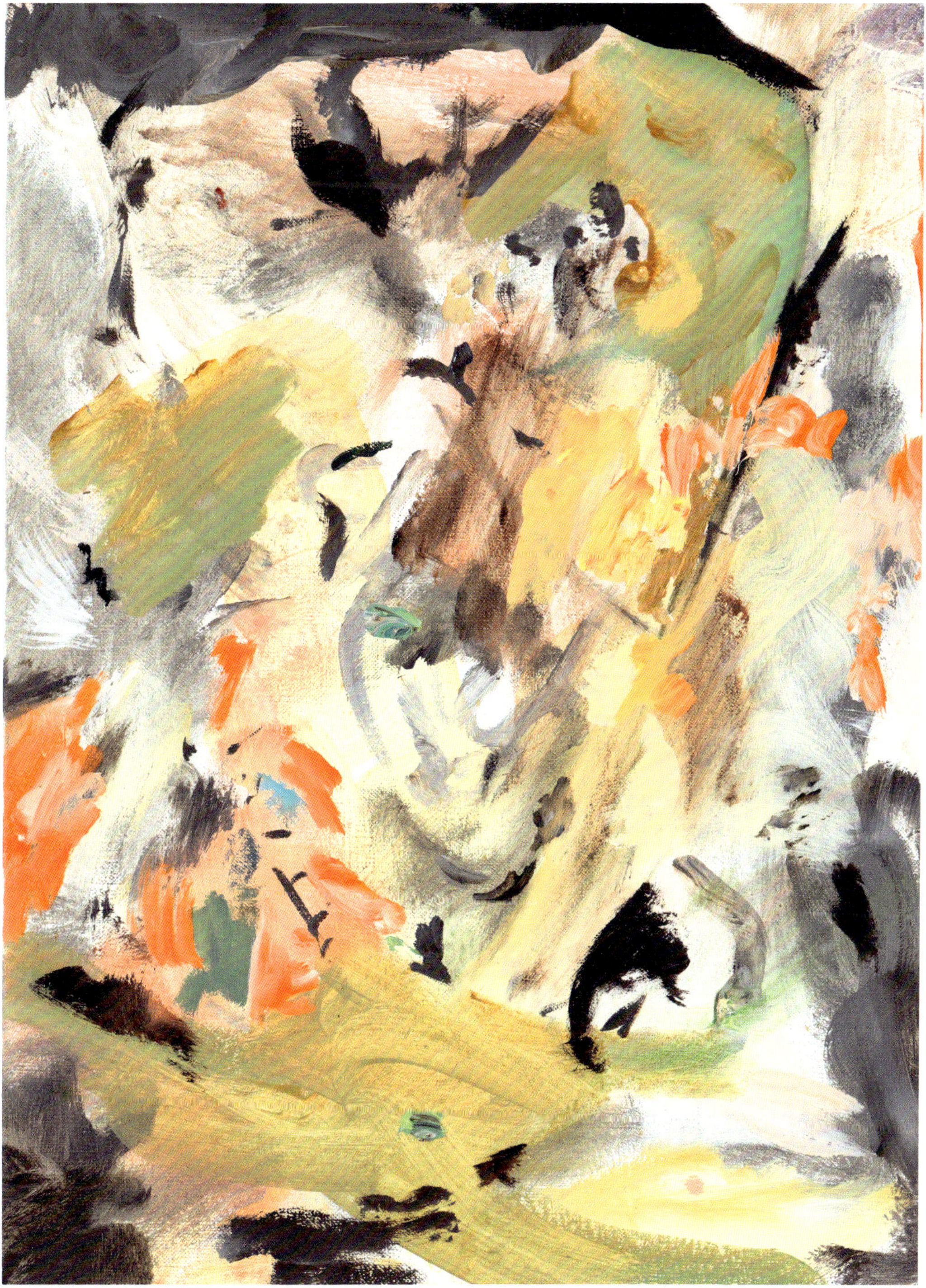

Untitled, 2009

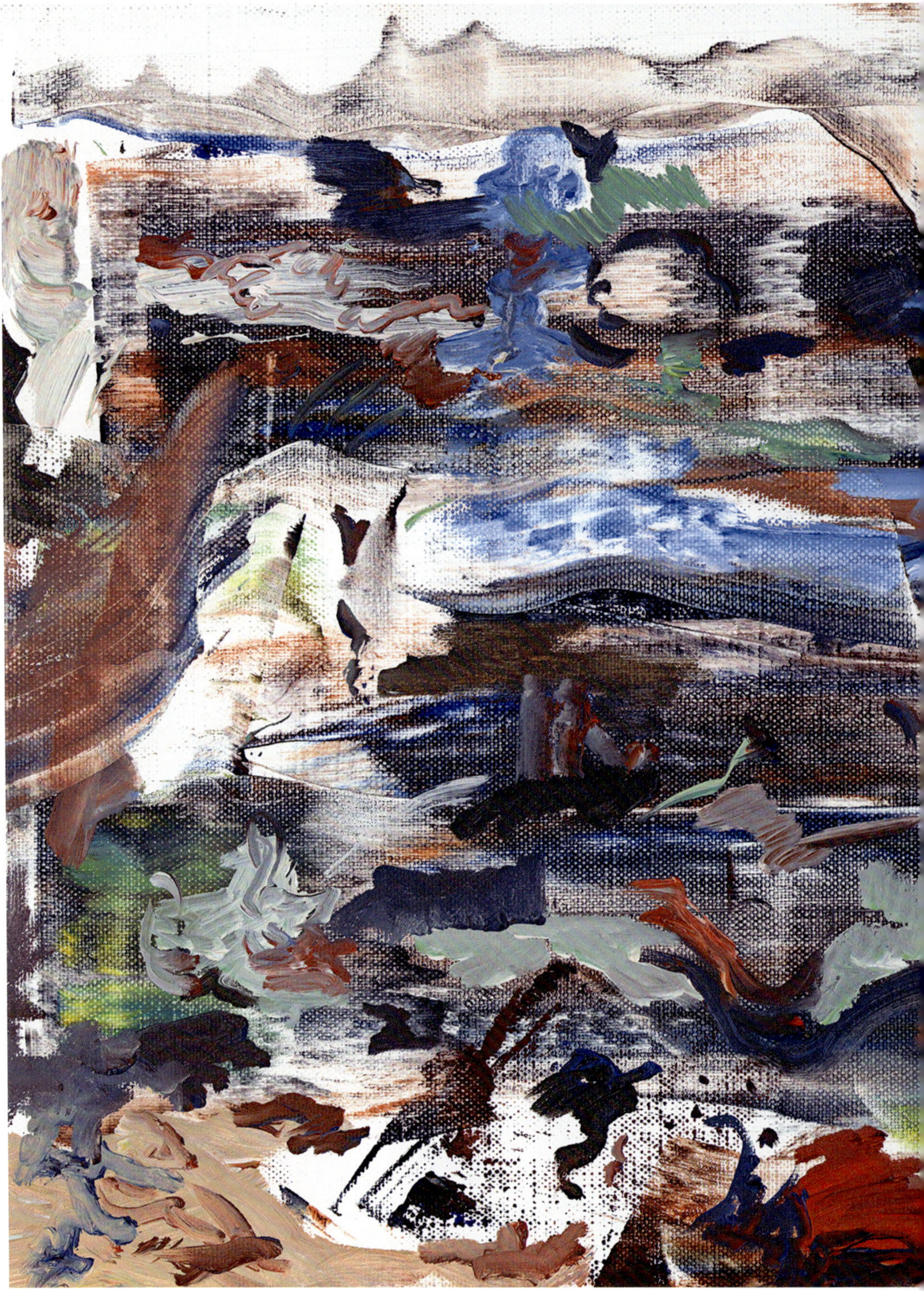

Untitled, 2016

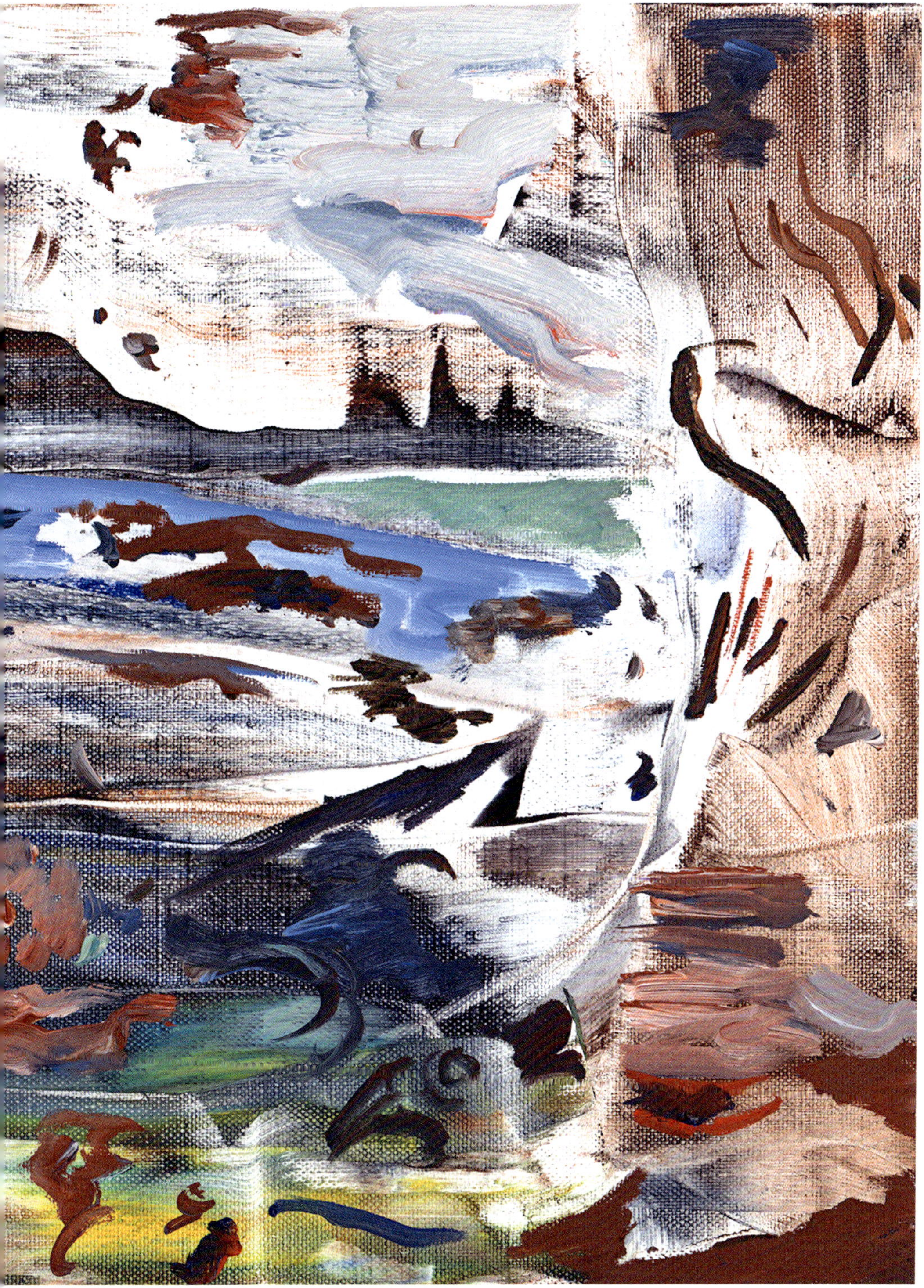

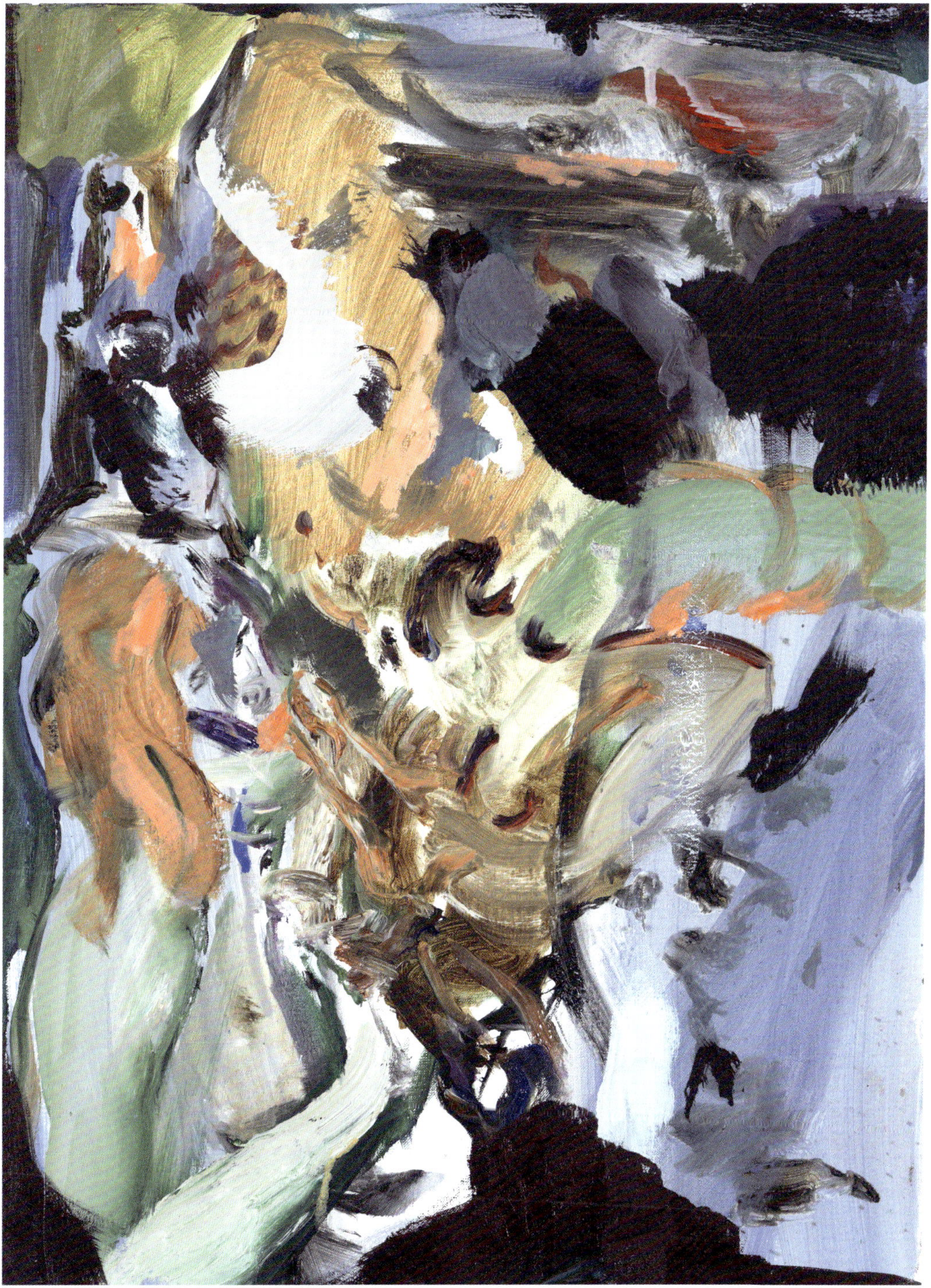

Are You Weary, Are You Languid?, 2010

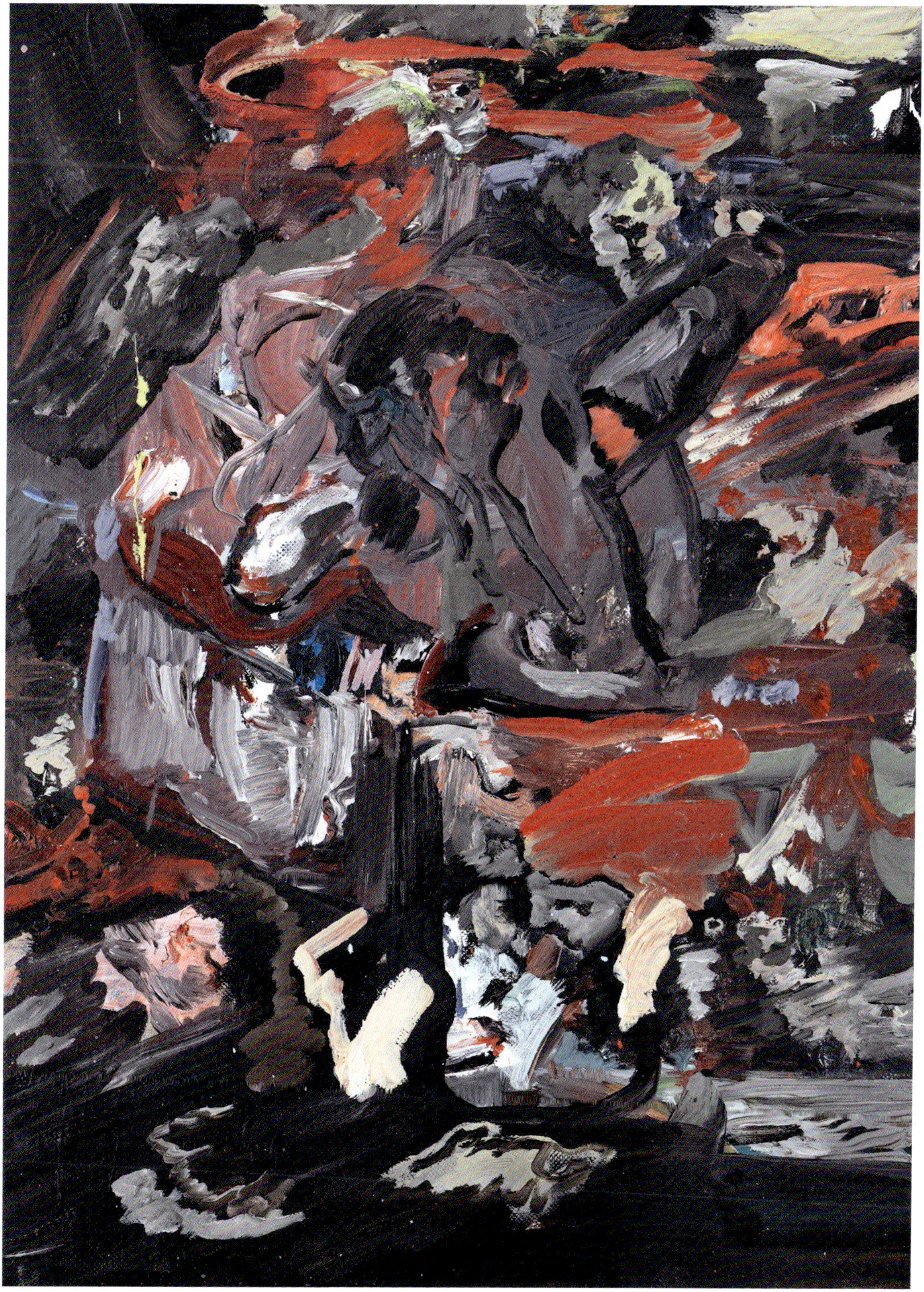

Untitled, 2013

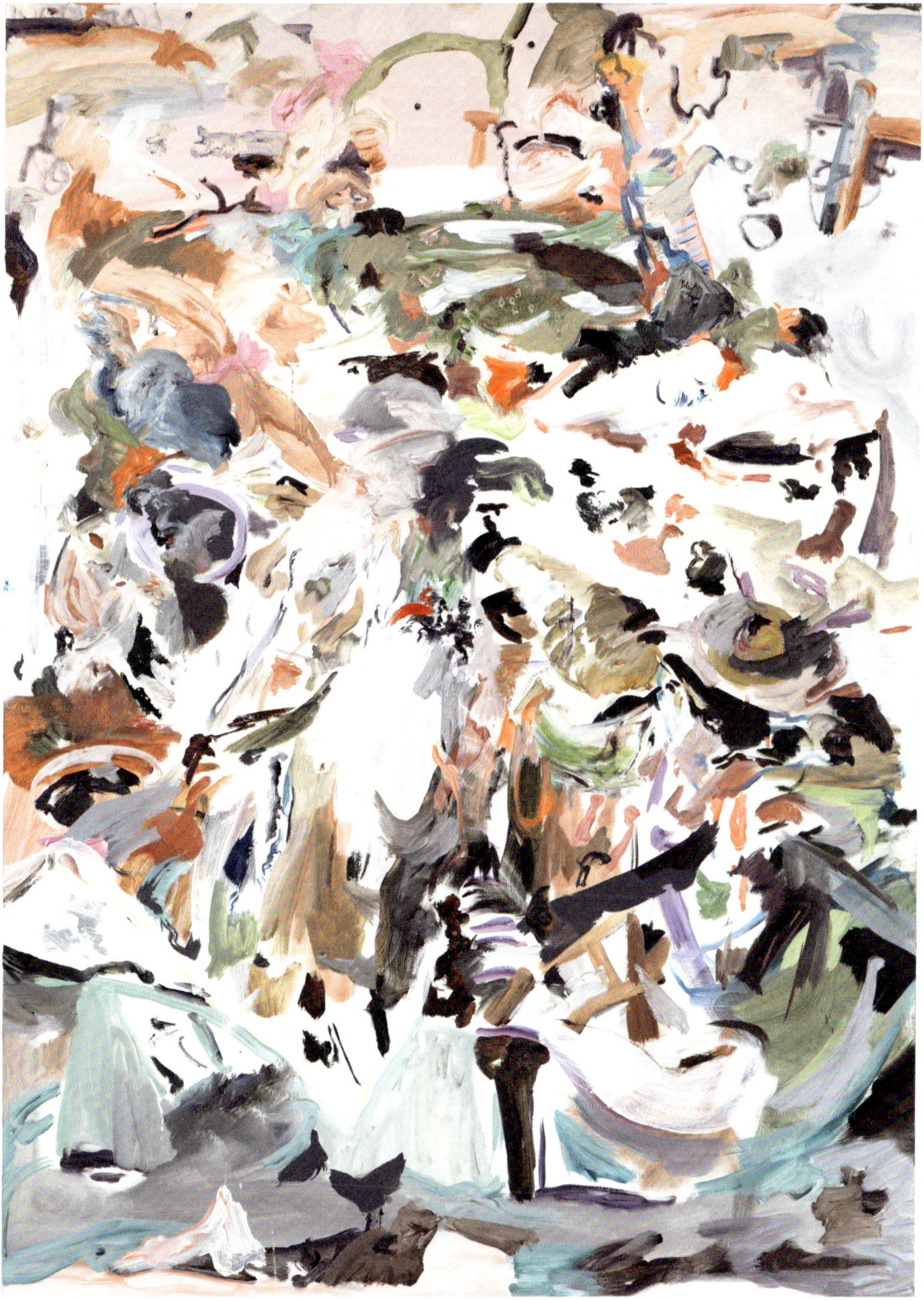

The Tribulations of the Tablecloth, 2011

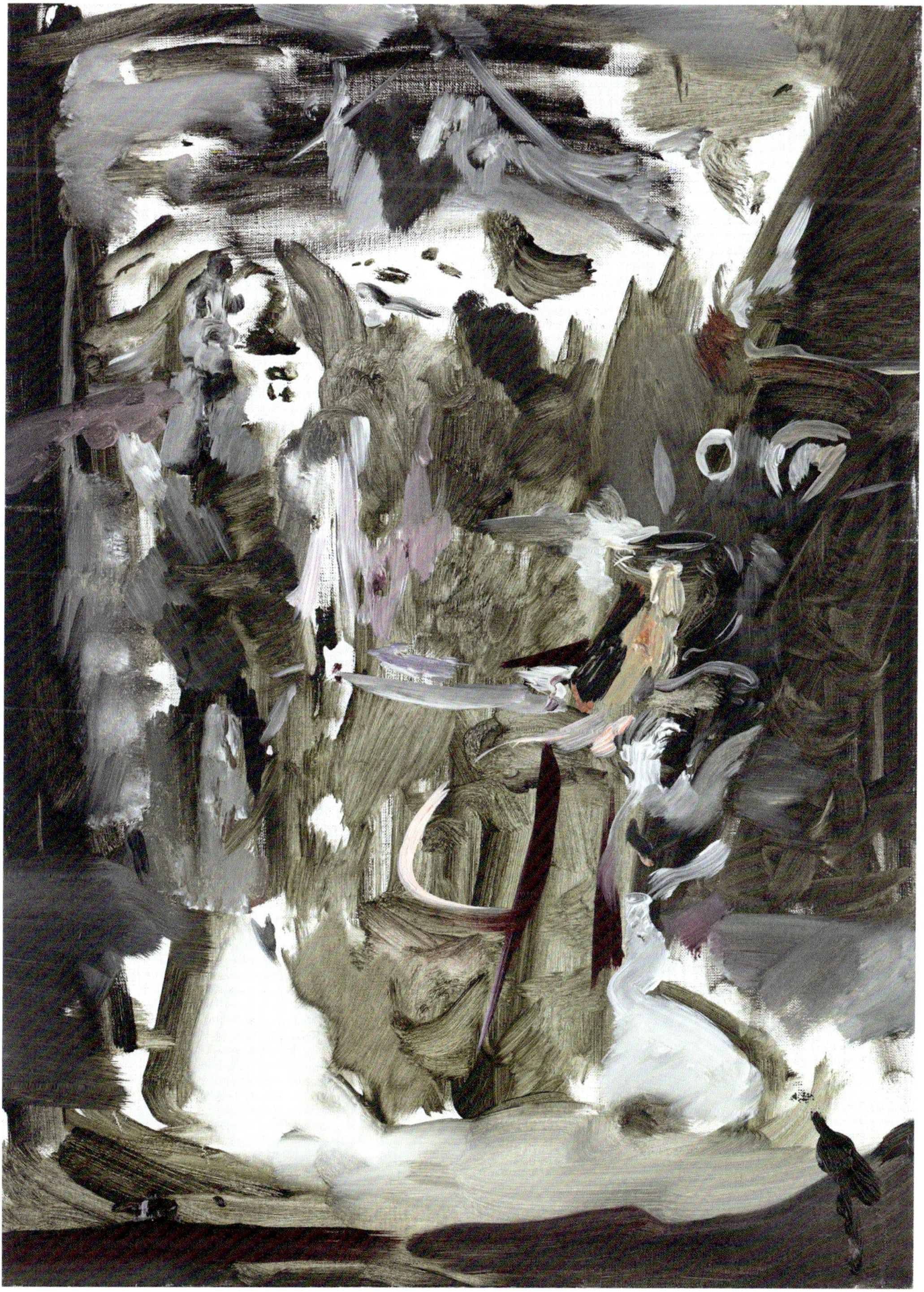

Untitled, 2016

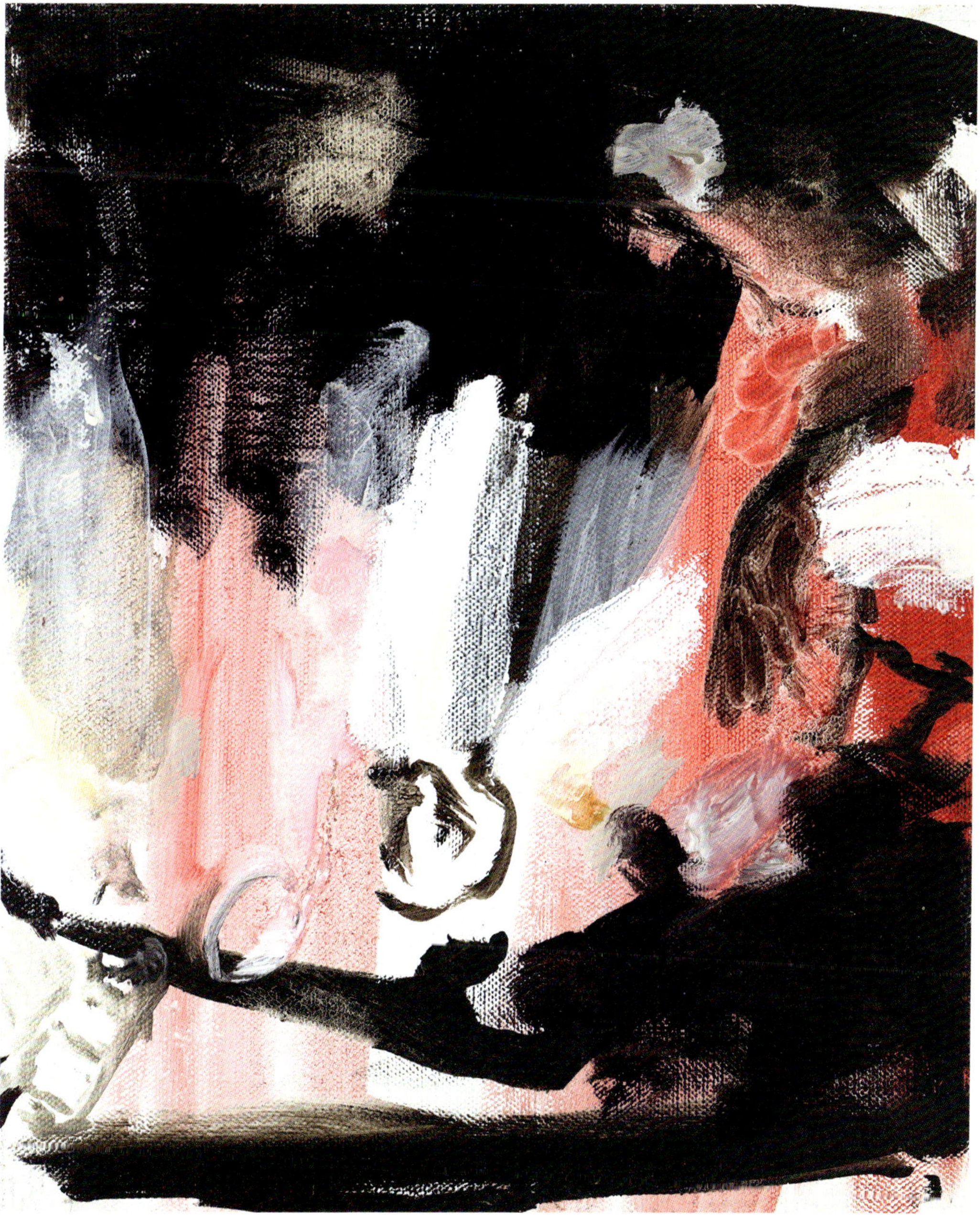

Untitled, 2009

SWIPE RIGHT

Terry R. Myers

Purity is exclusive and exercises choice; experience, nature for the purpose of art, invites anybody.
Elaine de Kooning, 1955[1]

You adjust the paints' values and hues not to the world, not to the vision, but to the rest of the paint. The materials are stubborn and rigid; push is always coming to shove.
Annie Dillard, 1989[2]

"Maybe the earlier paintings are like characters in the new paintings?" That's what slipped out of my mouth in late April during my last visit to Cecily Brown's studio in New York, and at the time we both thought it sounded pretty good, especially for a text intended to accompany a survey of her paintings and works on paper. However, it didn't take me long to ask myself what it actually meant. Great artists steal, it's true, and Cecily Brown is a great artist who has improved her work steadily if not exponentially by stealing from artists with abandon and a refreshing lack of guilt. Or as Elaine de Kooning wrote, also in the essay quoted from above: "The reason that artists can be endlessly enthralled by previous styles of painting is that they can bring new motives to them and thereby confiscate them."[3] Brown's head-on take-no-prisoners approach to painting over all of these years makes postmodern anti-painting appropriation art come off weaker than it seemed back when it dominated critical discourse.

Brown has exposed her thievery the most in her audacious works on paper by making her sources as graphic as her subject matters, not to mention the multitude of marks, strokes, and, yes, *swipes* needed to get these images on the paper, but the stealing is in the paintings as well.[4] Maybe the nature of paint itself contributes to the slipperiness required to get away with this? If so, it wouldn't be the first time, and no way will it be the last. But "stealing" is such a boring word, susceptible to such lame things as fake outrage. That's one of the reasons I'm sticking with "swipe." One of the other reasons has to do with what seems to have emerged in Brown's work over the past few years to magnificent impact: she is doing some of her best swiping from her very own work. Take, for example, *The Baptism* (2016), and put it next to *Handsome Stranger* (2010), two paintings that are roughly the same size and proportion. Even though they are only six years apart, and they share

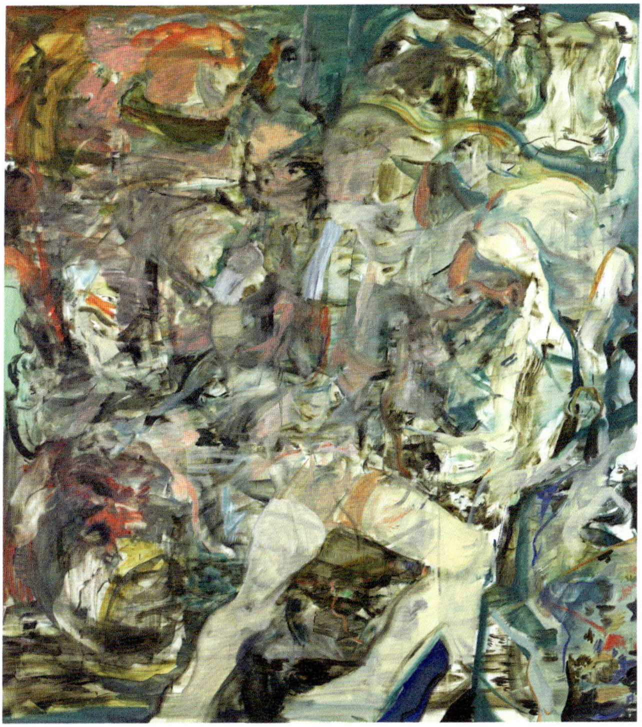

The Baptism, 2016

a great deal in terms of composition, the later painting performs the kind of confident gestural borrowing from the earlier work (and, to be clear, from others – I'm not trying to push an exclusively one-to-one connection) that often emerges with painters who keep plugging away at such, let's say, *action*. I think this is also a key reason why many of the latest paintings are capable of integrating legible body parts into the flow of the picture without sacrificing them completely to representation or narrative: put another way, it is because of the muscle memory of Brown's swiping that those legs at the bottom of *The Baptism* give the painting legs. (I also believe that this is intended to be funny.)

True to form, I have taken "swipe" from a text by Elaine de Kooning, who in 1959 wrote one of the best lines regarding the never-ending "crime" of painting: "Frank O'Hara: Bob says we're a generation of swipers."[6] Whether the poet Frank O'Hara actually said that Robert Rauschenberg said this, or whether Rauschenberg himself said it in the first place is of minor consequence here. What matters the most here is that swipe is a perfect user-friendly word for unpacking the complexities of Brown's paintings. I have foolishly assumed the various meanings of swipe were pretty universal, however, one key nuance doesn't make the cut to be translated into other languages: that "to swipe" can mean "to steal." Of course it doesn't only apply to painting, but a painter can swipe at the painting, can put down a swipe of paint (or swipe away paint), can take a metaphorical swipe at another painter, but she can also swipe from another painter, not unlike the way in which Rauschenberg went to Willem de Kooning, the "king" of painterly abstract expressionism, and convinced him to give up a heavily-worked drawing of a woman that the younger artist worked hard to erase and then claim as his own.[7] "I know what you're doing," is one of the things de Kooning supposedly said to him. There is plenty of evidence that Rauschenberg wanted to have things both ways: to "kill the father" and to preserve him in the literal presence of his absence (and there is a ghost left on that paper). Brown has the advantage of the distance of time that has guaranteed that she didn't have to have such a complicated relationship to de Kooning, or, for that matter, any historical painter that has caught her painterly attention. Over the years of her development she has figured out how to have them stick around without letting them win.

It is worth admitting that much of the power of the swipe as a thing or an action has come from the privileging of what we still call originality, especially within the expanded yet far from abandoned boundaries of painting. This is the reason why when I first saw Brown's paintings in the late 1990s, I was at the very least receptive to the assertion that the work was derivative of the likes of de Kooning. More Willem than Elaine in this instance, but it is interesting to consider Elaine de Kooning's paintings, especially her portraits, in relation to Brown's. A portrait like *Harold Rosenberg #3* (1956), for example, anticipates not only the particular activity of Brown's painterly gestures, but also (and more importantly) the daring attitude (it's hard not to see the portrait as being as more about the famous art critic's crotch than his face) and the goal of keeping the figure in action painting. Much of Elaine

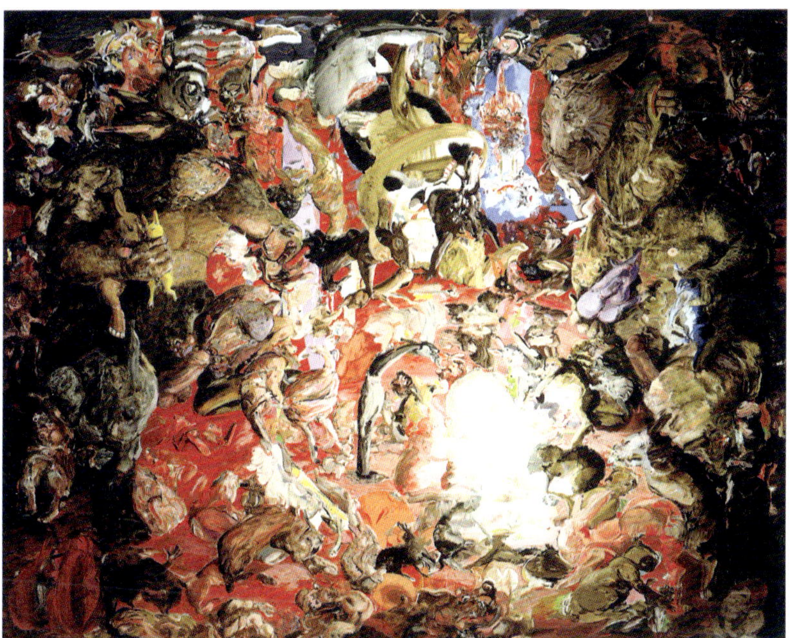

Untitled, 1997

de Kooning's passion about this was fueled by just how taboo it was at the time for a painter to admit that they were looking at dead artists – she also wrote in 1959 that "Living artists have become snobs about being alive."[8] Take, then, an early painting of Brown's like *Untitled* (1997) which, despite its plethora of imagery that would quickly be identified as hers – her early work incorporated such creatures as stuffed rabbits – so readily brings to mind Eugène Delacroix's epic Romantic canvas *The Death of Sardanapalus* (1827), with its overwhelming red-hotness, dramatic lighting, and, of course, its outrageously sensual presentation of something horrible.[9] His painting is also packed with stuff, including an elephant head. My memory of the late 1990s is that no one else was daring enough to attempt such a thing, much less pull it off, despite the likes of John Currin and Lisa

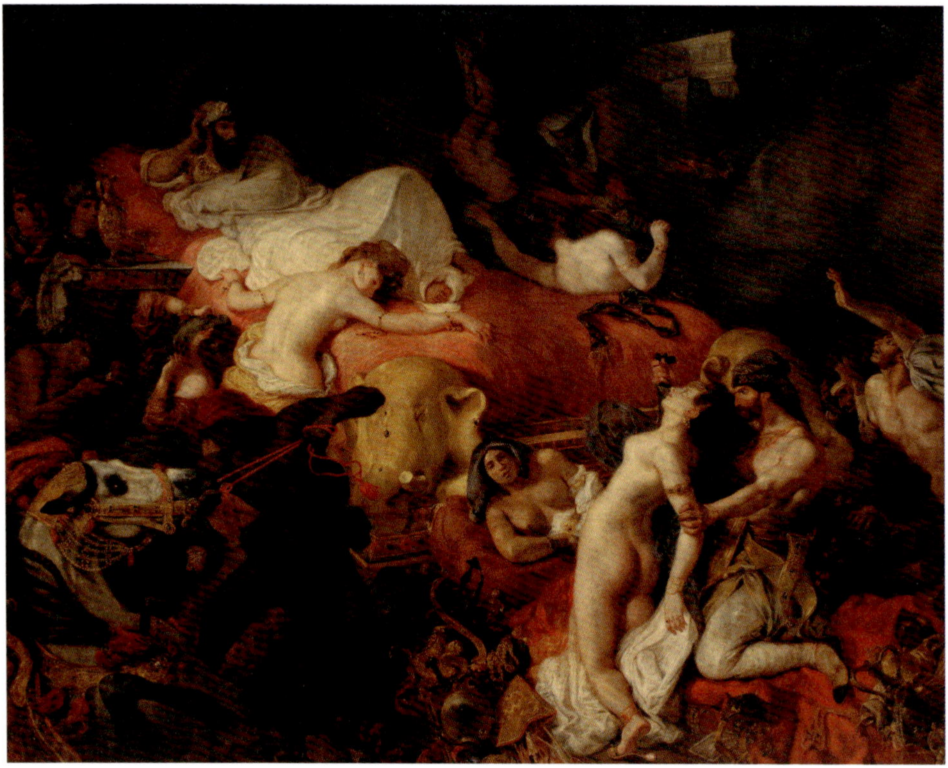

Eugène Delacroix: Mort de Sardanapale, 1827. Oil on canvas, 392 x 496 cm. Musée du Louvre

Yuskavage and their incredibly aggressive and skilled takes on the history and influence of figurative painting. Back then it seemed as if those two painters were still winking at us from a certain postmodern distance, while Brown was willing to clear all of that away to stick to what was being misrepresented at the time as the retrograde limitations of painterly figuration. I've previously written that this was the bugaboo nailed by Willem de Kooning's assertion that "Flesh was the reason why oil paint was invented," and his notion of the "slipping glimpse" that made it difficult if not impossible to meld the materiality of paint-as-flesh with the intangibility, if not distractedness of our vision.[10] Brown has become more and more focused without narrowing the parameters of her work. Now it seems clear that she had what I have called "the long view" from the very beginning, all the while working with critical aspects of painting that had been suppressed too quickly (and even the fastest painting is slow) by the domination of abstraction within the narrative of modernism, as well as the presumptions of postmodernism that attempt to wish painting into a perpetual endgame or premature death. And, keeping in mind Elaine de Kooning's claim at the very beginning of this essay, originality, particularly during modernism, went hand in hand with purity and exclusion, while "experience, nature for the purpose of art, invites *anybody*." It is the vital connection of that "anybody" to any *body* that continues to fuel Brown's work, the paint-as-flesh that will stick with us as long as we have flesh. Her paintings thrive on *inclusion* in the painterly and the social senses of the term, and her small canvases (of which there are many) have been crucial to her ability to borrow even more freely from her own moves.

This brings me to the relationship between Brown's more recent paintings, and the latest connotation added to the meaning of "swipe" by the introduction of smartphone "hookup" apps (Tinder, Grindr, etc.) into current life. At a time in which the figure as a material body remains under as much pressure from the virtual as the actual (all indications are that this pressure will increase, from social media manipulations to the impact of climate change), Brown's has diversified the ways in which she is painting the figure in relation to the now fully cross-pollinated if not completely fluid categories of figuration and abstraction. That we can now swipe right or left to express (even if in a deficient way) interest or desire or the immediate lack thereof, provides all the more fuel, to my mind, for malleable yet unapologetically tangible painting as a contemporary enterprise. Put another way, her paintings are packed with swipes in all directions driven by interest and desire (as well as such likely things as frustration and frivolity, confusion and clarity, and so on) but they can't be swiped left or right.

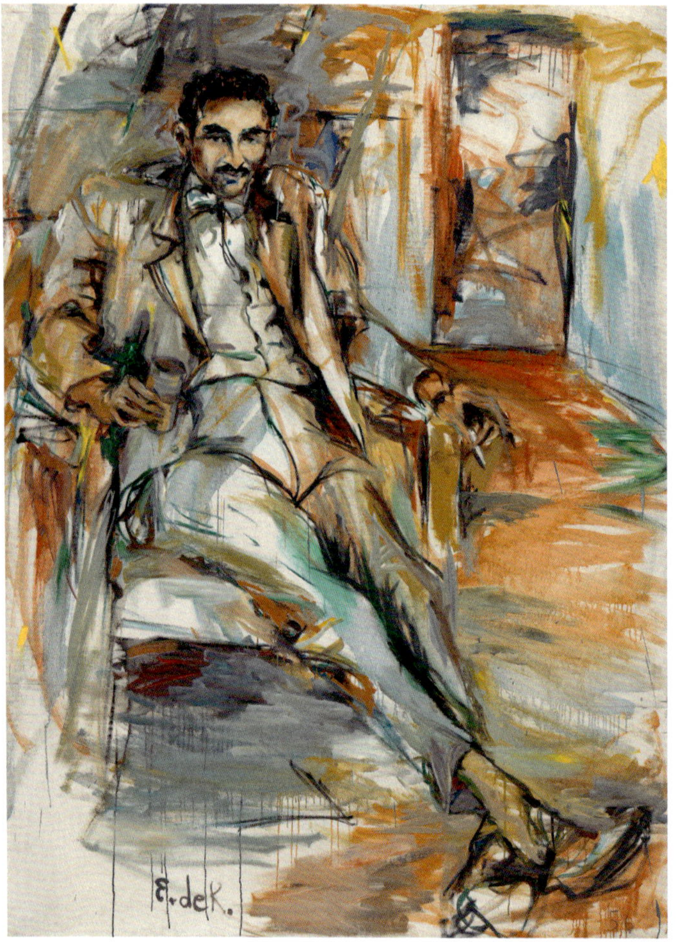

Elaine de Kooning: Harold Rosenberg #3, 1956. Oil on canvas, 203 x 150
National Portrait Gallery, Smithsonian Institution. Courtesy Elaine de Kooning Trust

Even when any figure (or, to be more accurate, a part of any figure) is perfectly readable in one of Brown's more recent paintings—for example, those legs in *The Baptism* (2016), mentioned above, or even more emphatically *Study of a Man* (2015) that is straightforwardly a figure painting, dominated by a man's backside, like the title claims – it still isn't released enough from its swipes and strokes of paint to be delivered completely over to narrative. As I've said slightly differently before, the stories of Brown's paintings are painting stories, a surprising form of narrative that comes from, as Annie Dillard claimed above, adjusting the painting not to the rest of the world or even the vision that may have instigated it, but rather to the "rest of the paint." This is yet another way to consider why those legs in *The Baptism* keep working the way they do, a way of behaving that I first recognized was

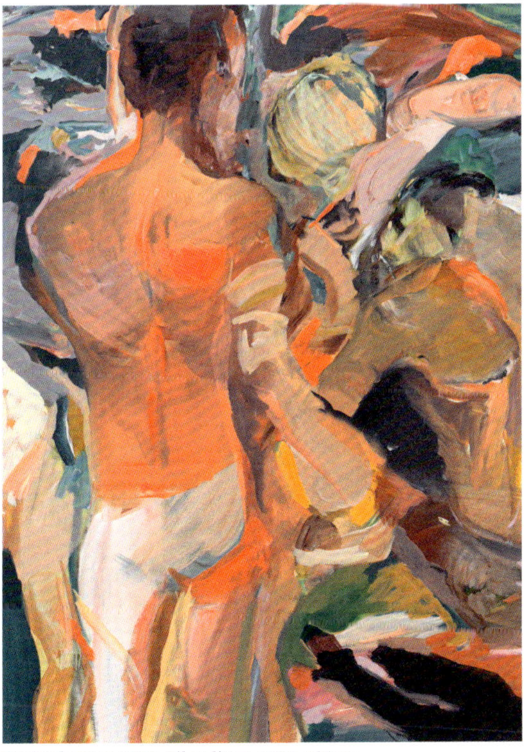

Study of a Man, 2015. Oil on linen, 129.5 × 94 cm
Collection of Michael Ballack

happening in her work in a slightly earlier painting called *The Triumph of Virtue* (2014-15). In it, a pair of well-built legs are literally stopped mid-run in and through a vibrant painterly field that evokes landscape but is resolutely abstract. Brown didn't invent this way or working, but the point is that she didn't have to, Now, even when attempting to take in her most overwhelming paintings like *Where, When, How Often and with Whom* (2017), it is clear that de Kooning (Willem, again) is no longer the patriarch to be killed, if in fact he ever was as far as Brown was concerned. Part of this emerging phenomena is the natural progression of an artist's development (in other words, she *has* gotten better), but it also comes from there now being enough distance between her work and his. Already in 1955, when Elaine de Kooning deployed the term nature, there was an increasing move away from expressionism to a more objective interest in light, nature, and the materiality of paint being played out in the work of artists like, for example, Joan Mitchell. Then, of course, came Pop and what seemed at first to be its desire to end the kind of swiping going on in so-called painterly painting for good. That, of course, didn't happen – largely because of the Germans: Gerhard Richter and Sigmar Polke, Martin Kippenberger and Albert Oehlen. Brown has been one of the key beneficiaries of the landscape they held open (not just) for her.

1. Elaine de Kooning, "Subject: What, How, or Who?" (1955), in *The Spirit of Abstract Expressionism: Selected Writings*, New York 1994, p. 144. **2.** Annie Dillard, *The Writing Life*, New York 1989, p. 57. **3.** Elaine de Kooning, p. 148. **4.** The essays by Claire Gilman ("Cecily Brown: Rehearsal") and David Salle ("Cecily Brown and the Non-Anxiety of Influence") in *Cecily Brown: Rehearsal*, New York 2016, provide numerous examples of the range of artists that Brown has looked at and worked from. **5.** Terry R. Myers, "Slip Swiping Away," in *Cecily Brown: The Sleep Around and the Lost and Found*, Berlin 2015. **6.** Elaine de Kooning, excerpt from "5 Participants in a Hearsay Panel," *It Is*, no. 3, 1959, p. 60. **7.** Rauschenberg's work is *Erased de Kooning Drawing*, 1953, traces of drawing media on paper with label and gilded frame, 25 1/4 in. x 21 3/4 in. x 1/2 in. (64.14 cm x 55.25 cm x 1.27 cm), San Francisco Museum of Modern Art. **8.** Elaine de Kooning, 1959, p. 60. **9.** Delacroix's 1824 journal entry, written three years before he would complete this painting, is germane: "what moves men of genius, or rather, what inspires their work, is not new ideas, but their obsession with the idea that what has already been said is still not enough." In Eugène Delacroix, *The Journal of Eugène Delacroix*, ed. Hubert Wellington, London 1995, p. 41. **10.** Willem de Kooning, "The Renaissance and Order" (1950), in Thomas B. Hess, *Willem de Kooning*, New York 1968, p. 142.

Terry R. Myers is the author of *Mary Heilmann: Save the Last Dance for Me* (2007), and the editor of *PAINTING: Documents of Contemporary Art* (2011). He has organized several exhibitions, most recently *Candida Alvarez: Here* at the Chicago Cultural Center in 2017. He has held faculty positions at Pratt Institute, Otis College of Art and Design, Art Center College of Design, the Royal College of Art in London, and at the School of the Art Institute of Chicago.

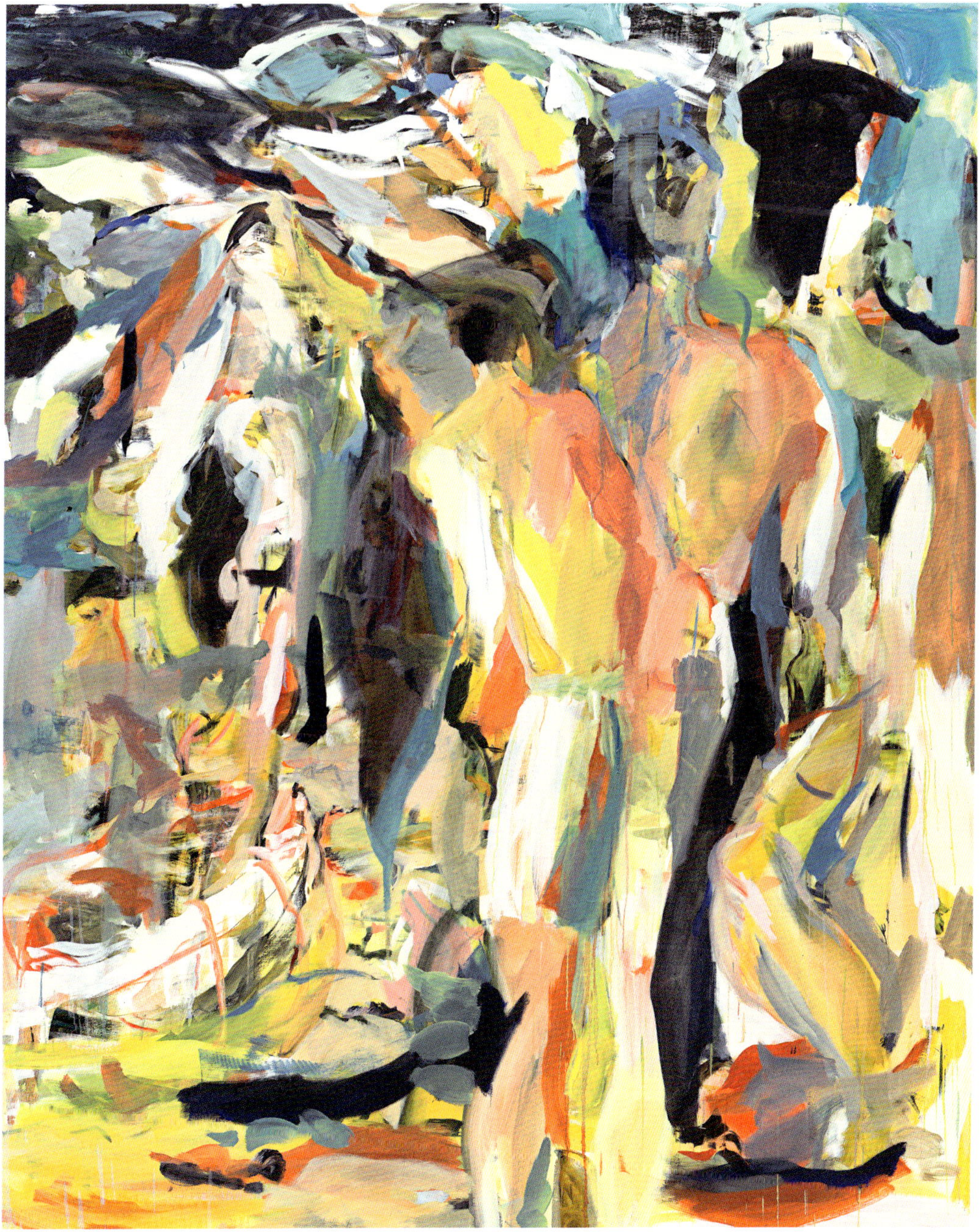

Lucky Beach, 2017

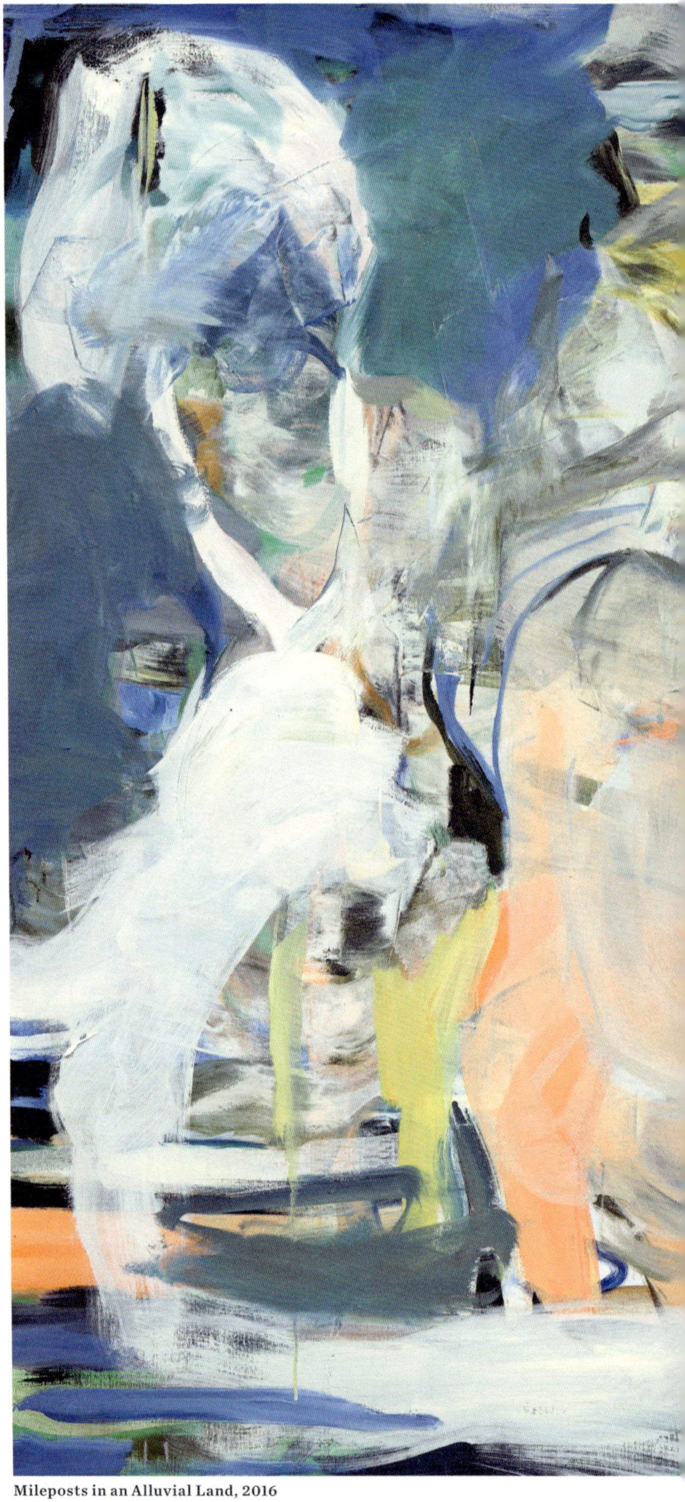

Mileposts in an Alluvial Land, 2016

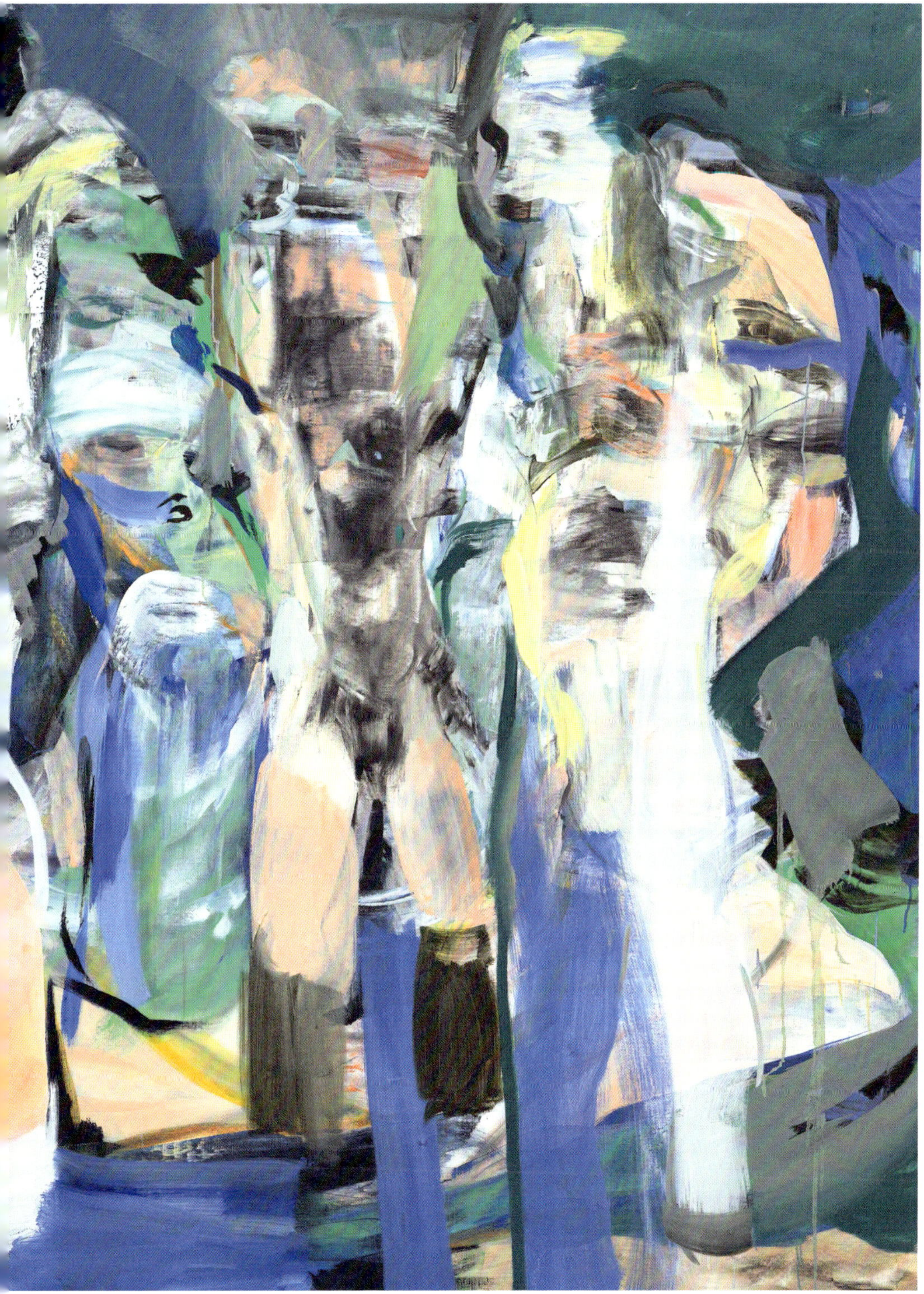

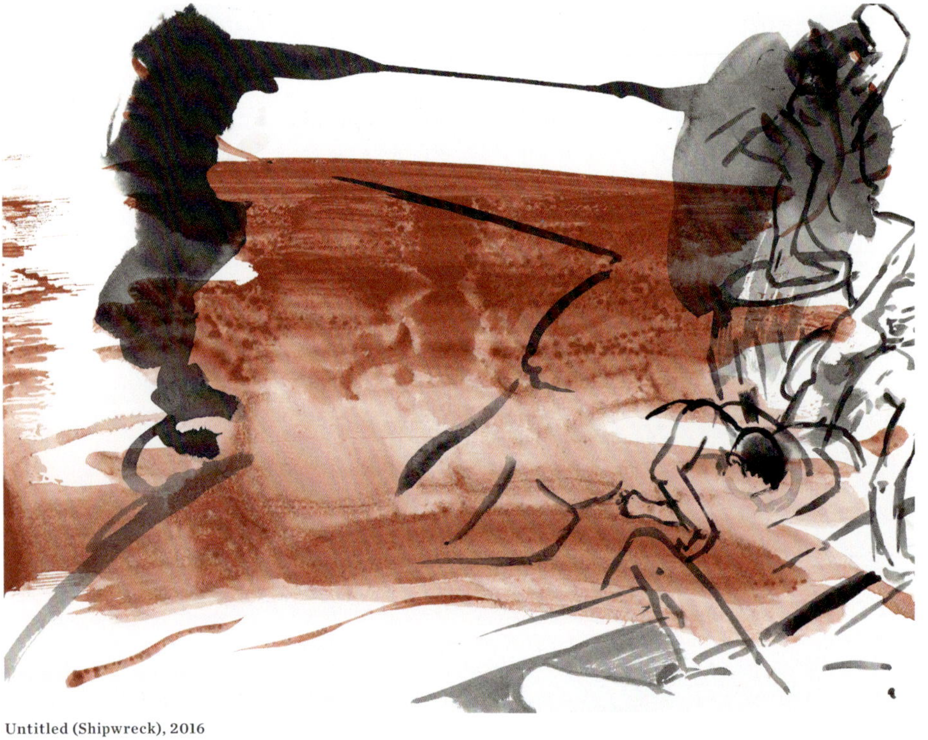

Untitled (Shipwreck), 2016

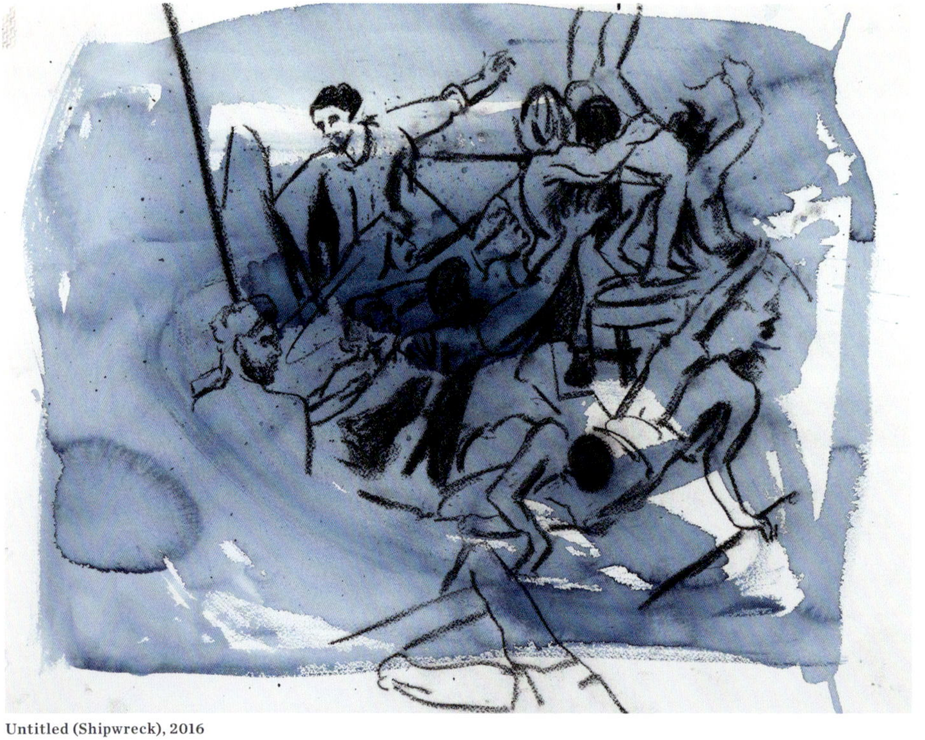

Untitled (Shipwreck), 2016

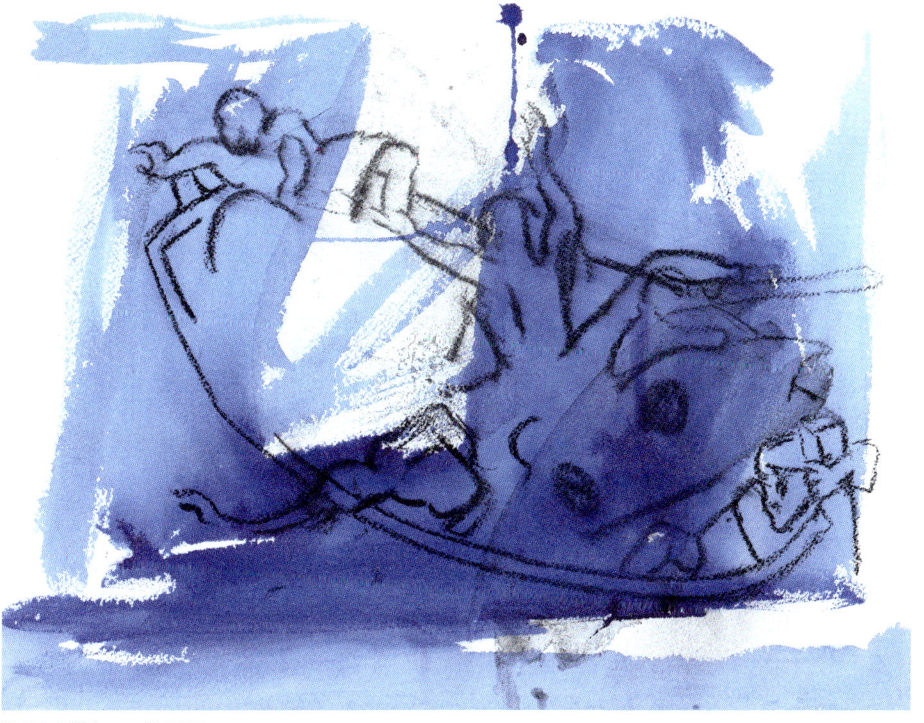

Untitled (Shipwreck), 2016

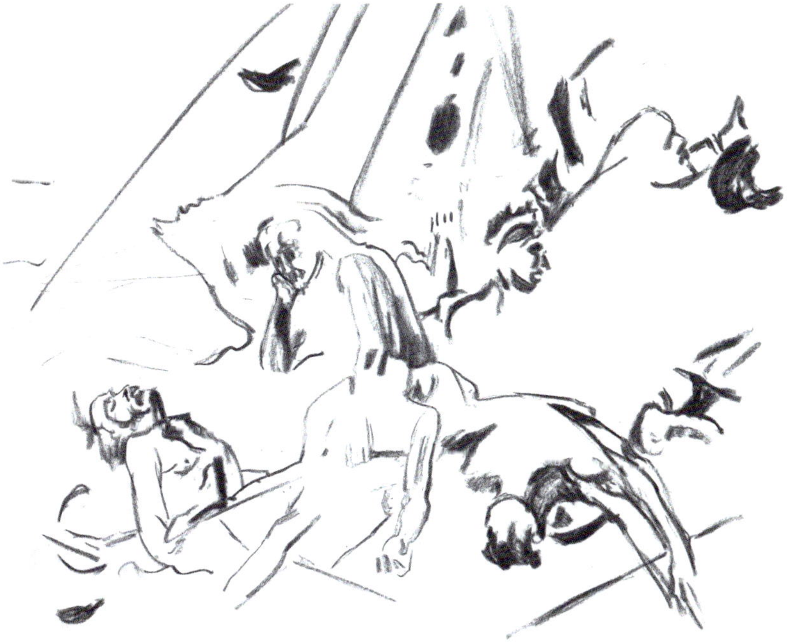

Untitled (Shipwreck), 2016

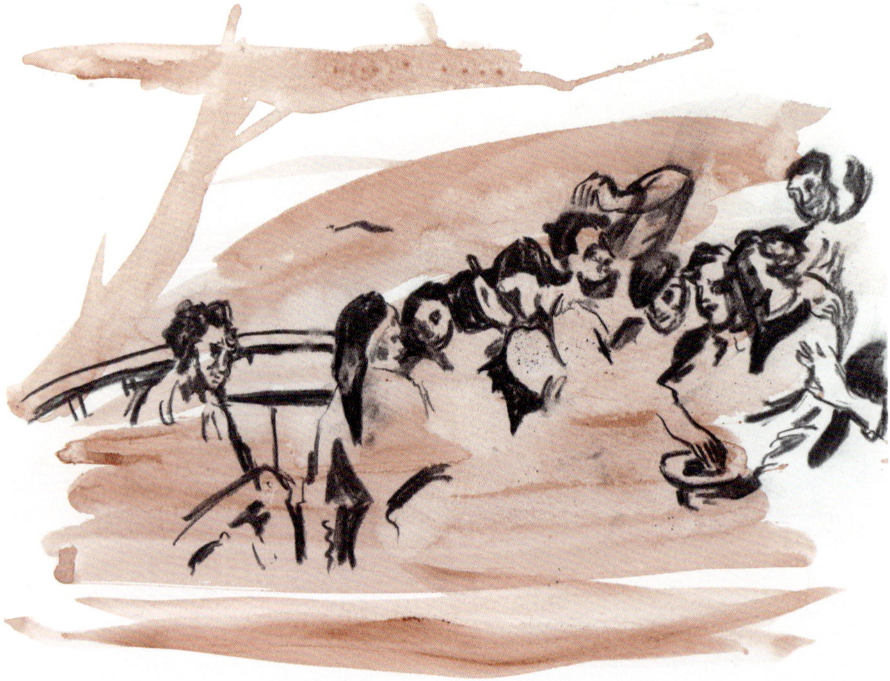

Untitled (Shipwreck), 2016

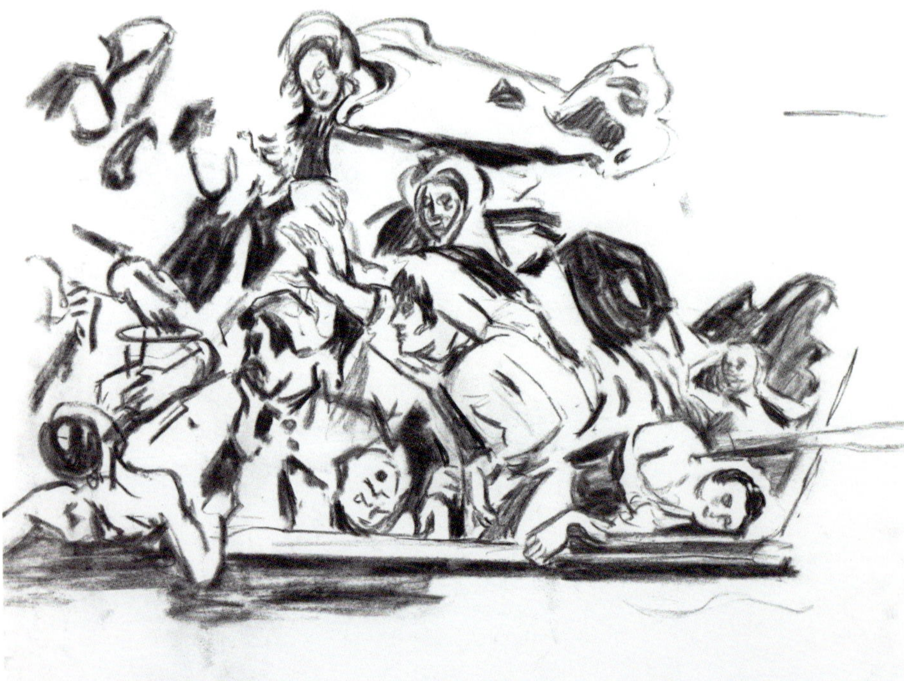

Untitled (Shipwreck), 2016

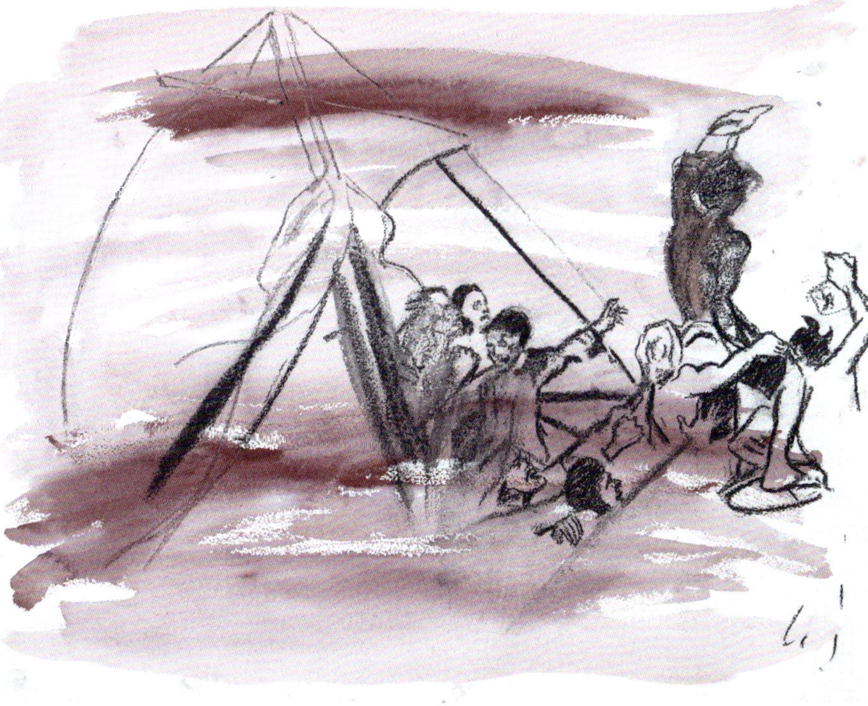

Untitled (Shipwreck), 2016

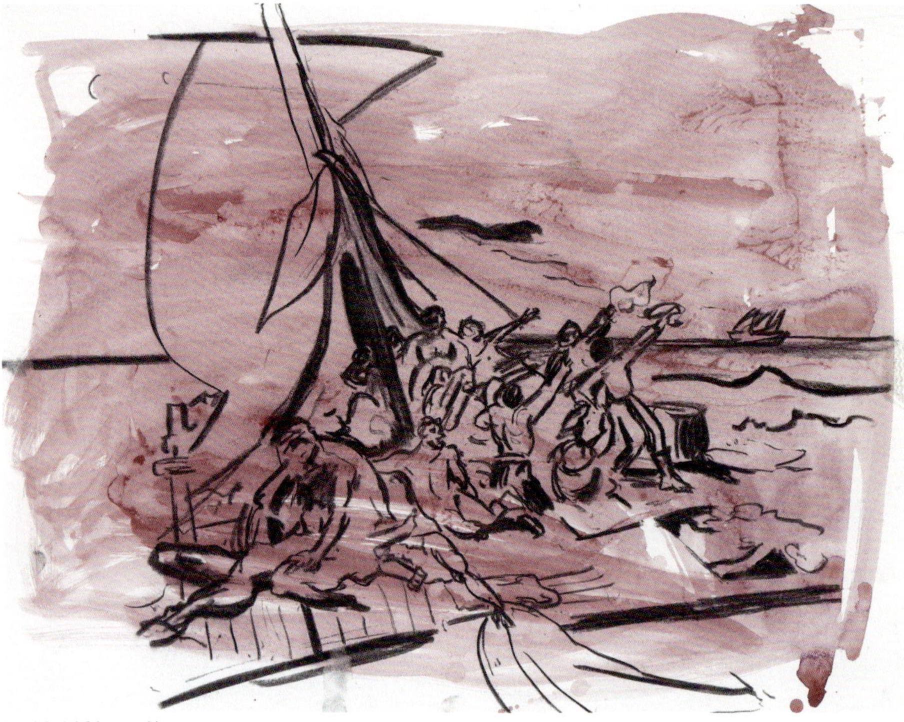

Untitled (Shipwreck), 2016

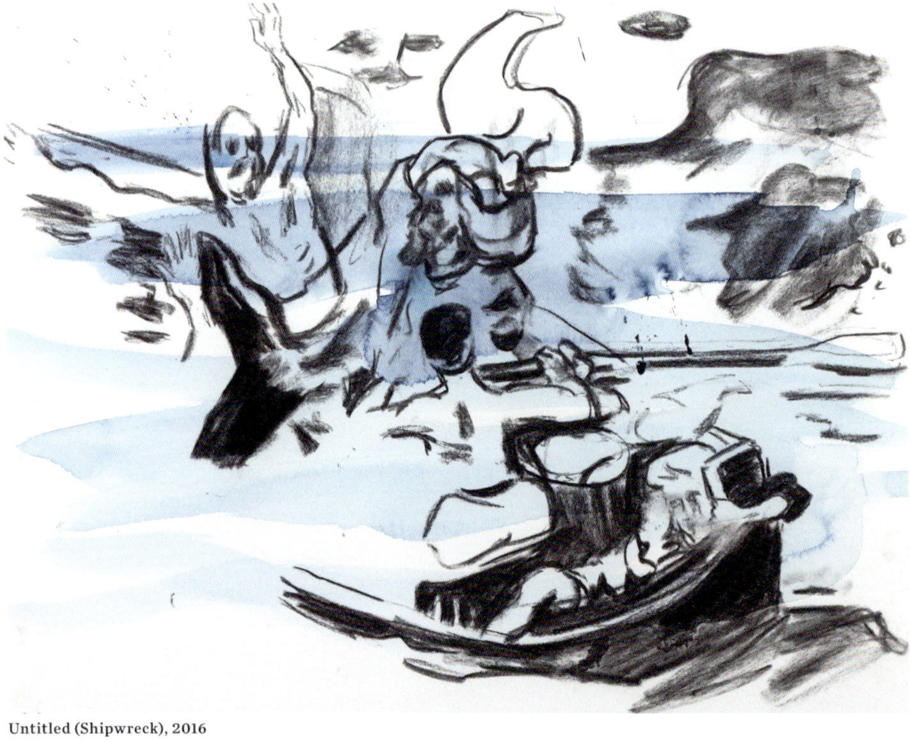

Untitled (Shipwreck), 2016

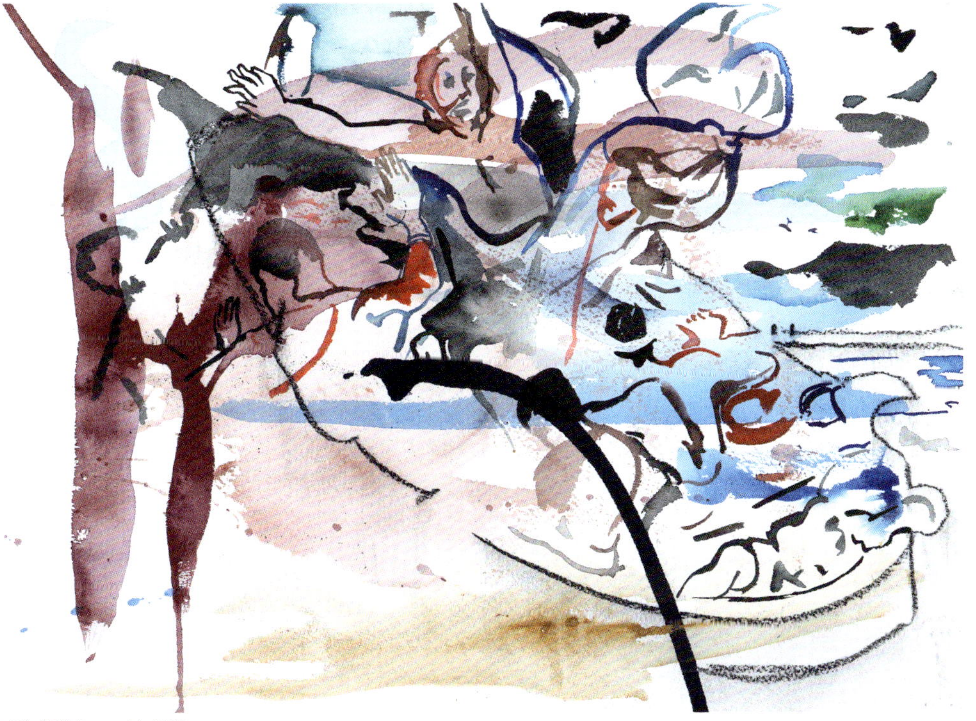

Untitled (Shipwreck), 2016

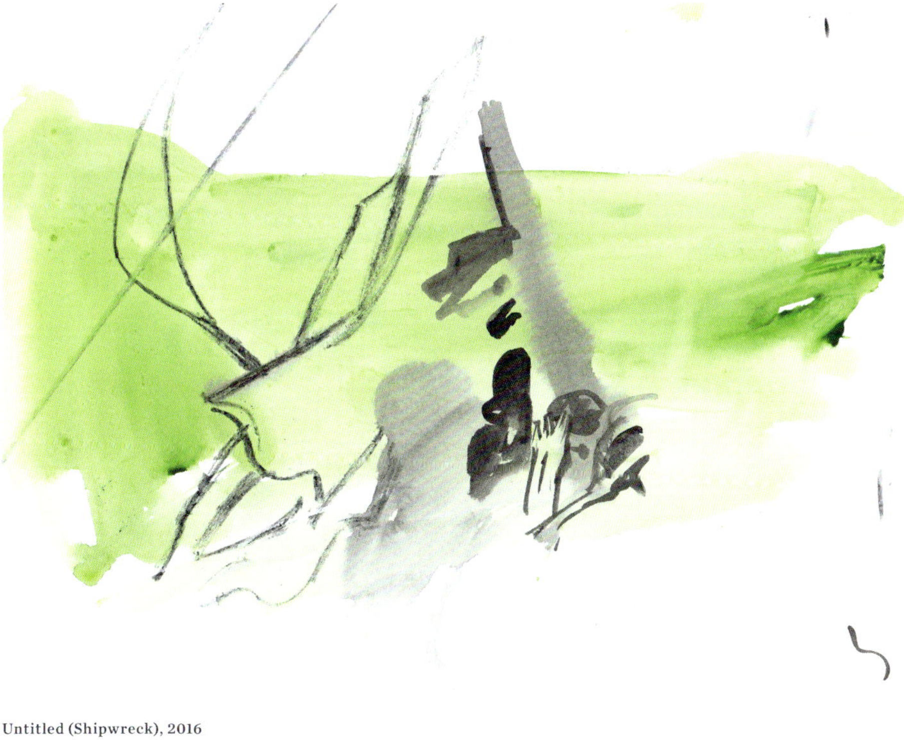

Untitled (Shipwreck), 2016

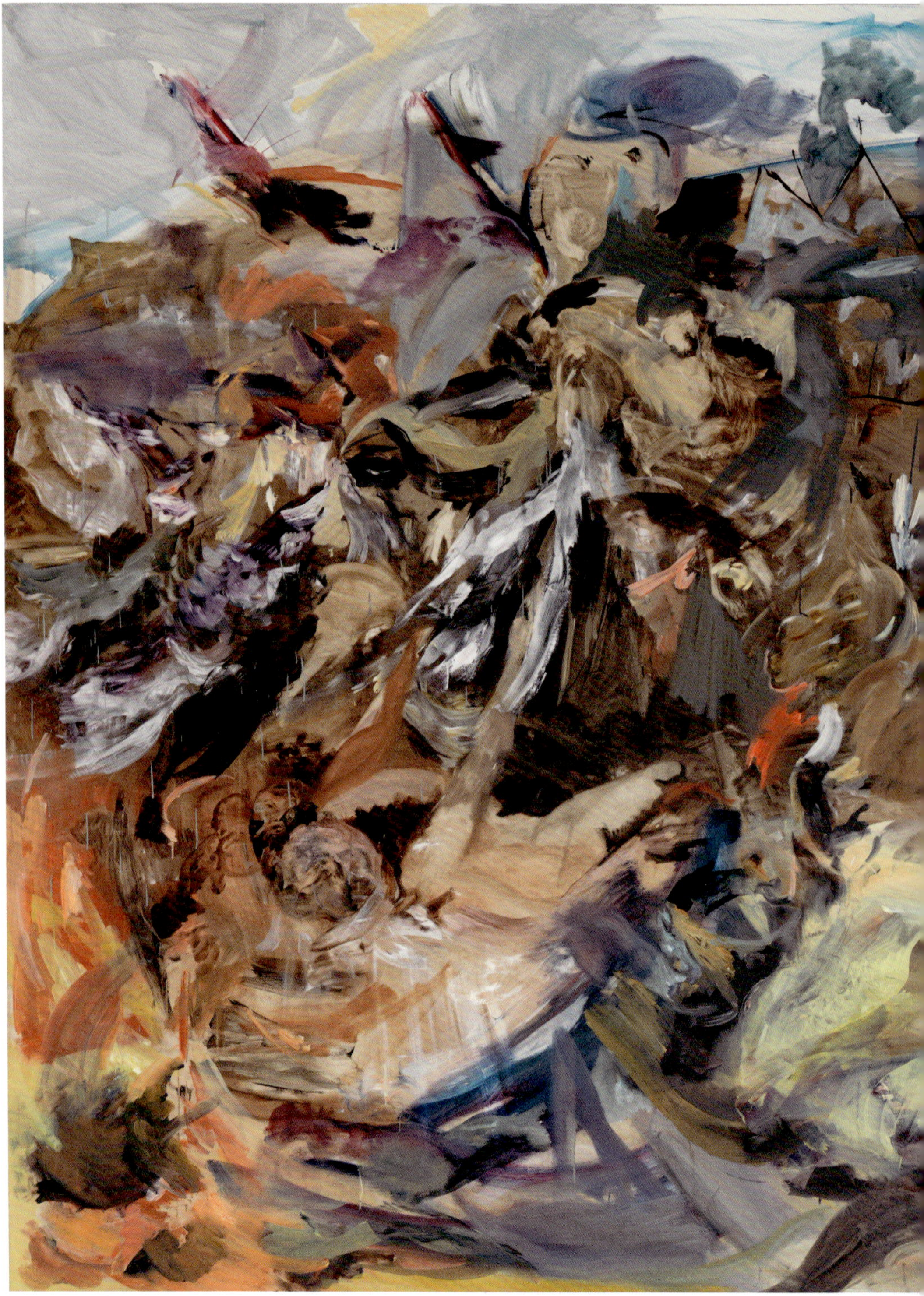

Wake, Awake, for Night is Flying, 2010

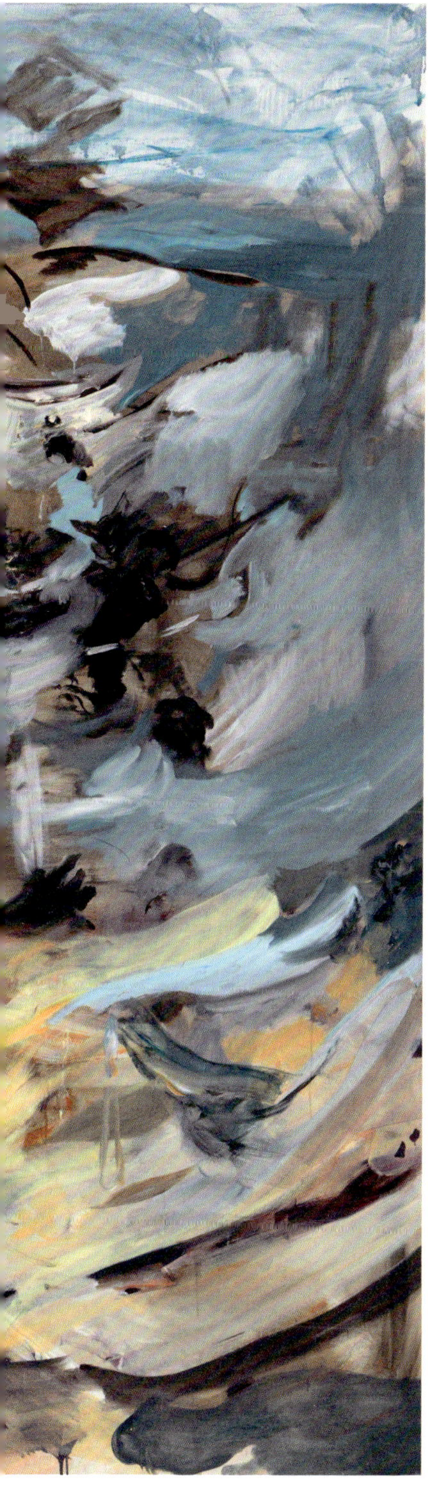

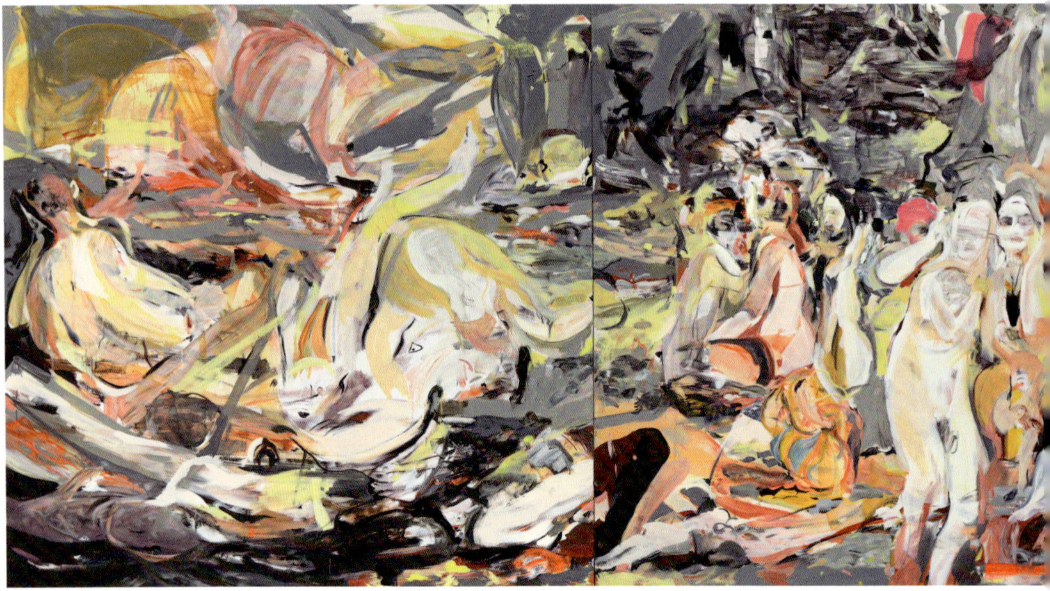

Where, When, How Often and with Whom, 2017

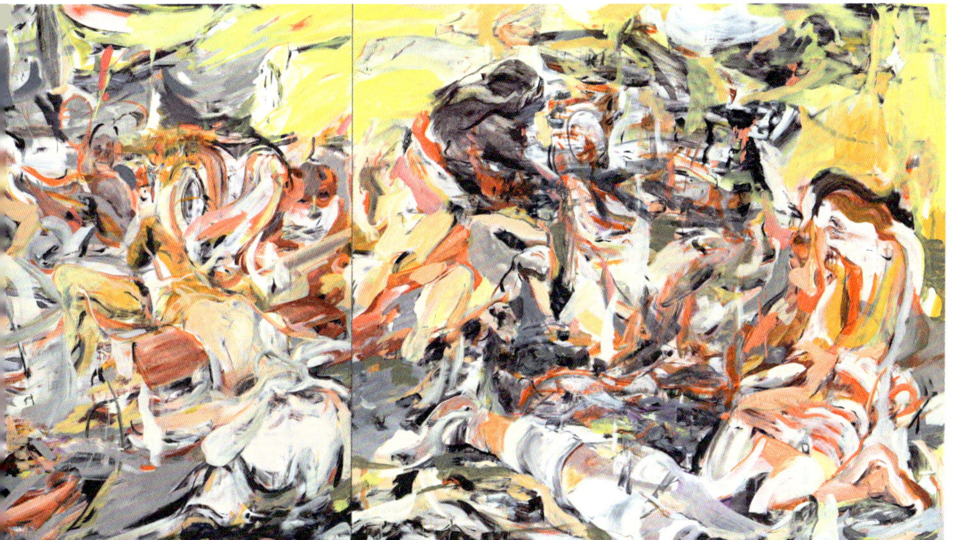

LIST OF WORKS

Paintings

Untitled, 1997
Oil on canvas
130 × 152 cm
Private Collection
Courtesy Faurschou Foundation
(pp. 10-11)

Figures in a Landscape 1, 2001
Oil on linen
229 × 254 cm
Private Collection
(pp. 12-13)

Girl on a Swing, 2004
Oil on linen
183 × 244 cm
National Gallery of Art, Washington
Gift of the Collectors Committee, 2015
(pp. 18-19)

Couple, 2004
Oil on linen
229 × 203 cm
Private Collection
(pp. 14-15)

Canopy, 2004
Oil on linen
203 × 203 cm
Private Collection
(pp. 16-17)

Study after Two Paintings by William Hogarth, 2004
Oil on linen
104 × 277 cm
Private Collection
(pp. 72-73)

Shadow Burn, 2006
Oil on linen
246 × 262 cm
Private Collection, Berlin
Courtesy Contemporary Fine Arts Berlin
(pp. 8-9)

Untitled, 2009
Oil on linen
38 × 31 cm
Courtesy of the artist
(p. 133)

Untitled, 2009
Oil on linen
43 × 32 cm
Courtesy of the artist
(p. 117)

Untitled, 2009
Oil on linen
43 × 32 cm
Private Collection
(p. 121)

The Green, Green Grass of Home, 2010
Oil on linen
246× 384 cm
Private Collection
Courtesy Guggenheim, Asher Associates, Inc.
(pp. 98-99)

Wake, Awake, for Night is Flying, 2010
Oil on linen
226 × 246 cm
Collection of Kay Harrigan Woods, San Francisco
(pp. 152-153)

Handsome Stranger, 2010
Oil on linen
245 × 262 cm
Gemma de Angelis Testa Collection
(pp. 92-93)

Are You Weary, Are You Languid?, 2010
Oil on linen
43 × 32 cm
Collection of Gina and Stuart Peterson
(p. 125)

Untitled (#102), 2010
Oil on canvas
43 × 32 cm
Nicole Hackert & Bruno Brunnet, Berlin
(p. 119)

Jicky, 2010
Oil on canvas
With frame: 220 × 229 cm
216 × 226 cm
Karlheinz Essl, Klosterneuburg / Vienna
(pp. 88-89)

The Tribulations of the Tablecloth, 2011
Oil on linen
109 × 79 cm
Private Collection
Courtesy Alexandra Mollof Fine Art
(p. 129)

Name That Tune, 2012
Oil on linen
196 × 246 cm
Private Collection
(pp. 86-87)

All the Nightmares Came Today, 2012
Oil on linen
170 × 211 cm
Iris & Matthew Strauss Collection,
Rancho Santa Fe, California
(pp. 84-85)

Untitled, 2013
Oil on linen
43 × 32 cm
Courtesy of the artist
(p. 127)

Untitled, 2016
Oil on linen
43 × 32 cm
Courtesy of the artist
(p. 131)

Untitled, 2016
Oil on linen
28 × 43 cm
Courtesy of the artist
(pp. 122-123)

Thug in Landscape, 2015
Oil on linen
196 × 246 cm
Dr. Joselito Cariño Cabaccan
Courtesy Contemporary Fine Arts, Berlin
(pp. 94-95)

Torch, 2015
Oil on linen
170 × 211 cm
Contemporary Fine Arts
Nicole Hackert & Bruno Brunnet, Berlin
(pp. 94-95)

The Baptism, 2016
Oil on linen
262 × 226 cm
Private Collection
(pp. 96-97)

Imaginary Calamities, 2016
Oil on linen
43 × 31 cm
Courtesy the artist and Thomas Dane, London
(p. 115)

Mileposts in an Alluvial Land, 2016
Oil on linen
135 × 211 cm
Arora Collection
(pp. 144-145)

Where, When, How Often and with Whom, 2017
Oil on linen
277 × 1008 cm
Courtesy of the artist
(pp. 154-155)

Lucky Beach, 2017
Oil on linen
202 × 170 cm
Laura and Barry Townsley, London
Courtesy Contemporary Fine Arts, Berlin
(p. 143)

Frenchy on a Swing, 2017-2018
Oil on aluminium
135 × 109 cm
Private Collection
(p. 5)

Works on paper

Untitled (After Jeux des Dames Cruelles),
1997-1998
Watercolour, gouache on paper
31.8 × 31.8 cm
Courtesy of the artist
(p. 39)

Untitled (After Goya), 1997-1998
Ballpoint pen on paper
31.8 × 31.8 cm
Courtesy of the artist
(p. 38)

Untitled, 1998
Ballpoint on paper
27 × 23.2 cm
Courtesy of the artist
(p. 41)

Untitled, 1998
Ballpoint pen on paper
35.2 × 27.9 cm
Courtesy of the artist
(p. 42)

Untitled, 1998
Ballpoint pen on paper
31.8 × 31.8 cm
Courtesy of the artist
(p. 40)

Untitled, 1998
Ink on paper
38.1 × 27.9 cm
Courtesy of the artist
(p. 43)

Untitled, 2003
Gouache, watercolour, ink on paper
31.1 × 41 cm
Courtesy of the artist
(p. 59)

Untitled, 2004
Gouache, watercolour, ink on paper
30.8 × 41 cm
Courtesy of the artist
(p. 58)

Chairing the Members (After Hogarth), 2004
Watercolour, ink, gouache on paper
22.9 × 31.1 cm
Courtesy of the artist
(p. 66)

Chairing the Members (After Hogarth), 2004
Watercolour, ink, gouache, oil on paper
24.1 × 54.6 cm
Courtesy of the artist
(pp. 70-71)

Carnival and Lent (After Bruegel), 2007
Gouache, watercolour, ink on paper
46 × 61 cm
Courtesy of the artist
(pp. 52-53)

Carnival and Lent (After Bruegel), 2007
Gouache, watercolour, ink on paper
30.8 × 41 cm
Courtesy of the artist
(pp. 50-51)

Untitled (After Bruegel), 2007
Gouache, watercolour, ink on paper
31.1 × 40.6 cm
Courtesy of the artist
(p. 54, bottom)

Untitled (After Bruegel), 2007
Gouache, watercolour, ink on paper
31.1 × 41 cm
Courtesy of the artist
(p. 54, top)

The Temptation of St. Anthony, 2010
Gouache, watercolour, ink on paper
31.1 × 23.2 cm
Courtesy of the artist
(p. 48)

The Temptation of St. Anthony, 2010
Gouache, watercolour, ink on paper
31.1 × 23.2 cm
Courtesy of the artist
(p. 55)

Untitled, 2010
Gouache, watercolour, ink on paper
35.9 × 50.8 cm
Courtesy of the artist

Untitled, 2010
Gouache, watercolour, ink on paper
36.2 × 50.8 cm
Courtesy of the artist

Daphne and Apollo (After Bernini), 2010
Gouache, watercolour, ink on paper
26 × 36 cm
Courtesy of the artist
(p. 56)

Untitled (After El Greco), 2012
Gouache, watercolour, ink on paper
46 × 61 cm
Courtesy of the artist
(p. 67)

Untitled, 2012
Gouache, watercolour on paper
27.9 × 38.1 cm
Courtesy of the artist
(p. 57)

Untitled (After Beckmann), 2012
Gouache, watercolour, ink on paper
51.3 × 36.2 cm
Courtesy of the artist
(p. 61)

Untitled (Ladyland), 2012
Gouache, watercolour, ink on paper
35.9 × 51.1 cm
Courtesy of the artist
(pp. 78-79)

Untitled (Ladyland), 2012
Pastel on paper
30.5 × 45.7 cm
Courtesy of the artist
(pp. 74-75)

Untitled (Ladyland), 2012
Gouache, watercolour, ink on paper
35.9 × 26 cm
Courtesy of the artist
(p. 49)

Untitled (Ladyland with Bestiary), 2013
Watercolour, gouache on paper
41.9 × 31.1 cm
Courtesy of the artist
(p. 77)

Untitled (After Jeux des Dames Cruelles), 2013
Watercolour, gouache on paper
61 × 46 cm
Courtesy of the artist
(p. 37)

Young Spartans (After Degas), 2013
Watercolour on paper
30.5 × 40.6 cm
Courtesy of the artist

Analysis of Beauty (After Hogarth), 2014
Watercolour, ink, oil on paper
35.8 × 50.8 cm
Courtesy of the artist
(pp. 68-69)

Untitled (After Bosch), 2015
Oil, pastel, watercolour on paper
110.5 × 160 cm
Courtesy of the artist
(pp. 34-35)

Untitled, 2015
Pastel on paper
119.4 × 88.9 cm
Courtesy of the artist
(p. 36)

Untitled, 2016
Gouache, watercolour, ink on paper
35.9 × 50.8 cm
Courtesy of the artist
(pp. 44-45)

Beach Blanket Babylon, 2016
Oil, charcoal on paper
46 × 61 cm
Courtesy of the artist
(pp. 64-65)

Untitled (Shipwreck), 2016
Gouache, watercolour, charcoal on paper
30.5 × 40.6 cm
Courtesy the artist and Thomas
Dane Gallery London

Untitled (Shipwreck), 2016
Charcoal on paper
30.5 × 40.6 cm
Courtesy the artist and Thomas
Dane Gallery, London
(p. 151, bottom)

Untitled (Shipwreck), 2016
Watercolour on paper
30.5 × 40.6 cm
Courtesy the artist and Thomas
Dane Gallery, London
(p. 146, top)

Untitled (Shipwreck), 2016
Watercolour, charcoal on paper
30.5 × 40.6 cm
Courtesy the artist and Thomas
Dane Gallery, London
(p. 147, bottom)

Untitled (Shipwreck), 2016
Charcoal on paper
30.5 × 40.6 cm
Courtesy the artist and Thomas Dane Gallery, London
(p. 148, top)

Untitled (Shipwreck), 2016
Watercolour, charcoal on paper
30.5 × 40.6 cm
Courtesy the artist and Thomas Dane Gallery, London
(p. 148, bottom)

Untitled (Shipwreck), 2016
Watercolour, charcoal on paper
30.5 × 40.6 cm
Courtesy the artist and Thomas Dane Gallery, London
(p. 147, top)

Untitled (Shipwreck), 2016
Gouache, watercolour, charcoal on paper
36.2 × 50.8 cm
Courtesy the artist and Thomas Dane Gallery, London
(p. 151, top)

Untitled (Shipwreck), 2016
Charcoal on paper
45.7 × 61 cm
Courtesy the artist and Thomas Dane Gallery, London
(p. 149)

Untitled (Shipwreck), 2016
Watercolour, charcoal on paper
45.7 × 61 cm
Courtesy the artist and Thomas Dane Gallery, London
(p. 146, bottom)

Untitled (Shipwreck), 2016
Watercolour, charcoal on paper
45.7 × 61 cm
Courtesy the artist and Thomas Dane Gallery, London
(p. 150, top)

Untitled (Shipwreck), 2016
Watercolour, charcoal on paper
45.7 × 61 cm
Courtesy the artist and Thomas Dane Gallery, London

Untitled (Bather with Cops), 2017
Gouache, watercolour, ink on paper
36.2 × 51.1 cm
Courtesy of the artist
(p. 46)

Untitled (Bather with Cops), 2017
Gouache, watercolour, ink on paper
46 × 61 cm
Courtesy of the artist
(p. 47)

Untitled (Bathers), 2017
Gouache, watercolour, ink on paper
30.8 × 41.3 cm
Courtesy of the artist
(p. 60)

Untitled, 2018
Pencil on paper
31.1 × 41 cm
Courtesy of the artist
(pp. 62-63)

Untitled (CB 1350), 2018
Monotype, oil on Lanaquarelle paper
78.7 × 109.2 cm
Courtesy of the artist and Two Palms Press, New York
(pp. 168-169)

Untitled (CB 1352), 2018
Monotype, oil on Lanaquarelle paper
109.2 × 78.7 cm
Courtesy of the artist and Two Palms Press, New York
(p. 175)

Untitled (CB1353), 2018
Monotype, oil on Lanaquarelle paper
78.7 × 109.2 cm
Courtesy of the artist and Two Palms Press, New York

Untitled (CB 1354), 2018
Monotype, oil on Lanaquarelle paper
78.7 × 109.2 cm
Courtesy of the artist and Two Palms Press, New York
(p. 170)

Untitled (CB 1356), 2018
Monotype, oil on Lanaquarelle paper
78.7 × 109.2 cm
Courtesy of the artist and Two Palms Press, New York

Untitled (CB 1360), 2018
Monotype, oil on Lanaquarelle paper
78.7 × 109.2 cm
Courtesy of the artist and Two
Palms Press, New York

Untitled (CB 1361), 2018
Monotype, oil on Lanaquarelle paper
78.7 × 109.2 cm
Courtesy of the artist and Two
Palms Press, New York
(p. 171)

Untitled (CB 1364), 2018
Monotype, oil on Lanaquarelle paper
78.7 × 109.2 cm
Courtesy of the artist and Two
Palms Press, New York
(p. 164)

Untitled (CB 1366), 2018
Monotype, oil on Lanaquarelle paper
78.7 × 109.2 cm
Courtesy of the artist and Two
Palms Press, New York

Untitled (CB 1367), 2018
Monotype, oil on Lanaquarelle paper
58.4 × 78.7 cm
Courtesy of the artist and Two
Palms Press, New York
(p. 162)

Untitled (CB 1370), 2018
Monotype, oil on Lanaquarelle paper
58.4 × 78.7 cm
Courtesy of the artist and Two
Palms Press, New York

Untitled (CB 1372), 2018
Monotype, oil on Lanaquarelle paper
58.4 × 78.7 cm
Courtesy of the artist and Two
Palms Press, New York

Untitled (CB 1375), 2018
Monotype, oil on Lanaquarelle paper
58.4 × 78.7 cm
Courtesy of the artist and Two
Palms Press, New York
(p. 165)

Untitled (CB 1377), 2018
Monotype, oil on Lanaquarelle paper
58.4 × 78.7 cm
Courtesy of the artist and Two
Palms Press, New York
(pp. 172-173)

Untitled (CB 1378), 2018
Monotype, oil on Lanaquarelle paper
58.4 × 78.7 cm
Courtesy of the artist and Two
Palms Press, New York
(p. 163)

Untitled (CB 1382), 2018
Monotype, oil on Lanaquarelle paper
58.4 × 78.7 cm
Courtesy of the artist and Two
Palms Press, New York

Untitled (CB 1386), 2018
Monotype, oil on Lanaquarelle paper
58.4 × 78.7 cm
Courtesy of the artist and Two
Palms Press, New York

Untitled (CB 1388), 2018
Monotype, oil on Lanaquarelle paper
78.7 × 58.4 cm
Courtesy of the artist and Two
Palms Press, New York
(p. 166)

Untitled (CB 1389), 2018
Monotype, oil on Lanaquarelle paper
78,7 × 58.4 cm
Courtesy of the artist and Two
Palms Press, New York
(p. 167)

Untitled (CB 1390), 2018
Monotype, oil on Lanaquarelle paper
58.4 × 78.7 cm
Courtesy of the artist and Two
Palms Press, New York

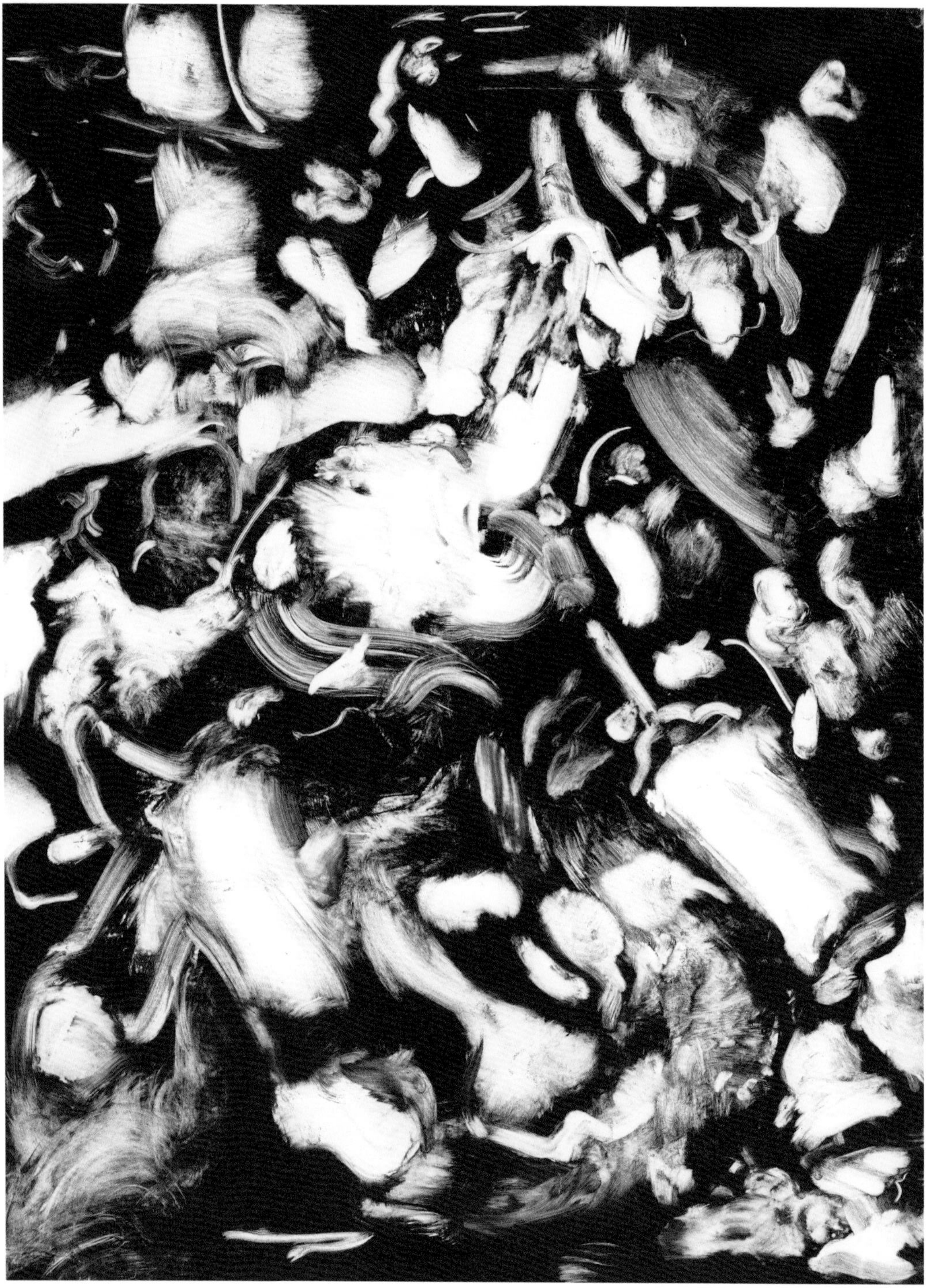

Untitled (CB 1367), 2018

Untitled (CB 1378), 2018

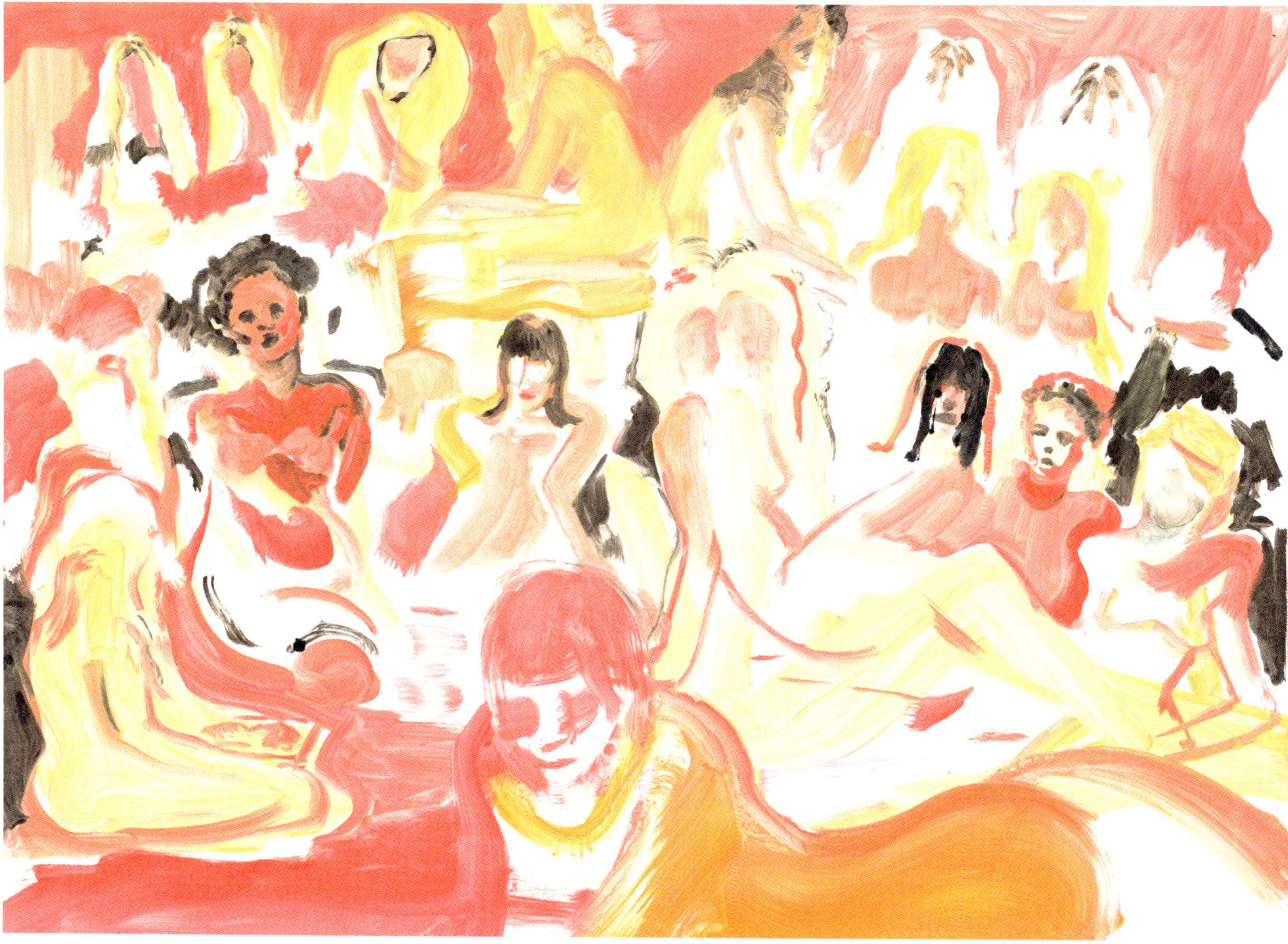

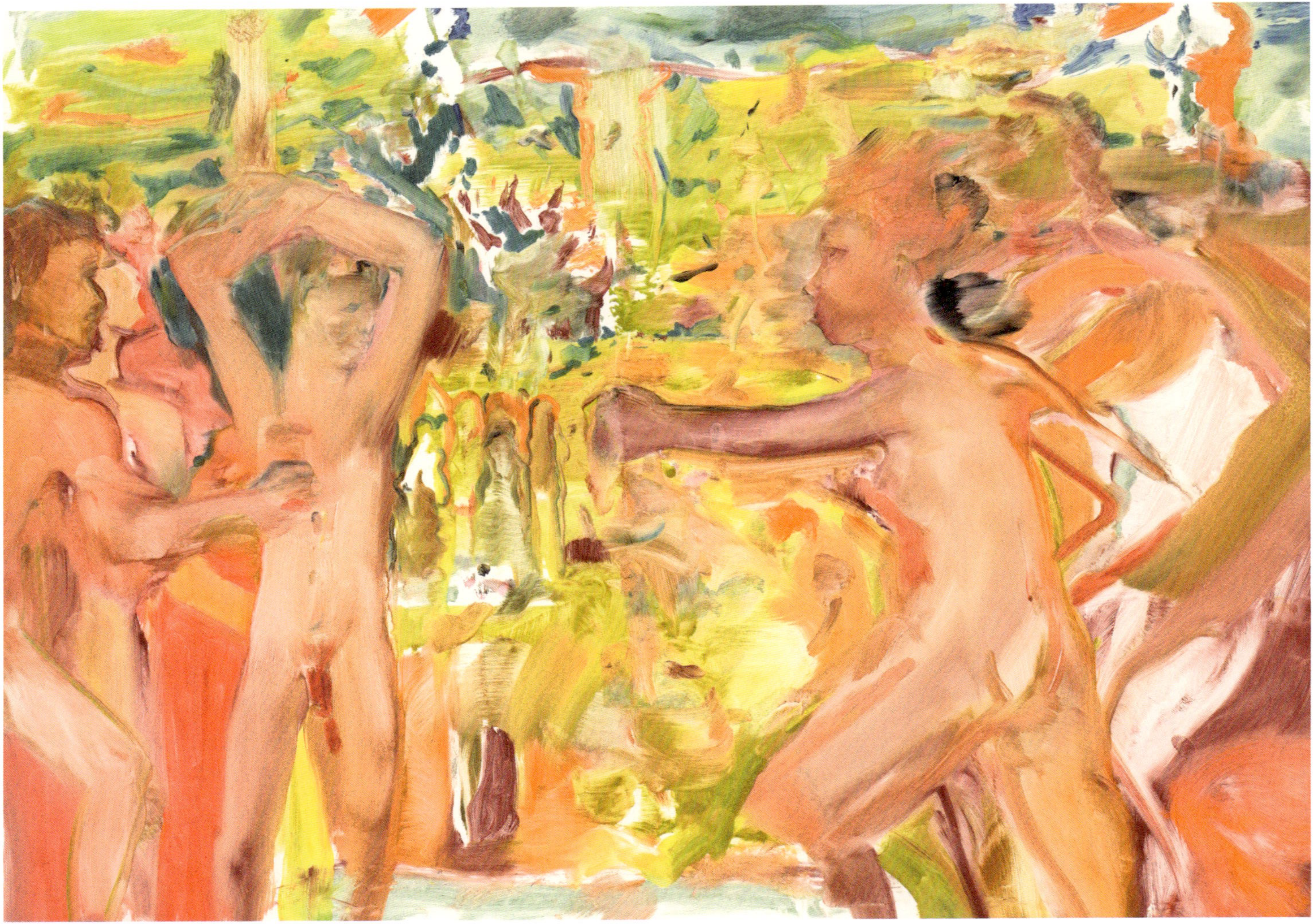

Untitled (CB 1364), 2018

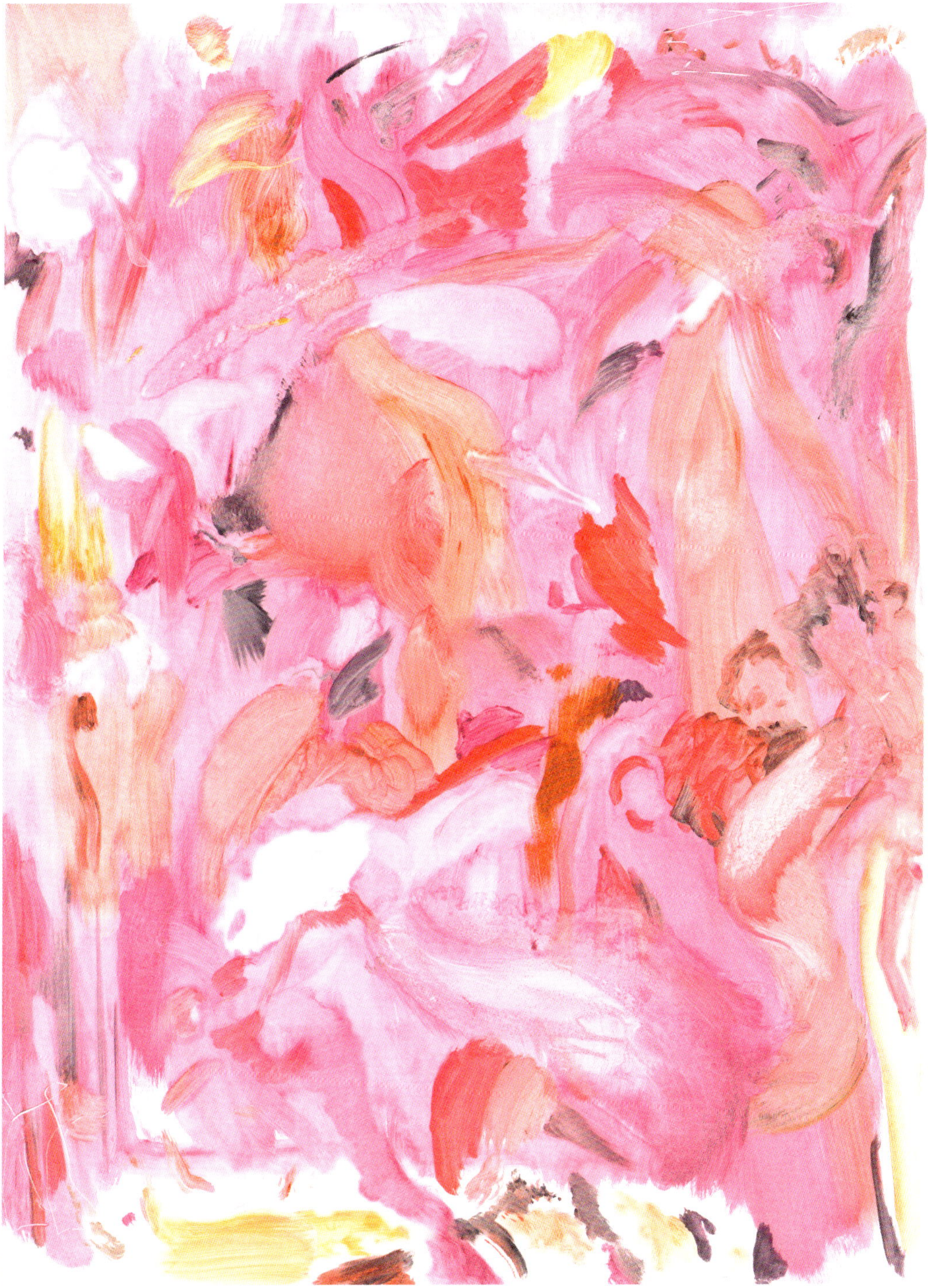

Untitled (CB 1375), 2018

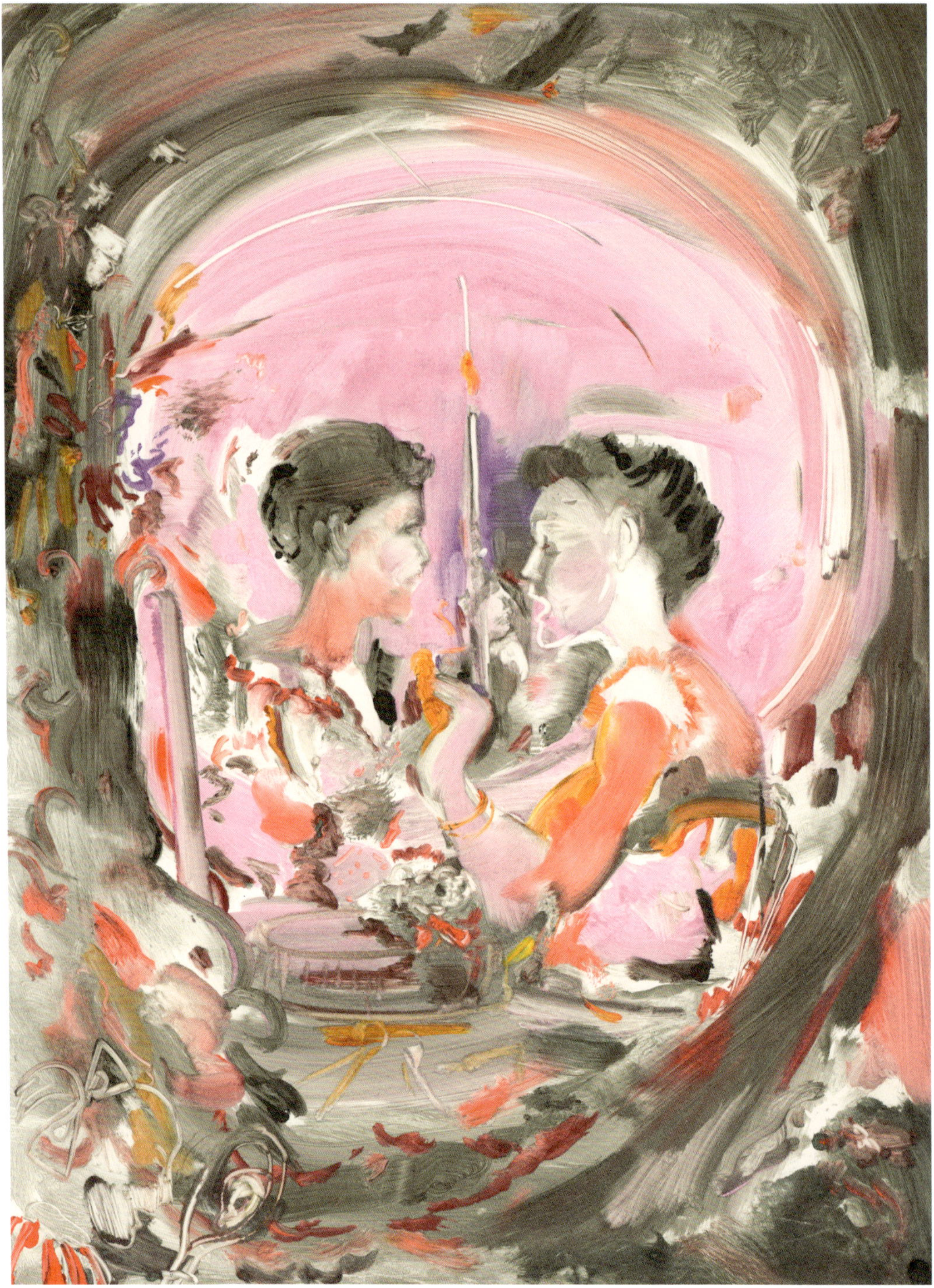

Untitled (CB 1388), 2018

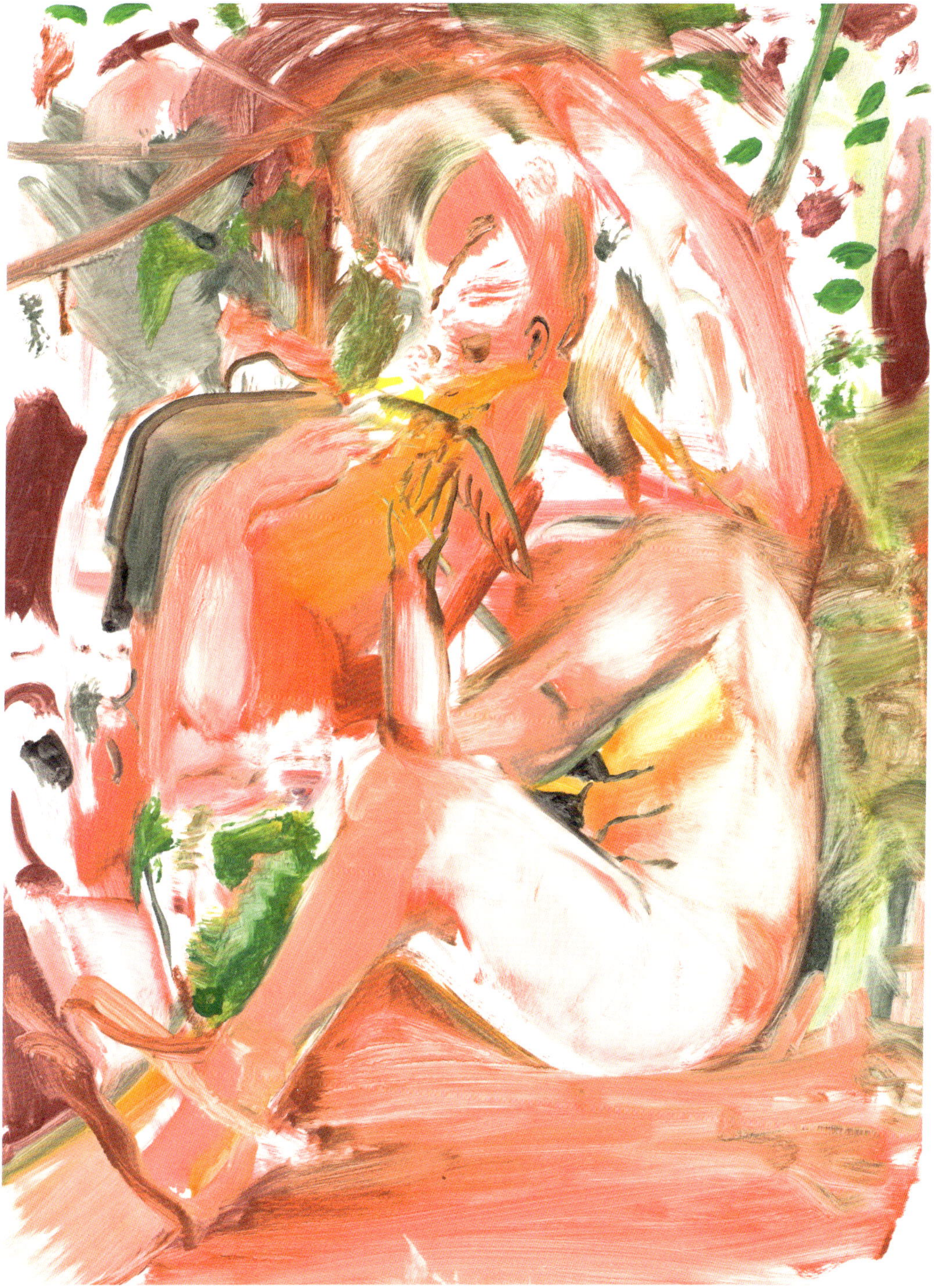

Untitled (CB 1389), 2018

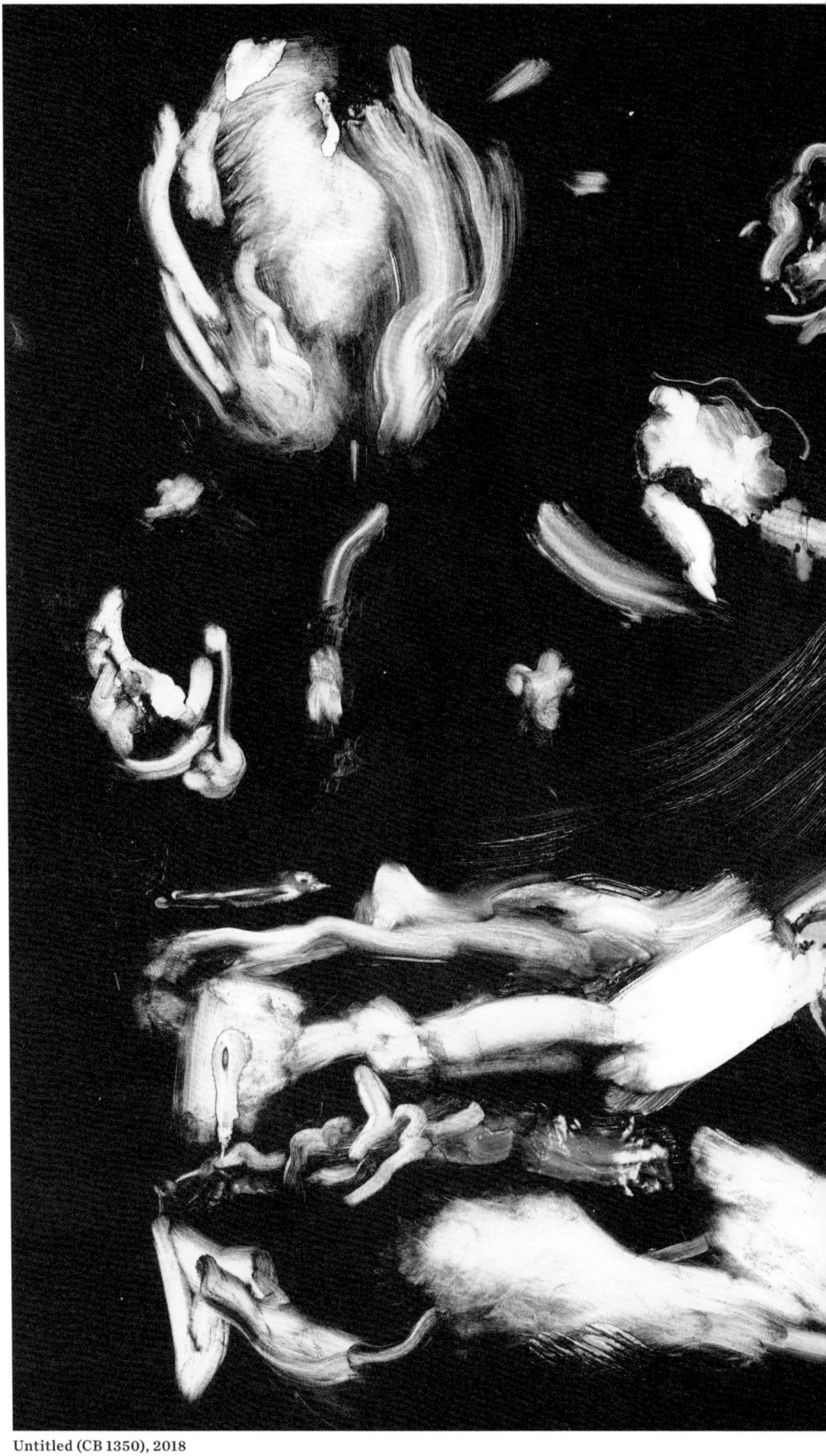

Untitled (CB 1350), 2018

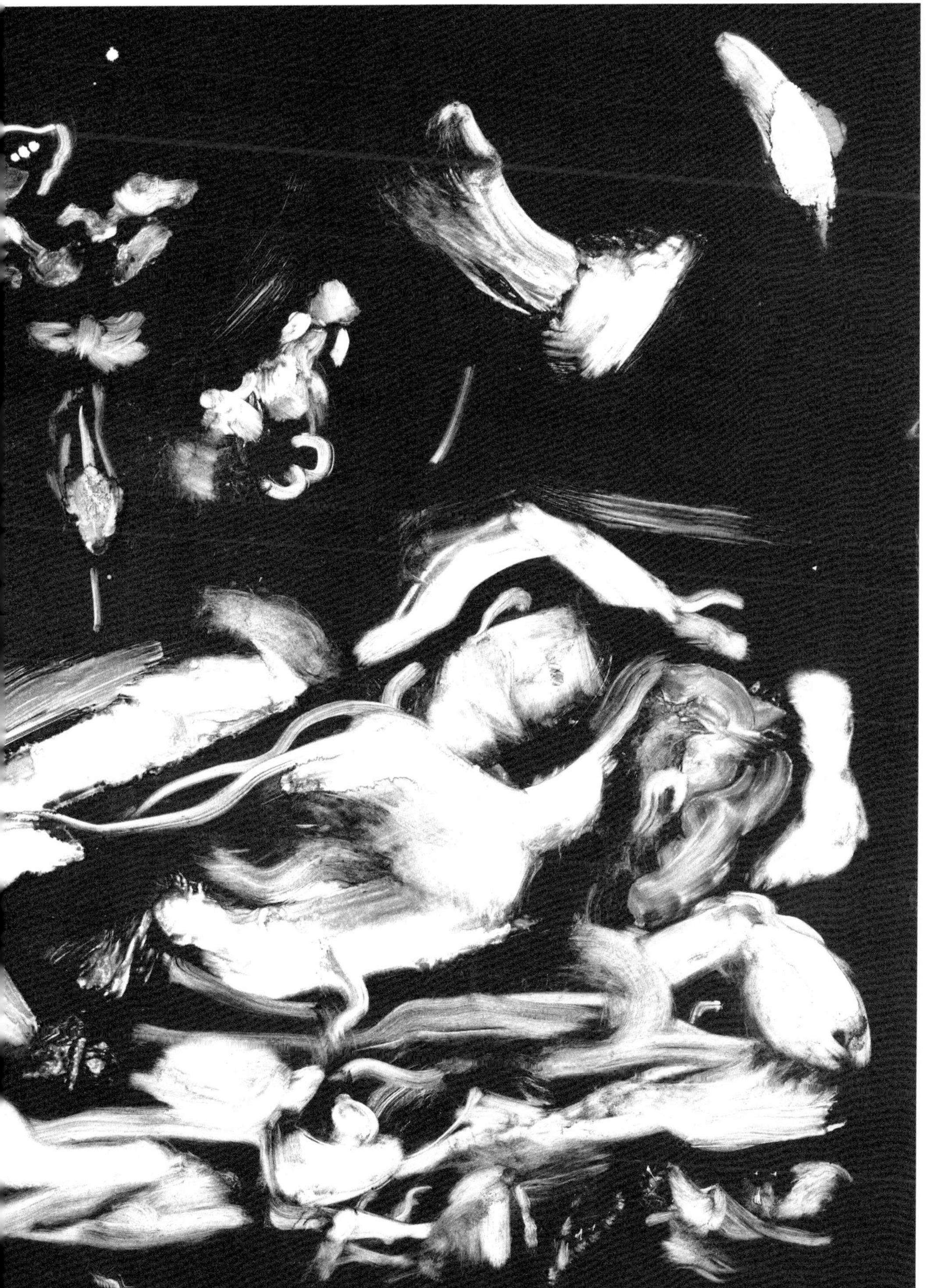

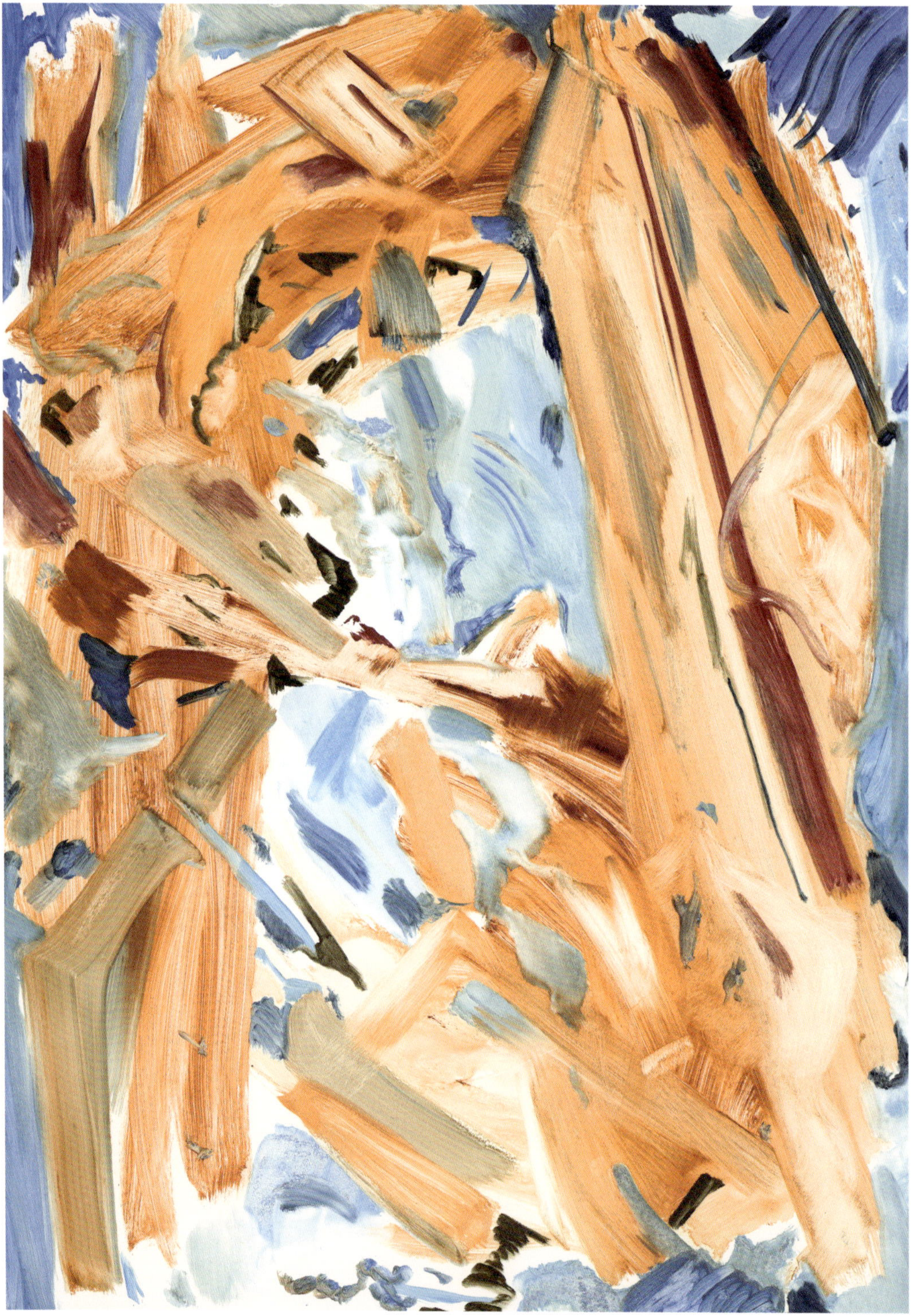

Untitled (CB 1354), 2018

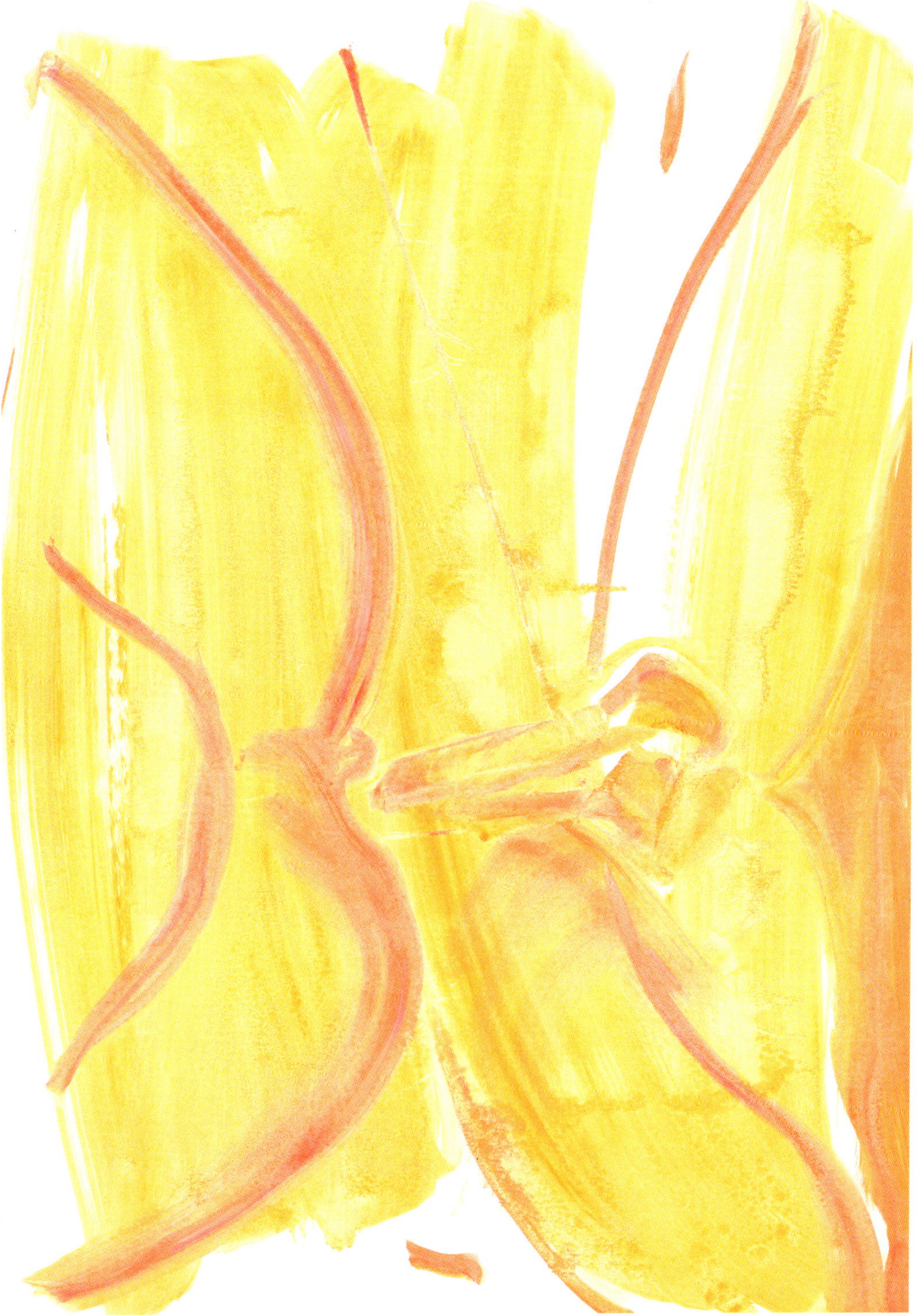

Untitled (CB 1370), 2018

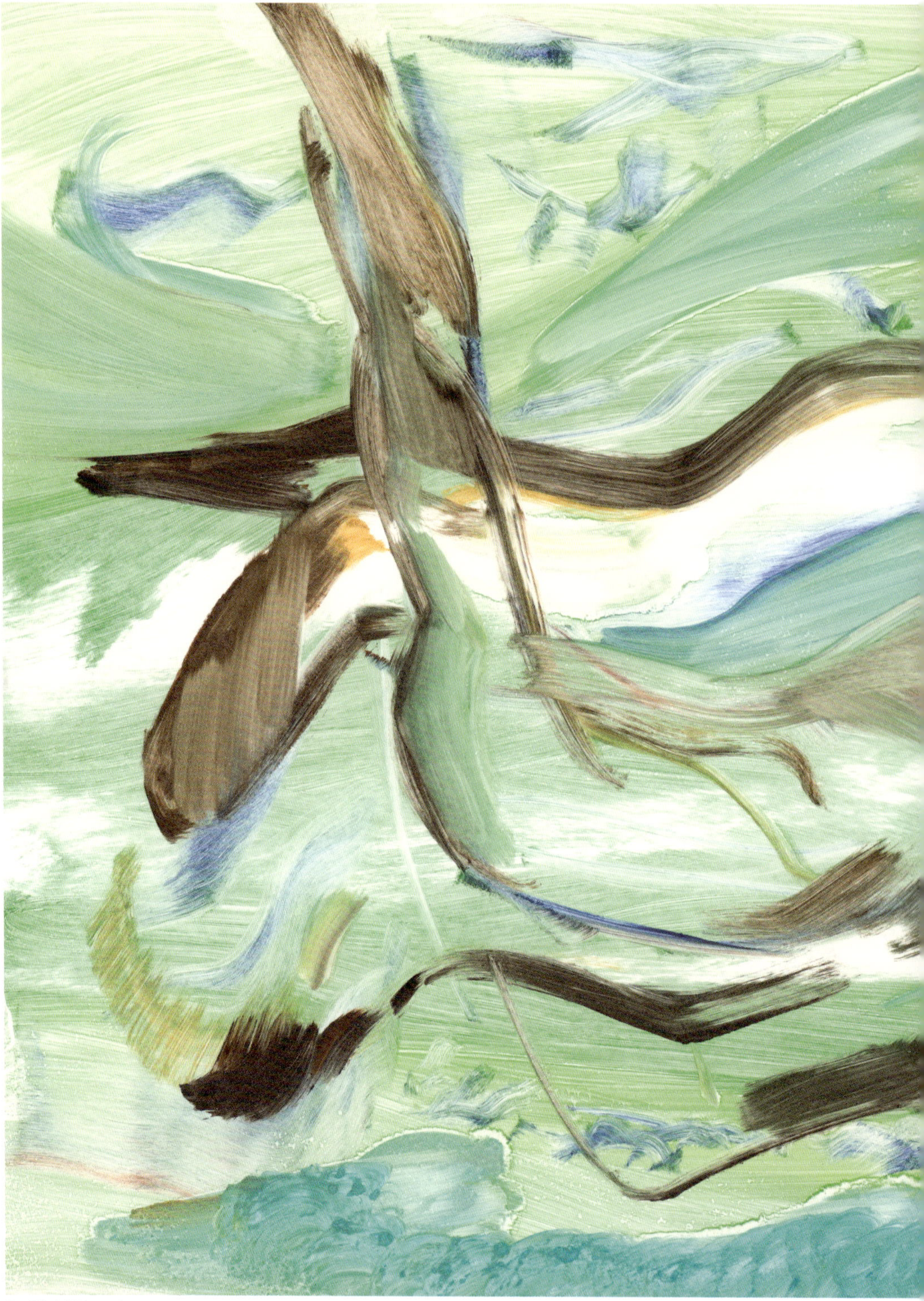

Untitled (CB 1377), 2018

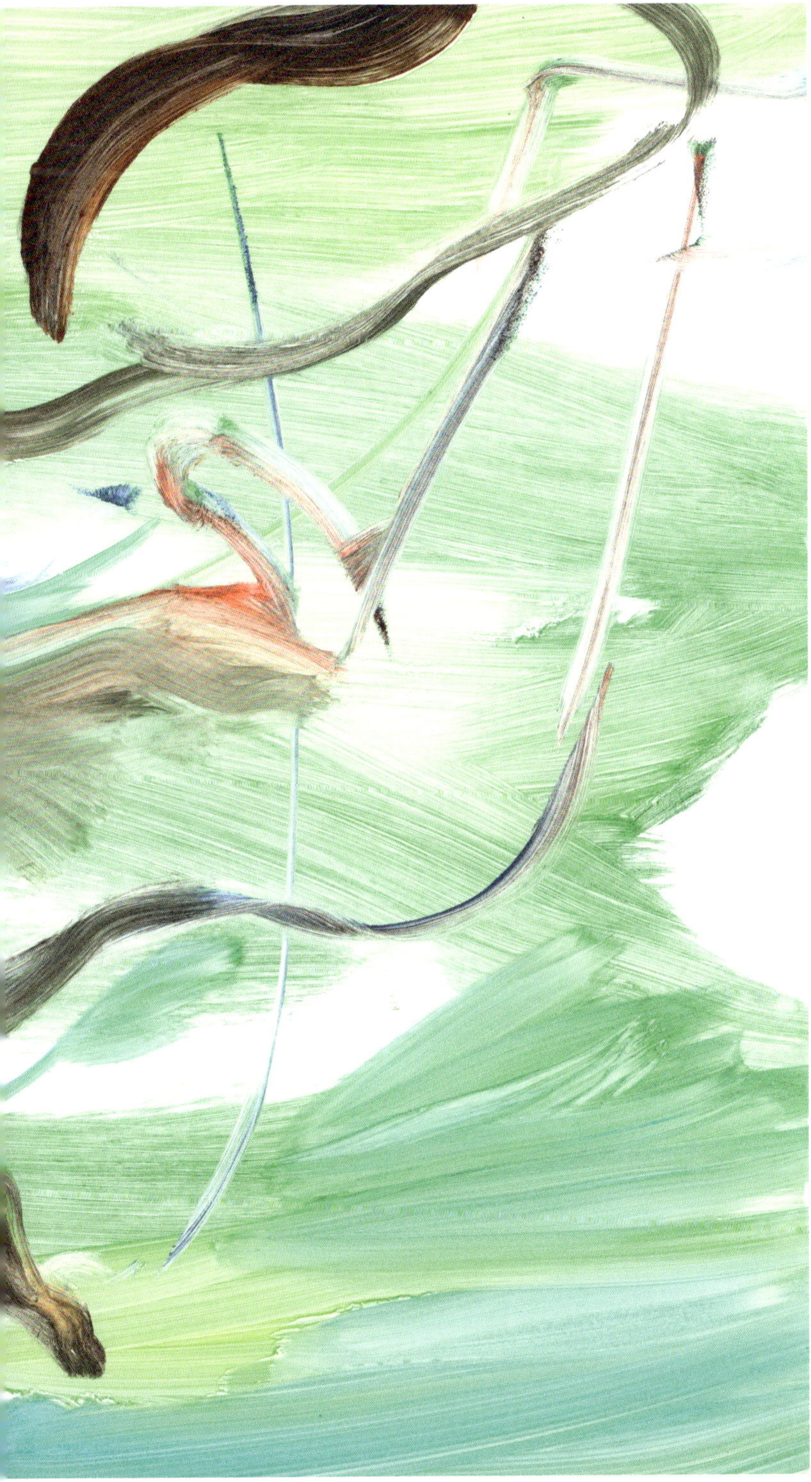

The catalogue has received
generous support from

Contemporary Fine Arts, Berlin
Thomas Dane Gallery, London
Paula Cooper Gallery, New York

and from

De Ying Foundation
Federico Martin Castro Debernardi

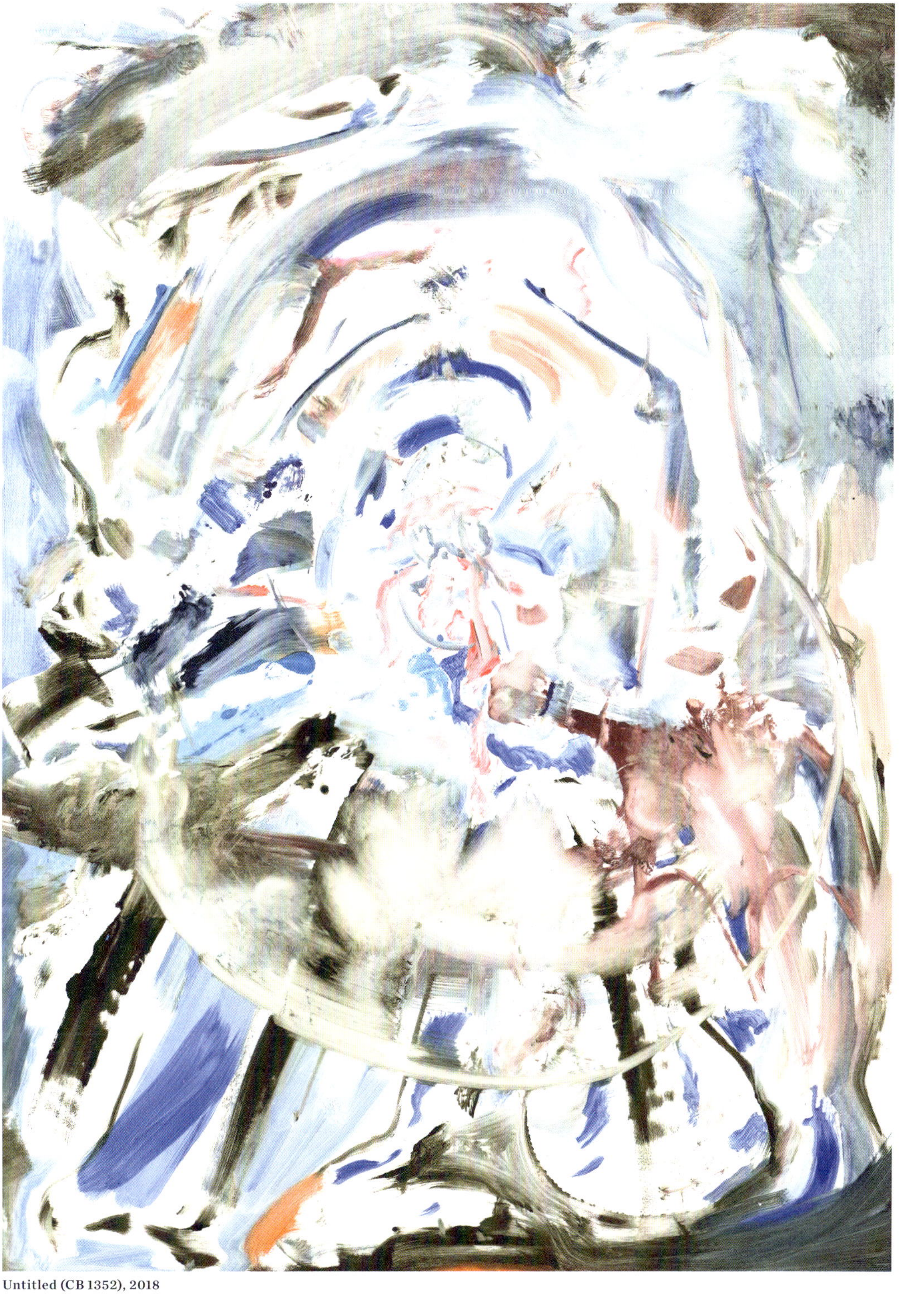

Untitled (CB 1352), 2018

CECILY BROWN: WHERE, WHEN, HOW OFTEN AND WITH WHOM

Edited by Lærke Rydal Jørgensen
and Anders Kold
Graphic Design: Michael Jensen
Photo Editor: Sidse Buck
Translations: Glen Garner
(Poul Erik Tøjner and Anders Kold)
Proofreading: James Manley

Cover and endpapers: Cecily Brown:
Where, When, How Often and with
Whom, 2017. Oil on linen, 277 × 1008 cm
(detail). Photo: Genevieve Hanson
Back cover: Cecily Brown in Two
Palms studio, New York, 2018

Litho: Narayana Press
Print: Narayana Press
ISBN: 978-87-93659-12-4
Printed in Denmark 2018

Distributed by D.A.P.
in North and Latin America
and Thames & Hudson in
the rest of the world

www.louisiana.dk

Photo: Florian Kleinefenn: p. 30; Genevieve
Hanson: p. 2-3, 5, 23 (top), 34-71, 74-79,
94-97, 115, 117, 122-123, 127, 131-135, 141, 143,
146-151, 154-155; Robert McKeever: p. 8-9,
14-17, 28, 31 (top), 72-73, 84-93, 98-99, 119-121,
125, 129, 144-145, 152-153; National Gallery
of Art, Washington: p. 18-19; National Portrait
Gallery, Smithsonian Institution / Mark
Gulezian: p. 140; RMN-Grand Palais (Musée
du Louvre) / Angèle Dequier: p. 138; RMN-
Grand Palais (Musée du Louvre) / Stéphane
Maréchalle: p. 25; Vantagenews.com: p. 23
(bottom); Brandon Israels & Doug Volle:
p. 162-175

The catalogue is published
on the occasion of the exhibition
Cecily Brown: Where, When,
How Often and with Whom
Louisiana Museum of Modern Art,
Humlebæk, Denmark
8 November 2018 – 10 March 2019

Curator: Anders Kold
Curatorial Coordinator / Registrar: Eva Lund
Exhibition Architect: Jens Kamp
Graphic Design: Marie d'Origny Lübecker
Conservators / Exhibition Producers:
Jesper Lund Madsen & Pernille Højmark

Louisiana's Main
Corporate Partners

NØRGAARD PÅ STRØGET

REPUBLIC OF Fritz Hansen®

Realdania

Supports Louisiana's
architectural exhibitions

UBS

Supports programs and exhibitions at
Louisiana Museum of Modern Art

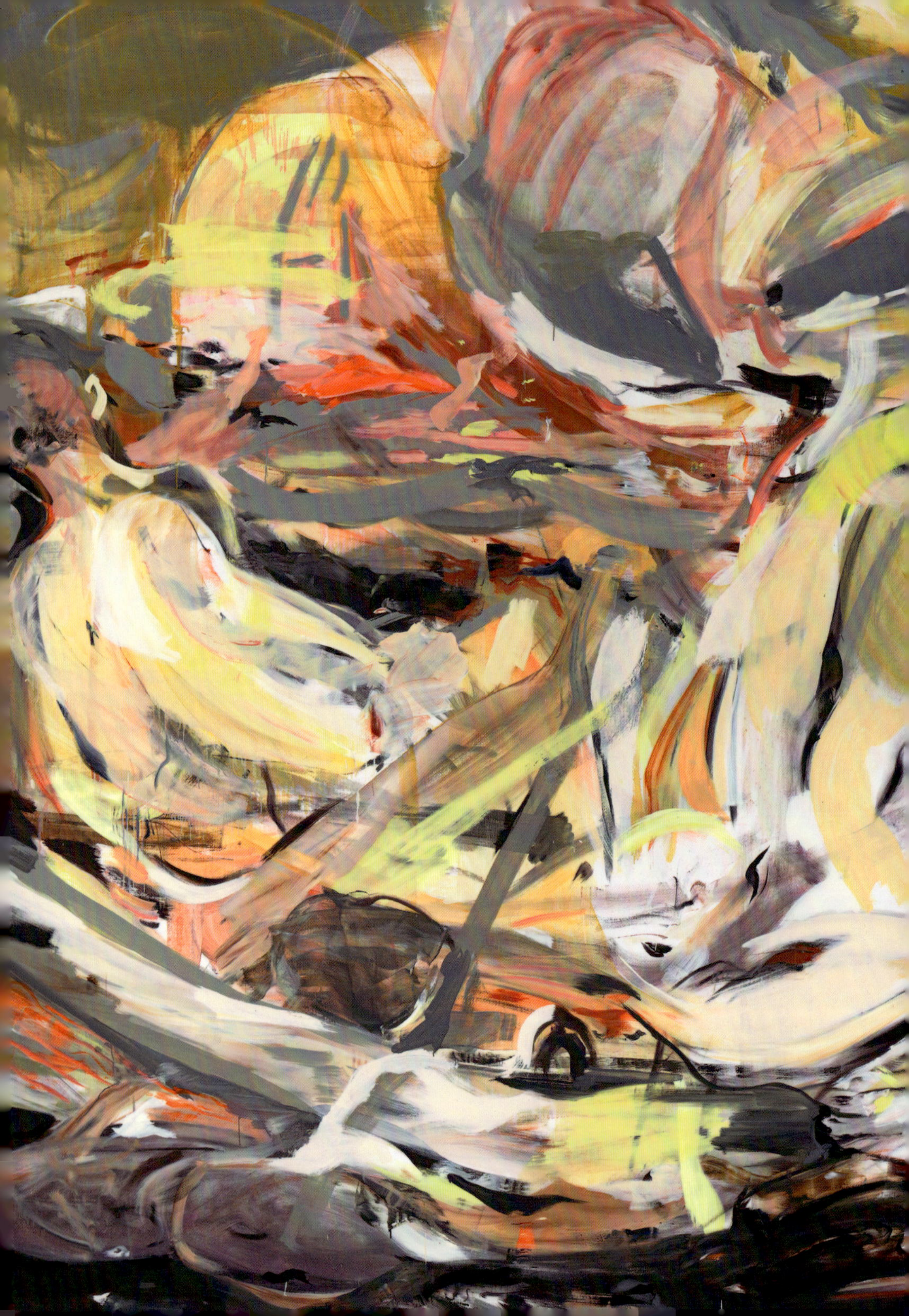